SALES
PROMOTION

PRAISE FOR THE FIRST EDITION OF
SALES PROMOTION

Sales Promotion is one of those books which manages to make the subject interesting, readable and informative, which can explain just what the sales promotion is for the novice, and still find something new to say to the professional ... it is all these in an almost compellingly readable form ... as a basic text for students and novices and a revision for practitioners, the book could go far.

Faith Leigh in *Incentive Today*

This book spells out how to create and implement campaigns that really work, detailing offers that win and keep new customers in every type of business, be it large or small.

Association of British Executives

Sales Promotion spells out the methods companies use to build their sales. It details the offers that win new customers and keep them buying – in every type of business, large or small. Full of practical examples, the book is designed to be a DIY sales promotion kit ... Sales Promotion is placed to become a fundamental text both for students of sales and marketing and for marketing professionals in companies large and small.

Merseyside Chamber of Commerce

I've been reading the book with pleasure and profit. I think it's an excellent contribution to the literature on the subject, and deserves to be widely read.

Alan Toop, Chairman TSM Group and author,
Successful Sales Promotion

Julian Cummins' book is a most welcome addition to the all too slim library of sales promotion books. It fills one of those classic gaps in the market: it is a book for practitioners ... If read and digested it can only raise the level of professionalism of consultants and promoters alike. It is written from a position of experience and also from a position of perception. Indeed, it should be prescribed reading for all consultancy personnel from account manager director down, and all promotion personnel from marketing manager down.

Aubrey Watson in *Marketing*

SALES PROMOTION

How to Create and Implement Campaigns that Really Work

Second Edition

Julian Cummins

KOGAN PAGE

econd edition is dedicated to
George Cummins.

YOURS TO HAVE AND TO HOLD

BUT NOT TO COPY

First published in 1989
This edition published in 1998

Kogan Page Limited
120 Pentonville Road
London N1 9JN

© Julian Cummins 1998

British Library Cataloguing in Publication Data

A CIP record for this book is available from the British Library.

ISBN 0 7494 2447 8

Typeset by JS Typesetting, Wellingborough, Northants.
Printed and bound in Great Britain by Creative Print & Design Group.

CONTENTS

ACKNOWLEDGEMENTS

In preparing the second edition, I would like to thank the many sales promotional practitioners who have offered invaluable help and advice, notably Jim Porteous, Trade Communications Manager at Nestlé UK, who was for many years Nestlé Rowntree Sales Promotion Manager; Colin Jarvis, Director, ITEM Group plc; Simon Mahoney, Joint Managing Director, SMP; Charles O'Reilly, Managing Director, PIMS; David Williams, Chairman, POPAI Europe; Sallyann Betts, Business Development Manager, Granby Marketing Services; Carole-Ann Guy, Director of Sales, Brevis Marketing Services; Teresa Barker, Director of Client Services, NCH Promotional Services; Chris Reed, External Affairs Manager, Advertising Standards Authority; and Robert Silver, business journalist and author.

I am also grateful to the agencies and companies that have provided case study material and in many cases commented helpfully on my drafts, notably Joan Hay, Account Director, The Communications Agency; Ellis Watson, Marketing Director, *The Sun*; Simon Mahoney, Joint Managing Director, SMP; David Croydon, Chairman, Marketing Principles; Dai Davis, Partner, Eversheds; Tim Bonnet, Tequila Option One, and Louise Wall; Morella Heanley, Lovell Vass Boddey; David Walters, Director, The Blue-Chip Marketing Consultancy; Elizabeth Baker, Business Planning Director, Triangle Communications; Debbie Smith, Group Managing Director, Promotional Campaigns Group; Alastair Duncan, Account Director, Ammirati Puris Lintas; Mike Todd, The Continuity Company; Michelle Hocking, Clarke Hooper Consulting; and Steve Bell and Alex Legge, Account Managers, IMP. (The addresses of the agencies and supplier firms are in the Useful addresses list should you wish to see what they could do for you.)

Finally, I am grateful to my colleagues at Avista, in particular my secretary Maureen Hatton. All faults remain my own responsibility. I would be delighted to hear about any you find and your suggestions for improvement. Write to me at Avista, Beech House, Troy Road, Horsforth, Leeds LS18 4HX; fax on 0113 259 1102; or e-mail me at julian@avista.co.uk

Julian Cummins

PREFACE TO THE SECOND EDITION

When *Sales Promotion* was first published in 1989, it met an immediate need for a concise, practical guide to creating and implementing promotional campaigns that really work. Adopted as a course text by the Institute of Sales Promotion (ISP) and the Communications, Advertising and Marketing Foundation (CAM), it helped thousands of managers pass their exams and put their knowledge into effect. Businesses small and large have used it as a handy reference to the nuts and bolts of sales promotion.

Why a second edition? A great deal has changed in the last nine years. Loyalty schemes are universal, the codes of practice have been rewritten, lotteries have changed in style, and there are hundreds of new and exciting case studies to illustrate sales promotion in practice. There's also been a change in how we think about marketing. There's more stress on relationships, less on mechanistic rules and structures. There has also been an expansion in the range of activities embraced by the sales promotion practitioner, to include events, sponsorship, loyalty and often media relations. So, its been necessary to look again at every chapter, every line. I've also taken the chance to introduce more case studies and a new and more logical structure.

However, there are important continuities. The sales promotions run by Thomas Lipton in the 1890s remain a classic example of imaginative, effective promotion. The core of sales promotion – influencing behaviour – is unchanged. The importance of sales promotion was growing in the 1980s. I said it would continue to grow – and it has. More than ever, it is important for managers to know how to influence the behaviour of their customers and prospects cost-effectively and efficiently. And it remains the case that there is far less written on sales promotion than its importance warrants.

I hope this second edition will provide inspiration to a new generation of marketing practitioners.

INTRODUCTION

SALES PROMOTION IN ACTION

Long Row Fisheries in Horsforth, Leeds, is not in the same league as Harry Ramsden's, the internationally known fish and chip restaurant five miles down the road in Guiseley. It is a single, privately owned chippie, of the kind familiar in towns everywhere. It is also a fine example of sales promotion in action.

Three offers were on display on professionally signwritten posters in March 1997. One offered extra peas, beans, curry or breadcake for just 10p with a full meal on Tuesday evenings, the normal price of 30p slashed through. Another offered a lunchtime special of free chips with two pieces of chicken at £2.05, the normal price of £2.70 slashed through. A third offered another lunchtime special – fish and chips and beans or peas at £1.90 instead of £2.10, plus free tea or coffee.

This is an unusually price-focused range of promotions for Long Row Fisheries. Others have included free Creme Eggs for children at Easter; Jurassic Park dinosaurs for sale at the price they cost from the cash and carry; spooky jellies at Hallowe'en; and free raffle tickets to win seasonal fare at Christmas.

'It's about watching it all the time, keeping people's interest and never being blasé', says one of the partners, Robert Smithies. He changes promotions when people stop taking notice of them, roughly every two months. They also feature on an automatic message machine, which is sometimes switched off for months at a time. When it is switched on again, people take notice. He prefers promotions that offer something extra: 'We go for that bit more rather than slashing the price. People are wary of things being cheap.' One of his most successful promotions was a kids offer of two sausages, chips, peas and pop for £1 – a saving of 55p against a full price of £1.55. In practice, it offered more for the £1 that children would normally spend.

Long Row Fisheries is my usual chippie. I drive past several others to reach it. The hours are long and never change, so I don't need to wonder if it will be open. The staff are friendly, and the fish is good. That much is true of many of its competitors. The buzz of its promotional offers adds to its attractiveness. It also reflects something deeper than the offers themselves: a business that is alive to its customers, and gives them good and constantly refreshed reasons to buy. That is sales promotion in action, the subject of this book.

Harry Ramsden's is equally but differently imaginative. It offers a series of 'Opera and Chips' evenings – fish and chips with Verdi and Puccini sung by the chorus of Opera North. The first evening was set up for the CBI's annual conference in November 1996, and was a sell-out to delegates staying in Harrogate, 15 miles away. Other promotions include singalongs for senior citizens, tea dances and sportsmen's dinners. The Manchester restaurant, located on the canal, offers canal trips with fish and chips, and has run joint tours with the nearby Manchester United and Granada Studios. The Dublin restaurant invited 20 Elvis Presley lookalikes to eat with them following a 'Chip Challenge' to find the best fish and chips in Dublin that was set up with Radio Telefis Éireann.

What do these examples have in common? Jim Porteous, who was responsible for sales promotion at Rowntree Mackintosh and then Nestlé for years, comments, 'No one buys chocolate to be miserable: make your promotions add to the fun.' The same is true of buying any other product or service. If the fun goes out of it, so does the spirit that makes buying and selling part of our lives as customers and businesspeople alike.

There's a more serious point, too. Much of this book necessarily talks about detailed mechanics (see page 43) and codes of practice. It's impossible to look at price promotions without some reference to economics. There's hard graft and detail in sales promotion. At its heart is the serious business of building long-term, profitable customer relationships. It's no surprise to discover that Harry Ramsden's is an Investor in People, the winner of a National Training Award, and highly regarded for its management skills. Good promotions are not a sub-stitute for serious thinking or for building deep staff and customer relationships, but part of the same process.

Managers start with a serious disadvantage in engaging with sales promotion. They're too busy to get involved in promotions, to collect coupons, send in for offers, seek out special offers – or think they are. It's a big mistake. The best basis for understanding sales promotion is from inside. Collect sales promotions and participate in them. Above all, enjoy them as much as my daughters Olivia and Caroline enjoyed the Hallowe'en jellies at Long Row Fisheries.

THE EXTENT OF SALES PROMOTION

A cursory check at your supermarket, in your local paper or pub, and in the direct mail sent to both your home and business address will give an immediate feel of the extent of sales promotion today. Sales promotion is found whenever a supermarket offers 'three for the price of two', whenever a pub offers a happy hour, whenever an insurance mailer offers a free pen for replying, whenever a product offers a free draw, competition or mail-in.

Philip Kotler, the American marketing academic, estimates that a decade ago the advertising to sales promotion ratio was about 60:40. In 1997, he estimated that in many consumer goods companies, sales promotion accounted for 65 to 75 per cent of expenditure, and had been growing annually for the last two decades.[1]

Research by Harris International Marketing/*Marketing Week* in 1986 showed that over 70 per cent of the population had taken part in competitions or games on products and services. Over a third had done so in the last month. Further, 40 per cent had sent off packet tops or tokens for a free gift in the last month, and 54 per cent had used a money-off coupon.[2]

Taking these figures together, almost 60 per cent of the population actively participate in some form of promotion in any given month – whether it be entering a competition, sending in for a free gift or using a money-off coupon. This makes participating in sales promotions one of Britain's biggest active leisure activities.

The General Household Survey regularly measures participation by adults in the last month for a wide range of leisure activities. The 1994 data showed that 10 per cent had been cycling, 13 per cent had been swimming, 9 per cent had played bingo and 12 per cent had played pool or snooker. Active participation in sales promotion is higher than many highly publicized activities. It is as extensive as visiting a pub once a month or more.[3]

These measures are one indicator of the size and extent of sales promotion. Some parts of sales promotion are readily measurable. NCH, which dominates the coupon redemption business, reports that more than four billion coupons were distributed in 1995, enough for nearly 200 per household.[4] But that is just one part of the total. Attempts to put a figure on the amount spent by companies on sales promotion always founder on difficulties of definition and measurement.

It is easy enough to measure the amount spent on TV and press advertising (£3.1 and £3.5 billion respectively in 1995). It is possible to get a reasonable measure of the amount spent on direct mail (£1.1

billion in 1995). Much smaller areas of marketing expenditure have generally agreed estimates of expenditure. For example, sports sponsorship was estimated to be worth £285 million in 1995, and telemarketing £108 million.[5] But sales promotions are so varied in their form, and expenditure goes on so many different things, that there is no agreed way of arriving at an estimate.

In 1988, the Advertising Association and the Institute of Sales Promotion conducted an initial study to identify the criteria for measurement. It did not get far, and has not been followed up. In the first edition of this book in 1989, I cited estimates from that study that sales promotion was worth as much as £6 billion, more than TV and press advertising put together. Today, the Institute of Sales Promotion puts the figure at £7.5 billion. This is a proportionately greater increase than the growth of advertising, but it is very much a guesstimate.

In the autumn of 1997, the European Promotional Marketing Association (EPMA) announced a major research programme to establish the money and resources put into sales promotion across Europe.[6] It may provide a clearer answer. However, it faces a fundamental problem of categorization. Sales promotion uses advertising, direct mail, telephone response and printed literature as media. It is part and parcel of the expenditure quoted for these activities rather than separate from them. Price promotions – a large part of sales promotion – may not even be counted as expenditure, but as lost income. Expenditure on altering packs and products for a promotion may not be counted as promotional expenditure at all.

The significant measures are two-fold:

- the extent of consumer and trade participation in sales promotion

- the use of media from TV to press to events to put across promotional messages.

Together they demonstrate that sales promotion is not an also-ran in the business of marketing products and services, but one of the most important tools available to companies, and a major part of our day-to-day lives. It is likely to become more important in the future.

WHY SALES PROMOTION HAS GROWN

There are four main reasons for the extensive growth of sales promotion and for managers finding that promotions are essential to building customer relationships.

First, firms are getting better at what they do. The European Vice-President of a major toiletries group commented recently, 'It's no longer enough to have an excellent product at an excellent price; I need a tie-breaker.' Companies everywhere are facing declining real differences between products and services, increased distributor power and faster communication of alternatives. They have to fight harder and faster for every sale. Sales promotion offers a tie-breaker in markets in which most products are excellent.

Second, firms are rethinking the relationship between attitude and behaviour. Consumers are increasingly fickle in their brand choice and look for more from the brands they buy. Trying to create awareness of and a positive attitude to a brand by means of advertising is seen as less effective than encouraging a sale that may lead on to just such a positive attitude to the brand. Sales promotion offers novelty, excitement and humour at the point of purchase, which customers respond to.

Third, the pressure to achieve short-term results is growing. The fortunes of brands and companies are increasingly volatile. Sales promotions can be devised, implemented and take effect in the market far more quickly than other forms of marketing. This is of growing importance as demands for short-term profit performance grow.

Fourth, TV audiences are fragmenting as the number of channels grow, making it more expensive to reach certain audiences; the decline in community identity at a local level is making it more difficult to reach particular groups (such as the young) via local media; and the growth in the sheer number of competing brands and products is leading people to switch off from many of the advertising messages beamed at them. The ad agency chief Winston Fletcher points out that there are 9500 brands advertised sufficiently for their ad spends to be measured; few people will buy more than 400 in a year. He suggests, tongue in cheek, that maybe 96 per cent of advertising is wasted.[7]

There is a more serious side to it, however. Recent advertising research has shown that the sales effects of TV advertising over a four-week period are between two and seven times greater when they coincide with promotions. This important finding came from a survey of 21 different brands in 8 different consumer goods markets that integrated the shopping behaviour of 9000 households with TV viewing data.[8] In the case of 2 out of 11 established brands where the effect of TV advertising with and without promotional activity could be measured, TV advertising was only effective when promotions were also happening.

These are the reasons sales promotion is taking a growing share of marketing budgets, and managers should be proud to be involved in sales promotion. Far from being the Cinderella of the marketing world, it is one of the most useful tools for acquiring and retaining customers.

HOW TO USE THIS BOOK

There are three parts to this book:

- Part 1 deals with structure
- Part 2 with techniques
- Part 3 with the context of sales promotion.

They are designed to be read and used differently.

Chapter 1 deals with the business purpose of promotions. It sets out how they contribute to building long-term customer relationships – and can sometimes damage them. Chapter 2 spells out how to use promotions, from the identification of a business task to the specification of the promotional brief. These first two chapters are crucial for understanding what sales promotion can and cannot do.

The next two chapters deal with two crucial inputs into promotional planning:

- creative ideas
- supplier resources.

Creative ideas are an essential part of good promotions. Chapter 3 sets out how to go about identifying them. Chapter 4 deals with sales promotion agencies, handling houses, specialist printers and other suppliers.

Whether promotions stand or fall turns on the details of their implementation. Chapter 5 describes how to implement a promotion, avoid disaster and ensure that all the elements work together. Chapter 6, on research and evaluation, is a must for ensuring that your promotions meet the business objectives you set.

If you are tempted to dive straight into the techniques and skip Part 1, resist it. You can use the techniques to best effect only if you are clear about the why, when and how of sales promotion.

Part 2 deals with a wide range of promotional techniques. Chapter 7 covers offers such as free flights, holidays and film processing that are available 'off the shelf'. It spells out how they work, and how to make the best of them. Chapter 8 looks at the important area of joint promotions – teaming up with another firm to your mutual advantage.

Chapter 9 covers promotions that use discounts, coupons, price reductions, cheap finance and other price-related tools. A massive area of sales promotion, it is one that carries dangers as much as benefits. Premiums, whether with a product or available as a mail-in item, are another major area. They are discussed in Chapter 10, along with what to watch for in identifying and sourcing premiums. Chapter 11 sets out the range of prize promotions available, including competitions, draws and instant wins.

You will find Part 2 useful for years to come. You may not want to read it all at once. You will probably want to dip into it and refer to it for the nuts and bolts of techniques you may want to use now or in the future. If you are studying for a marketing course, you will find the data you need on the range of techniques available to you.

Part 3 of the book deals with the context in which promotions take place in a global economy with significant national regulations. In larger companies, promotions span national boundaries. International promotions are covered in Chapter 12. Even if your concerns are local, the chapter is full of ideas of international applications.

Chapter 13 sets out the principles behind the UK Code of Sales Promotion Practice and discusses recent case studies of promotions from the Advertising Standards Authority (ASA). It also discusses the variety of rules that apply in other countries. It is a must as a reference for any promotion you run.

Chapter 14 sets out details of books, magazines and courses to help you find out more about sales promotion, and gives a set of self-study questions to help you make the most of this book. Finally, there is a list of addresses of organizations that can help you set up and run promotions.

There are 25 case studies throughout the book, illustrating the best (and in one case the worst) in sales promotional practice. Use these for ideas for your business sector, and your business challenge. They have been placed at the end of the chapter to which they mainly refer, but they illustrate the many types of sales promotions and their use in different business sectors as well. With each case study there is a set of questions to get you thinking. Table 1 sets out how they refer to particular business sectors and challenges.

Table 1   *Case study index*

Case	Page	Promotion	Type	Business sector
1	25	Maxwell House	Free draws	Consumer goods
2	25	Bovril	Sampling	Consumer goods
3	26	Sainsbury's	Collector	Retail
4	46	Kleenex Facial Tissues	Various	Consumer goods
5	48	Zantac 75	Games	Pharmaceuticals
6	49	Music for Schools	Collector	Confectionery/retail
7	64	Eversheds	Creativity	Business to business
8	65	Rover Group	Competitions	Motors
9	129	Tango	Events	Soft drinks
10	130	*The Sun*	Travel	Newspapers
11	131	Hoover	Travel	Consumer durables
12	145	NatWest/BT	Joint promotions	Services
13	146	Shell	Loyalty	Petrol
14	147	Sellotape	Lotteries	Business to business
15	175	Tesco	Price	Retail
16	177	Gale's Honey	Coupons	Consumer goods
17	178	Worcestershire Sauce	Coupons	Consumer goods
18	193	Procter & Gamble	Premiums	Consumer goods
19	194	Clearblue One Step	Premiums	Health products
20	195	Electrolux	Premiums	Trade promotions
21	196	Smirnoff	Premiums	Youth markets
22	216	Sarson's	Instant win	Consumer goods
23	216	Faber & Faber	Competitions	Bookshops
24	227	Tony Stone Images	Competitions	Business to business
25	228	Umbro	Instant win	Consumer goods

Part 1

Structure

1

BUSINESS PURPOSE

Sales promotion can be thought of as a marketing function. It is far better to think of it as part of the creation and strengthening of relationships that contribute to the success of the business. This chapter spells out the particular ways that sales promotion strengthens (and sometimes weakens) a company's relationships.

The leading management thinker John Kay writes 'I see the firm as a set of relationships between its various stakeholders – employees, customers, investors, shareholders. The successful firm is one which creates a distinctive character in these relationships and which operates in an environment which maximizes the value of that distinctiveness.'[1]

What characterizes these relationships? Money plays a large part – whether in salaries for staff, dividends to shareholders or invoices to customers. However, there is much more to it than that – like loyalty, expectation and human feeling. Whether people buy a product or work for a firm, they are engaged in a relationship that satisfies their needs to a greater or lesser extent. The task of business is to maximize the value of that relationship.

There was a time when business was thought of as a series of functions. Sales promotion was one among many things companies did, one of the responsibilities of a marketing department. Drawn as a hierarchical chart, the marketing manager knew exactly where sales promotion fitted into the scheme of things. Unfortunately, this neat scheme did not really describe how businesses achieve and sustain competitive advantage.[2] It certainly didn't describe the contribution of sales promotion.

Separate functions, such as finance, production and marketing, continue to exist in firms, and they can be managed well or badly. A good marketing department, however, does not create a competitive advantage on its own. Its work is part of a process that takes place every time someone buys or uses the company's products or services. It is part of the process by which relationships are strengthened, and by which customer and other stakeholder needs are satisfied. Good sales promotion supports that process.

CUSTOMERS AND OFFERINGS

At the heart of every successful business is a close understanding of customer needs and how to anticipate and meet them. For many years, people understood this unconsciously. Long before 'marketing' was invented, it was the genius of every great entrepreneur. Later, it was thought to be part of the task of a marketing department. Now people are going back to seeing customer needs as everyone's concern, not just the concern of a marketing department. Increasingly, firms are sharing responsibility for thinking about customer needs among line managers in every functional discipline. It's not that marketing has gone out of fashion, it's been generalized across the firm as a whole.

Customer needs in any particular area are met by product or service offerings that are a bundle of characteristics. Some the firm entirely controls, and some not. They can be summarized as three elements:

- **functional** what the product or service actually does; its physical characteristics or service components

- **economic** what the product or service costs; the time and other costs involved in obtaining and using it

- **psychological** the image of the product or service; the added values associated with it in the minds of the consumer.

In everyday language, these three elements are:

- quality
- value
- image.

The bundle of characteristics is the 'brand'. Truly great brands achieve leadership in all three dimensions – having superlative quality, unbeatable value and outstanding image.

Most people do not manage mega brands such as KitKat or Coca-Cola. Few manage totally undifferentiated commodities. Even if you do, you will be part of a firm that is unique – that has brand values at the company level, if not the product level. Making the most of 'brand equity' – the sum of quality, value and image as customers understand it – is one of the most crucial jobs for any manager. Sadly, many managers underrate the importance of the brand equity for which they are responsible.[3]

The most difficult element for any firm to manage is the psychological one. Companies often talk about 'creating an image'. They may do so in the minds of the staff who work long and hard to devise it. They only do so in customers' minds when customers adapt, develop and absorb that image as their own. Companies can offer an image, but they cannot make an image. If it is attractive and powerful, and accords with customers' own experiences, it will form part of their image of the product or service. Thoughts and images in our own minds are forever, thankfully, beyond anyone else's total control.

The relationship a firm has with its customers is conducted through the bundle of functional, economic and psychological benefits that its products and services offer. It's the job of management to ensure that they meet customer needs in a way that maximizes their satisfaction and creates a distinctive competitive advantage.

ATTITUDES AND BEHAVIOUR

Managing customer relationships focuses on two points:

- managing attitudes
- managing behaviour.

The two have a complicated relationship with each other. Psychologists vary in the priority they give to them. Some are inclined to stress that changing behaviour leads to a change in attitude. Others argue that changing an attitude leads to a change in behaviour. If this is disputed among psychologists, it is little wonder that marketing people also have different opinions.

Practical examples illustrate these points of view. Surveys show that far more people think that regular exercise is a good thing (attitude) than actually practise it (behaviour). Surveys also show that people drink more alcohol (behaviour) than they are prepared to admit (attitude). For years, government urged people to use seat belts (attitude) with only limited effect. They then passed a law making it a crime not to wear them (behaviour). People grumbled at first, but buckled up. Over time, their attitude changed to accord with the behaviour they had become accustomed to.

Some people believe that the primary task of marketing communications is to create awareness, interest and desire in the minds of potential customers. Action, they argue, follows from that. This is the classic theory of advertising developed in the 1950s and often called the 'persuasion model'. It is best known by the acronym AAIDA, which stands for awareness, interest, desire, action.

Others argue that people do not always work in such a logical way. We are all aware of products we never buy. We can even have positive attitudes to them, but not get around to buying them. Conversely, there are products we try out casually or on the spur of the moment – because we are given a free sample or because it is on special offer. Only after taking the action of trying and using it do we begin to take serious note of its advertising and form any attitude towards it. This second theory is called the 'involvement model' because it stresses the need to involve customers in the product or service by any means available.[4] Figure 1 summarizes these two models.

The persuasion model

Awareness → Attitude → Interest → Desire → Action

The involvement model

Usual brand out of stock
Sample dropped at the door } → Action → Notice ads → Attitude
Special price offer
Seen at friend's house

Figure 1   *Two classic theories of advertising*

Which comes first, attitude or behaviour? Few people will argue a black-and-white case, but most of us will stress one or the other. Those who stress attitude will tend towards the persuasion model of consumer behaviour. They will tend to argue for advertising campaigns aimed primarily at creating awareness and changing attitudes, and trust that the desired behaviour will follow. Those who stress behaviour will tend to the involvement model. They will tend to argue for marketing programmes that directly impact on the behaviour of customers, and trust that the desired attitude to the product or service will follow.

The involvement model is increasingly being seen as a more realistic description of the way in which consumers buy products and services.

The model extends well beyond marketing. The Church, for example, used to think that people started belonging to a church because they believed – often after a conversion experience. However, it is now understood that people belong before they believe.[5] Studies have shown that people become involved in a church because of friends or family. It is often quite casual at first. Only after a period of years do they come to realize that they believe. The process of 'belonging before believing' is about 'behaviour before attitude'.

Sales promotion is, first and foremost, about behaviour. It makes increasing sense in the light of evidence that behaviour precedes attitude. Encouraging someone to try a product or service is often the best way to begin the process by which they become a long-term customer and develop a relationship with your firm.

THE MARKETING MIX

For years, students have learnt that marketing consists of the 'four Ps' – product, price, place and promotion. If you don't want each word to start with a 'P', they can be called product, price, distribution and communication. Sales promotion's role in this scheme seemed clear cut. It was the part of a firm's communications efforts, concerned primarily with influencing the behaviour of its customers and potential customers in the short term. How does it fit with the rest of the communications mix? That mix is generally divided into five different tools:

- **advertising** paid-for space and time in broadcast or print media and other paid-for communications

- **sales promotion** incentives and offers that encourage people to behave in a particular way

- **publicity** information and opinion about your products or services carried by third parties

- **personal selling** personal presentation of your products or services to customers, prospects or intermediaries

- **direct marketing** non-personal presentation to customers or prospects to which they can respond directly.

This widely used division of communications tools helps in a number of ways. It gives a rough and ready definition of what each promotional tool is able to contribute to the mix, and helps companies to decide which will be most useful in achieving particular objectives. For example, an industrial company is likely to put most emphasis on personal selling. A company requiring short-term sales may put a priority on sales promotion. A company with a startling new product may go for publicity as its best bet. It also helps companies work out the balance between the different tools. Most of the time, there isn't one alone that will do the job, and we need a balance between all five.

Unfortunately, this way of thinking about the communications mix does not reflect the way sales promotion is used. It does not do justice to the role it plays in creating and building customer relationships – and sometimes putting them at risk. Like all time-honoured definitions, it is due for an update. Its inadequacy goes a long way to explaining why most marketing books give far less attention to sales promotion than people who are doing the job for real.

In 1992, two academics published an important article in which they pointed out that no one had ever properly researched whether or not the four Ps model actually reflected reality.[6] They argued that it didn't. In particular, they found that sales promotion was wrongly seen as just one part of the communications mix. It would not matter, they suggested, if sales promotion was a minor part of the mix. In fact, it is both large and continually growing – constituting, as Philip Kotler points out, 75 per cent of marketing expenditure.

The key point about sales promotion is that it can alter every part of the marketing mix. It can alter the product. For example, when a different-coloured Smartie is included in the pack for a short time period or KitKat is produced in a mint flavour. It can alter the packaging. For example, when a lager brand is sold as '33% extra free'. It can alter the price. For example, when a product is sold with a 10p off flash. It can alter the distribution. For example, when Guinness is sold at summer fêtes, well outside its normal licensed trade outlets. And it can alter the advertising. For example, when long-term advertising is altered to incorporate a promotional theme. The answer is a new classification that reflects reality rather better than the old four Ps (see Figure 2).

The logic of this way of thinking becomes clear when you look at how promotional offers are communicated. They invariably use one or more of the other communications tools. It is rare to see a piece of direct mail without an incentive for an early reply. It is rare for companies not to try to achieve media coverage of their promotions. It is increasingly common for promotions to be featured in advertising. Hybrid communications – combining sales promotion with advertising, direct mail, publicity and personal selling – are not the exception but the rule.

A sales promotional offer does not cease to be a sales promotional offer because you use advertising, publicity, personal selling and direct

The old four Ps

The new marketing mix

Figure 2   *The difference between the four Ps model and the
new model of marketing*

marketing to get it across to your target market. Does that mean, though, that they are all promotions and nothing else? Of course not: they are promotions-in-advertising, promotions-in-publicity and so forth.

Sales promotion is not one part of the communications mix. Rather, it is about making short-term changes to one or more parts of the whole marketing mix – to the product, the packaging, the price, the distribution and the advertising – all in the interests of influencing behaviour now. That is what makes it so effective – and also so risky.

VALUE AND PRICE

The Institute of Sales Promotion – the body that brings together all the major sales promotion practitioners in the UK – gives this definition: 'Sales promotion is a range of tactical marketing techniques designed within a strategic framework to add value to a product or service in order to achieve specific sales and marketing objectives'.

The key phrase is 'add value'. That is something that every business does in order to pay for its costs and make a profit. It is the basis for Value Added Tax – the tax on the difference between a firm's input and output costs. Unfortunately, not all sales promotions add value, and many reduce rather than add to the value of a product or service. They offer money off in one way or another.

Price promotions can seriously undermine the added value that years of advertising have built up. A study conducted by Andrew Ehrenberg at the London Business School in 1991 showed that most price promotions helped in the short term, but ended up lowering the price people were prepared to pay for brands.[7] Many advertisers believe that sales promotion is a short-term fix that detracts from long-term brand building. David Ogilvy, founder of Ogilvy & Mather, summed it up as follows: 'In 1981, US manufacturers spent 60 per cent more on promotion than on advertising, and distributed 1,024,000,000,000 coupons. Bloody fools.'[8]

Unfortunately, Ehrenberg looked at only one type of sales promotion – price promotion. This type of promotion affects the *economic* dimension of the product or service. It offers it at reduced price or with a favourable finance deal or on a buy-now, pay-later basis or with a coupon against the present or future purchase. In doing so, it can often have a negative impact on brand value – particularly if it is a 'me too' price offer.[9]

The second type of promotion affects the *functional* or *psychological* dimensions of the product or service. It offers it with extra features, such as a free mail-in item, a chance to win a prize, a special container or some other benefit over and above the normal product offering. In doing so, it often has a positive impact on brand value.

The difference between the two has been confused by the names people have given them. John Quelch, the Harvard academic, calls the first type 'price cut' and the second type 'added value'.[10] Jim Porteous at Nestlé calls the first type 'value' and the second type 'style'. I will follow Quelch in calling those promotions that essentially alter the price of the product 'price promotions' and those that essentially give an extra benefit 'value promotions'. The difference between the two can be seen clearly in this list of promotional techniques.

Price promotions:

- money off coupons
- pence off flashes
- buy one, get one free
- extra fill packs.

Value promotions:

- free draws
- mail-in premiums
- container promotions
- competitions.

Of course, any classification has an arbitrary side to it. Some people think that extra-fill packs ('33% extra free') belong in the 'value', not the 'price' category. If you want to put them there, you will be in good company – but remember that they can reduce the price people are prepared to pay for the standard size, and that can come to the same thing as a price cut.

The logic of value promotions is clear to see. There is evidence that these not only contribute to short-term sales, but to long-term brand value. The 'Hayfever Survival' campaign (Case Study 4) is an excellent example. The case for price promotions is more difficult, and the criticisms made by Ehrenberg, Ogilvy and others must be taken seriously.

Why do companies use promotions that can undermine brand value? The reason is competition. For most of the post-war period, the detergent manufacturers Procter & Gamble and Lever Brothers have been locked in a titanic battle. Their leading brands have competed for performance superiority, communicated by single-minded product-performance advertising. The classic 'side by side' comparisons of clothes washed in Daz against those washed in another powder were once considered a definitive form of TV advertising. Product innovation has been far-reaching and relentless.

These two giants have also spent massively on price promotion. In the early 1960s, 95 per cent of packs of Procter & Gamble and Lever Brothers' detergents carried a price promotion offer of one kind or another – from a pence off flash to a discount off next purchase. The situation was mad – and known to be mad. One day it stopped: Daz launched a 'near-pack' premium promotion involving plastic flowers (Case Study 18). Millions of families collected plastic roses from Daz in the following years. By the late 1970s, however, the majority of detergent packs once again featured pence off flashes and coupons. Retailers have also veered between price and value promotions. Case Study 15 looks at 20 years of Tesco's promotional activity, which has swung between the two.

Sometimes price promotions can be catastrophic for the company concerned. In 1996, the electrical retailer Comet made an offer for its competitor, Norweb. Norweb held out for more, which was refused, and then began an extensive campaign of 0 per cent finance offers (see Chapter 9 for details of how these work). Comet decided not to match them. Instead, whenever a customer asked about finance, they directed them to Norweb. Comet's margins went up, and Norweb was crippled by the cost of its promotion. Soon afterwards, Comet was able to buy Norweb at a lower price than it had offered before.

What do these stories tell us? Price promotions can drag a company or a whole industry into penury. However, they are not the cause of penury. Rather, they are the symptom of a competition that is so intense that it lays hold of every tool at its disposal – even if some of them are self-destructive. Price promotions are not the ideal way of competing. They are sometimes unavoidable in the marketplace. It makes it even more important to understand how they work, and the circumstances in which they can be less rather than more destructive (Chapter 9 explains how to do this).

One of the things to watch is the evidence from opinion polls that people prefer price cuts to any other form of promotion. Sometimes companies make use of this in their advertising. During the spate of petrol promotions in 1986–87, Jet ran a series of poster ads with the slogan '98 per cent of motorists prefer cheaper petrol'. Not for us, they were saying, all those tacky gimmicks; we just offer lower prices. Shell meanwhile achieved huge gains in market share with its 'Make money' promotion. People may say they prefer cheaper petrol (attitude), but they often buy more expensive petrol supported by promotional offers (behaviour). In 1997, Shell and Esso were taking two very different approaches to this – one with a value promotion, the other with a price promotion (Case Study 13). It's interesting to note that Jet was also actively engaged in value promotions, winning a European sales promotion award for its non-price collector promotion.

Keeping the distinction between price and value promotions clearly in mind is essential to making sense of the subject. The core of sales promotion is the attempt to influence behaviour here and now, and these are the two ways you can do it. It may contribute to a change in attitude, but that is not its primary task. A definition you may like to consider would run like this: sales promotion is a range of price and value techniques designed within a strategic framework to achieve specific objectives by changing any part of the marketing mix, normally for a defined time period.

TACTICS AND STRATEGY

Tactics

Sales promotion has often been seen as one of the short-term, tactical weapons available to businesses. As such, it has enormous strengths, but there is a real dilemma. Change the marketing mix too often, and the brand loses its identity. Change it too little, and you can be overtaken by more flexible competitors. Sales promotion is a tool that cuts across all the components of the brand. That is why the balance of tactics and strategy is so important in using sales promotion effectively.

Business success is always an interplay between short term and long term, tactical and strategic. Companies succeed by thinking about tomorrow, but they fail if, in so doing, they forget about today; and the reverse is also true. The best strategy is always adaptive.

Sales promotion shares with direct marketing the benefit that it can achieve short-term effects, that campaigns can be conceived and implemented in a matter of days, and that the result can be seen in a matter of weeks. As such, sales promotion fits well with a 'just-in-time' approach to business, which is already familiar in manufacturing stock control and delivery cycles.

Taking a tactical approach to sales promotion means having up your sleeve a number of promotional concepts that can be put into effect as and when they are called for. Large manufacturing companies approach this by issuing their salesforce with a range of promotions in concept form that can be put into effect with particular retailers whenever the sales situation demands. It also means having the imagination, speed and resourcefulness to react quickly to competitive pressure and to seize short-term market opportunities. These are tactics at their best, but does that mean sales promotion is not strategic?

Strategies

Any business activity benefits from being planned in a strategic manner. Strategy, as John Kay points out, is not another word for important. It is about identifying the firm's distinctive capabilities, and translating them into competitive advantage in the relationships the firm has with its customers and suppliers. It's about what you – and only you – do best.

Sales promotion is strategic if it enhances the firm's distinctive capabilities, increases its competitive advantages and builds its long-term relationships. It is the reverse if it undermines them. That can easily happen in sales promotion. A cut-price offer on a prestige brand, a promotion that is badly administered and leaves customers feeling aggrieved, an offer that promises more than it delivers – all these can undermine long-term relationships. A feeble 'me too' offer copied from a competitor can undermine distinctive positioning.

Frequently, the characteristics of a good tactical promotion are the characteristics of a good strategic promotion. A good promotion can be both tactical and strategic: ('Hayfever Survival', Case Study 4, is an example). A bad one can be both bad tactics and bad strategy (Hoover's free flights promotion, Case Study 11, is an example of this).

There are several reasons for taking a strategic approach to planning sales promotions. It enables one offer to build on the previous one, and to establish a continuity of communication. This makes it more possible to communicate long-term psychological values, making promotions work harder. It can produce considerable savings in time and money, and can speed up response times. Strategic planning also enables promotional offers to be fully integrated into the other activities in the marketing programme.

Sadly, this is not always done, even by the largest companies. This is often because responsibility for sales promotion is pushed down to junior staff, whose time horizons are shorter, who change jobs more frequently and who have not been briefed properly on strategic issues. This is a pity: it makes promotions less effective, and does not reflect the importance of sales promotion in business today. The remedy lies in the hands of senior management. Those charged with responsibility for sales promotion need to understand the relationships they are dealing with.

There are five things you should do in order to establish a strategic approach to sales promotion:

■ understand the strategic framework in terms of competitive advantage and positioning that should underpin every promotion

■ establish guidelines for each product or service, determining the style of sales promotion that will be appropriate to it

■ ensure that sales promotions are handled or overseen by a sufficiently senior executive so that they are conceived and implemented professionally

- insist that sales promotions are researched and evaluated in a way that enables you to assess their performance, and compare it to other types of marketing expenditure

- plan and budget for your use of sales promotion over the year ahead so that the promotions become integral to your marketing effort.

Most of this book details how to run promotions one by one. These are the building blocks for strategic promotional planning. It is well worth taking a look at the promotions your company has run over a longish period – say five years – and asking how they have contributed to its long-term differential advantage. Were they good tactics and good strategy? That is the goal to search for.

SALES PROMOTION AND ETHICS

In 1993, Hoover launched a 'free flights' promotion. There is nothing wrong in that. Free flights are a promotional evergreen (and are described in detail in Chapter 7). What characterized Hoover's promotion in the first instance was the unsustainably generous terms of the offer. What characterized it in the years that followed was the inadequate way in which the company handled its failure. Case Study 11 spells out the sorry tale.

There is always a temptation in sales promotion, as in many other areas of business, to cut corners, to promise more than you intend to give, to rely on the small print as a get-out. Is this good business if you can get away with it? Some people think so, but they are a declining minority. The reason is that relationships are increasingly seen as central to business success. It is unwise to treat badly those with whom you want to build up a long-term relationship.

In 1996, the Royal Society of Arts published a report entitled 'Tomorrow's Company' with backing from some of Britain's top business leaders.[11] This argued that successful companies are those that have a 'success model' that embraces the interests of all their stakeholders – shareholders, customers, suppliers, employees and community. A study of America's most visionary companies in 1996 found that those businesses that were consistently most successful were the ones that did not place profit first, but in second place to a core ideology that often stressed responsibility to others.[12]

Across the world, there is evidence that people prefer to deal with companies they trust. 'The company behind the brand' is increasingly important. Cadbury's has benefited from its association with enlightened social policies throughout its history – a point strongly made in its factory exhibition, 'The Cadbury Experience', visited by 450,000 people a year. Richard Branson's rating as Britain's most admired business leader has helped Virgin diversify from records to air travel to personal finance and drinks.

An ethic of enlightened self-interest guides companies not to abuse customer relationships by subjecting them to sharp sales promotional practice. However sales promotion practitioners have another and more specific ethical challenge to consider. If sales promotion is effective in changing behaviour, it is a powerful and double-edged weapon that can change behaviour for the bad as well as the good.

Some sales promotion agencies refuse to handle tobacco accounts on the grounds that promotions may reinforce a destructive form of behaviour. Other areas in which behaviour can be influenced to the detriment of wider social interests are the consumption of alcohol and participation in lotteries. On the other hand, sales promotion has been used for purposes that have a positive social benefit. Case Study 3 features a promotion for Sainsbury's that helped both schools and the re-use of plastic bags.

Sales promotion in the UK is largely guided by internal self-regulation, policed by the industry via the Advertising Standards Authority. In most of Europe, there are greater legislative controls. The UK Government elected in May 1997 is not convinced that self-regulation works as well as it could or should in every case. The cases of promotional malpractice cited in Chapter 13 indicate that there are legitimate grounds for concern. Every sales promoter needs to take the power to change behaviour seriously, and to think hard about the purposes to which it is put.

CASE STUDIES

The following three case studies have been chosen to illustrate the central points made in this chapter about relationships, behaviour and the capacity of sales promotion to change every other part of the marketing mix. As you read them, ask yourself the questions at the end of each case study, and then consider these two overall questions:

- What impact did each of these three promotions have on the quality of the relationship between the companies and their customers?

- In what ways were these three promotions both strategic and tactical?

CASE STUDY 1: MAXWELL HOUSE

Maxwell House competes in the highly competitive instant coffee market, dominated by Nestlé's Nescafé. It was relaunched in 1992 with an improved product formulation, a blue packaging theme, the proposition of 'mountain-grown taste' and TV advertising featuring the Maxwell House hot air balloon. However, the brand still faced the pressures that face number two brands generally. How was it to persuade repertoire purchasers (those who buy Nescafé and other brands from time to time) to buy Maxwell House? And how was it to persuade existing users to buy the brand more often?

Triangle Communications' answer was a major promotional event that took place on-pack, on TV and in events round the country. Its title was 'Out of the blue'. The basic mechanic was a free draw. Consumers were invited to win £500,000 of cash prizes by entering via on-pack coupons or 'plain paper' (which means those who had not bought the product could enter by writing in on a piece of paper). Noel Edmonds phoned 100 winners 'out of the blue' from the Maxwell House hot air balloon. The phone calls were featured on TV ads as a live dialogue, giving viewers the responses of winners to hearing they had won cash prizes of £2000 to £10,000. Meanwhile, the balloon made a series of visits to events round the country, creating a direct link between brand, balloon and offer.

The novelty of the delivery of the free draw created extensive PR coverage. 500,000 entries were received, the brand achieved its highest market share for six years, and in the promotional period its share was 50 per cent more than it had been the previous month.

This was a free draw on a massive scale, but the mechanic was simplicity itself. What characterizes it is the involvement of Noel Edmonds, the novelty of the means of contacting winners, the use of live dialogue on TV and the close link with the brand's mainstream advertising. The promotion won two ISP Gold Awards.

■ How did Maxwell House integrate the sales promotion into the rest of its marketing strategy?

■ What were the advantages/disadvantages of the Maxwell House promotion compared to spending the same amount on mainstream TV advertising?

Agency: Triangle Communications

CASE STUDY 2: BOVRIL

Everyone knows Bovril. It's one of those brands you can't remember not knowing. It's not constantly in your mind, though, and people lose the habit of drinking it. For some years, Bovril has had a strategy of reminding people that when you are cold, wet or in flagging spirits, a drink of Bovril cheers you up, sustains and nourishes you. It is one of those messages that can be put across by advertising, but is very much more powerful when it is experienced.

In 1995, the agency Promotional Campaigns Group tried a new tack. Bovril arranged to offer samples of Bovril at 467 bonfire nights. Bonfire nights are a popular British tradition, celebrated annually on 5 November in memory of a gunpowder plot in the seventeenth century. They are also cold, damp and often wet. Bovril linked with local radio stations and charities organizing firework displays. Kits of paste, cups and promotional material were supplied free. Charities could raise funds by accepting donations for cups of Bovril. Local radio stations were offered the opportunity to provide roadshows at the largest events, and to trail the events with both DJ plugs and paid-for advertising.

Two million people attended the sponsored bonfire nights, and over five million were reached by radio coverage. Thus, 520,000 people were sampled with Bovril at a fraction of the cost of doordrop methods. Sales rose by 4 per cent over the year.

Bovril did not have to create bonfire night – it was already there. The ingenuity of the promotion was recognizing it as a perfect sampling occasion at exactly the right time in the year to promote sales. The executional skill was to provide charities and radio stations with a reason to be involved in the delivery of the promotion. Extended over time, the promotion offered Bovril a direct link with a popular annual tradition.

■ What behaviour was Bovril seeking to change, and how did the promotion seek to change it?

■ What benefits/disadvantages would media advertising have had over the sampling programme Bovril adopted?

CASE STUDY 3: SAINSBURY'S

Sales promotion's capacity to impact directly on consumer behaviour can be used to good ends and bad. Sainsbury's 'Schoolbags' promotion is an example of a promotion that achieved business objectives along with social and environmental ones.

Sainsbury's faced two unrelated challenges in 1995:

■ it needed to increase its appeal to families, which lagged below that of competing supermarkets

■ it needed to tackle the financial and environmental cost of nearly 100 million carrier bags issued every year at a cost of £20 million.

These challenges were brought together by the agency Promotional Campaigns Group in a promotion which provided a reason for families with children both to shop at Sainsbury's and to re-use their carrier bags. The link was raising money to buy equipment for schools.

The mechanic was simple. Customers were offered a 'Schoolbags' voucher at the checkout for every carrier bag they re-used. These vouchers could be used by schools to obtain equipment, starting with a pack of crayons for 120 vouchers. Schools were recruited to the scheme via direct mail, and the promotion was advertised instore, on TV and in the press.

The promotion succeeded in all its dimensions. Over 10 per cent of Sainsbury's carrier bags were re-used, saving 900,000 litres of oil in their manufacture and £2 million in cost. A total of 12,000 schools (about half the total in the country) and a million families participated. The nature of the mechanic will have ensured a substantial incentive to making repeat visits to Sainsbury's. And the schools benefited too: about £4 million of equipment was claimed by them.

This promotion is a good example of hitting more than one objective at the same time, and doing so with a simple mechanic that is easy to communicate via a multiplicity of media.

■ How did Sainsbury's 'Schoolbags' promotion reflect on Sainsbury's core values?

■ What considerations would be involved in making this promotion a permanent feature of Sainsbury's trading?

SUMMARY

This chapter has set out how sales promotion fits into the central business challenge of building relationships that confer differential advantage. It does so as a process that focuses on behaviour, and in two different ways: price promotions and value promotions.

Promotions are primarily tactical in nature, but can be part of long-term strategy. They must be understood in the context of the functional, economic and psychological benefits with which firms seek to meet customer needs.

Promotions are a means of influencing behaviour, and alter every part of the marketing mix to do so.

There are reasonable criticisms of certain types of promotion that undermine rather than enhance brand value. Tacky and dishonest promotions have no place in long-term relationships. The manager who understands the place of sales promotion in the firm's strategy will be best placed to manage the risk of using the many techniques available.

2

HOW TO USE PROMOTIONS

Nobody in business likes giving away something for nothing. So, how do you decide on the objectives for a promotion? How do you work out what it can and cannot achieve? And how do you choose between the many techniques available?

The promotional planning cycle looks like that shown in Figure 3, and the stages are dealt with in turn in the next four chapters. As you go round the cycle in your promotional career, you'll find that you get better at each of the five elements.

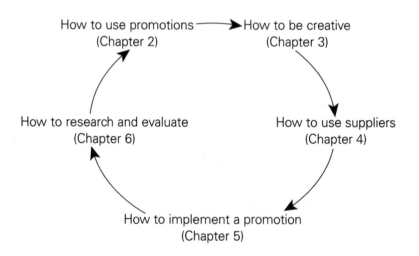

Figure 3 *The promotional planning cycle*

BUSINESS TASKS

This chapter starts with business objectives. There is a crucial distinction between business and promotional objectives.

The business objective is something that derives from your business or marketing plans – such as 'increase volume'. It could be met in many ways, of which sales promotion is just one. It provides the context for promotional thinking.

The promotional objective is much narrower in focus. It is concerned with persuading particular people to buy two of your products when normally they would buy one. It derives from the business objective you have set. It is specifically promotional.

Objectives we choose in our personal lives work in a similar way. You may be reading this book because you want to advance your career in business. Learning about sales promotion follows from that, but it is not the only way you could advance your career. Once you have decided you want to learn about sales promotion, you rightly focus on the best means of achieving it – of which reading this book is one.

This chapter identifies ten business objectives that are most commonly addressed by sales promotion, the mechanics available and how to put them together to achieve the behavioural change that you want. Following this process will not guarantee that your promotion will be a world-beater. However, it will ensure that it is fit for the task, that it logically connects with business objectives.

Whether you intend to devise a sales promotional offer yourself or to brief someone else, the first stage is the same. It involves setting down the answers to the six questions below, preferably on paper. It is just as valid as a brief to yourself as it is as a brief to someone else. And it should be brief – any more than two sides of A4 is long-winded.

- What is the *strategic* nature of the brand – its positioning and differential advantage, its strengths and weaknesses?

- What is the *task* for the promotion – the business problem or opportunity that you intend to tackle?

- Who are the *people* whose behaviour you want to influence? What are they like and what interests them?

- What *behaviour* do you want them to reinforce or change – in other words, what exactly do you want them to do?

- What are the *operational constraints* of the promotion – budget, timings, location, product coverage and logistics?

- How will you *evaluate* the promotion and know whether or not it has achieved the task you set for it?

Business tasks come in a variety of forms. Among the problems may be competitors taking business from you, stocks being slow to move, distribution being lost, sales being sluggish or an expectation that any of these may happen in the near future. Opportunities also come in a variety of forms: to take market share and volume from a competitor, to build awareness, to back up new distribution, to support other marketing activity at point of sale, to build on trial gains.

A clearly defined objective is the justification for spending time and money on promotional activity. Companies sometimes fail to identify that there actually is a business task to be done. A spring promotion may be run simply because there has always been a spring promotion. This may well be a waste of time and money.

Not all objectives are best met by promotional solutions. It may be that advertising is the answer or that there is a fundamental problem with the brand's price, distribution or physical characteristics. No promotion will solve that. However, there are various tasks that are particularly suited to promotional solutions.

It is often said that advertising brings the horse to water and sales promotion makes it drink. Consumers may be predisposed to buy a whole range of products and services now or in the future. Sales promotion focuses their attention on a particular product, at a particular time, in a particular place and provides the incentive to buy at that moment.

Every offer must start by specifying that one or more concrete objectives will be achieved. Time spent in thinking through the objectives, and relating them to your overall marketing strategy, is never wasted. There are ten core objectives that sales promotion typically addresses:

- increasing volume

- increasing trial

- increasing repeat purchase

- increasing loyalty

- widening usage

- creating interest

- creating awareness

- deflecting attention from price

- gaining intermediary support

- discriminating among users.

The three case studies in this chapter have been chosen because they illustrate the selection of promotional objectives and because of the way they make the link between business objectives on the one hand and promotional mechanics on the other. Other case studies in the book illustrate particular objectives, and they are referred to under the descriptions of each objective that now follow.

1 Increasing volume

The volume of product or service that you sell is, in the long run, dependent on a range of fundamental marketing factors, such as quality, price, distribution and value. Promotions geared to increasing volume can never overcome deep-seated competitive weaknesses, but they can be of considerable value in meeting short-term and tactical business needs.

Companies may need to increase volume in the short term for a variety of reasons: to shift stock of an old model prior to a new introduction; to reduce inventories prior to their financial year end; to increase stockholding by consumers and retailers prior to the introduction of a competitor's product; and to lift production on to a new and higher level.

Volume-generating promotions invariably bring in the marginal buyers, those who only buy when a product or service is 'on offer'. These buyers tend to be regarded by many companies with the distaste felt for the morally promiscuous, but they do not form an exclusive group. The more people buy of a particular product category, the more brands within it they tend to buy. We are all promiscuous purchasers to some extent. A volume promotion can bring in marginal buyers to an improved product or service who may well stay with you thereafter.

Almost any promotion that provides an incentive to buy will help to increase volume. Price promotions are often most effective in the short term. They can be aimed at trialists, regular users or new markets; they can put the emphasis on intermediaries or on the final customer; and they can use a very wide range of the offers described in this book. What must be provided is a real and genuine incentive: a low-budget self-liquidator may massage consciences, but it will do nothing to shift volume. Two case studies in this book are examples of non-price volume promotions: Maxwell House (Case Study 1) and Faber & Faber (Case Study 23).

The variety of techniques available to increase volume carries its own weakness. It is better to be specific about where you expect to find the extra volume. This means linking the increased volume objective with one of the other objectives listed below.

2 Increasing trial

A major source of extra volume is those who have not used your product or service before or not used it for a long time. In the case of retailers, they would be people who have not visited your premises before. Increased trial is also a self-standing objective that is fundamental to the growth of any business.

Potential trialists have, by definition, no personal experience of your product or service. They may be using one of your competitor's products or services or none at all in your category. A number of offers are particularly effective in gaining increased trial:

- providing a free sample or a trial coupon so that people can try out your product or service

- providing an additional benefit so that your product or service seems superior to others on the market

- providing short-term, financial benefits, such as good credit rates, so that it seems better value than others

- doing something different and imaginative, such as an open day or special event, that lifts it out of the general run.

Among the examples of trial promotions in this book are 'Bovril's Bang!', Bovril's sampling programme (Case Study 2), and the 'Tango Bash' (Case Study 9). These both focused on giving reasons for people new to (or lapsed from) the brand to try. Offers such as free extra product or those that require the purchase of large quantities of your product or service are unlikely to attract potential trialists. They will not, after all, want to buy it in volume until they know they like it.

3 Increasing repeat purchase

Repeat purchase promotions overlap considerably with volume promotions as existing customers are most likely to be prepared to bring forward their regular purchases and buy in bulk. Repeat purchase promotions are also effective in achieving other marketing objectives, such as spoiling the launch of a competitive product and getting your customers into the habit of using your product to the exclusion of others. This can be particularly important in markets such as the pub trade and frequently purchased confectionery products where people habitually use a range of different brands, chopping and changing between them from day to day (a pattern known as 'repertoire purchasing').

Here are some of the offers that are particularly effective in increasing repeat purchase:

- coupons on the product giving discounts off the next purchase
- specific incentives for multiple purchase – for example, 'buy three, get one free'
- collector promotions, such as collecting ten tokens and sending for a free merchandise or cash refund offer.

Maxwell House (Case Study 1) and Gale's Honey (Case Study 16) are both imaginative examples of promotions that target the need to increase repeat purchase. Promotions that are unlikely to be appropriate for increasing repeat purchase include door-to-door coupon drops and straight pence off flashes. They simply give the regular purchaser a discount without requiring any multiple purchase to take place. This is very nice for the purchasers, but of no use to the promoter.

4 Increasing loyalty

Loyalty to a product or service is a much more subjective and personal quality than repeat purchase. It is possible to buy something on a regular basis because it is the cheapest and best, without feeling any loyalty towards it. Loyalty keeps you buying when (perhaps temporarily) it ceases to be the cheapest and the best.

An example of loyalty occurred in the early 1980s, when Ford replaced the Cortina with the Sierra. The early Sierras suffered from a number of teething troubles, and although Ford did lose market share to Vauxhall's Cavalier, its extent was limited by Ford's high level of loyalty among motorists and fleet buyers. To paraphrase Winston Churchill, anyone can support you when you are right, friends are there to support you when you are wrong.

Loyalty promotions have been adopted by most supermarkets in the UK. They are designed to achieve a high level of personal identification and involvement with your company product or service beyond the collection of points. They tend to be long-running and to become integral to the way purchasers think about the product or service. There are a number of types of promotion that work well in building loyalty:

- long-term collector promotions – where a wide range of merchandise branded with the product or service can be collected

- clubs that people can join, and which offer a range of special benefits; these are particularly effective for children's products

- factory visits, roadshows and other direct-contact promotions, which bring purchasers into personal contact with the people behind the product or service.

A good example of a loyalty promotion is Shell's SMART card (Case Study 13), the two 'Music for Schools' promotions run by Jacob's Club and the Co-op (Case Study 6) are also relevant. In their different ways, they link closely to the interests of their consumers.

Immediate cash discounts to those who are not members of the scheme have no place in loyalty promotions. Their objective is to supersede immediate cash considerations by appealing to longer-term benefits. This is one of the major ways in which value promotions can contribute to long-term brand value.

5 Widening usage

Very often a product or service will be widely used in only one of the many possible ways it could be used. For example, honey is bought by most households very infrequently to use as a spread. A minority of households use it in great quantity as a cooking ingredient. Telling people how to use honey in cooking is therefore an important objective for honey processors.

Sometimes a company will have to widen the usage of a product or service because its original use is fast disappearing. The transatlantic shipping companies had to do this when people stopped perceiving ships as a mode of travel, and had to start perceiving them as a form of holiday. Sales promotions can be very effective in widening the usage of a product or service in a number of ways:

- by physically linking the product or service with something else already in the new usage area; for example, issuing trial samples with another product

- by offering books or pamphlets that are of value in themselves and explain new ways to use the product or service; for example, a 'cooking with honey' cookbook

- by creating a non-physical link with something else already in the new usage area, via coupons or joint promotions with another company; for example, coupons from a travel agent for winter ski gear.

Widening usage will almost always be achieved by a combination of promotional tools, including advertising and publicity. There is often huge consumer resistance to overcome – for example, to the idea that you should put Mars bars in the fridge or drink sherry with a mixer. The Lee & Perrins promotion for Worcestershire Sauce (Case Study 17) is a good example of extending usage of a very distinctive product.

Pence off or other cash-related promotions will not help at all in this. The right kind of value promotion can encourage purchasers to make the leap and try out the new usage of your product or service. Only when they've done that will they be convinced that what you have said in your advertising is true.

6 Creating interest

This can seem a very woolly objective, and is often avoided in favour of something that seems more specific, such as 'increasing volume'. Many consumer markets are mature and offer limited scope for product differentiation. Providing a reason to buy one product rather than another can be as simple as creating interest and excitement.

It is no accident that our ancestors punctuated the year with a series of festivals, fairs and holy days. Life becomes very boring if it proceeds at a regular, uninterrupted pace. Purchasing products and services is exactly the same. Out of sheer boredom, purchasers can decide to buy something else or go somewhere else. Creating interest in your product or service by means of sales promotion is a way of keeping purchasers with you. It is a matter of ringing the changes, having something fresh to offer, and keeping interest and enthusiasm on the boil.

The principle has long been understood by people who run success-ful businesses. One of Jesse Boot's colleagues recalled the early days of what became the Boots chemists chain in the 1880s: 'Always, Mr Boot had something striking, something to make people talk about Boots.' In our own day, Richard Branson of Virgin has similarly had people talking about his companies as a result of a constant stream of striking innovations, stunts, offers and promotions.

Value promotions that create interest are characterized above all by their humour, inventiveness, topicality and style. Examples include:

- being the first to offer a new product or service as promotional premium
- linking up with a celebrity or relevant charity
- finding a totally new way to do something that people enjoy doing.

British Airway's offer of tickets on Concorde in spring 1997 achieved a massive 30 million responses. Older examples include the treasure hunt for a buried hare featured in the book *Masquerade* and later copied (with disastrous results) by Cadbury's Creme Eggs; the telephone Trivial Pursuit game run by Heineken lager; and the enormously successful 'tiger in your tank' campaign by Esso in the 1960s, which had millions of cars driving around with a tiger tail hanging from their petrol cap. Case studies in this book that share these qualities are the promotions by solicitors Eversheds (Case Study 7) and Smirnoff (Case Study 21).

7 Creating awareness

For new or relaunched products, creating awareness is a key objective. This is a different challenge to that faced on mature brands where the aim is to maintain interest. It is often assumed that creating awareness is a job for media advertising. Sales promotion, it is said, should restrict itself to nuts and bolts matters such as shifting volume and gaining trial. In fact, there are a number of sales promotions that are very effective at making people aware of products:

- joint promotions with another product or service that is already well known in a particular market

- link-ups with charities or voluntary groups that have a relevant image

- the production of books or educational materials for schools and the general public.

Generating awareness is a wholly legitimate business objective, particularly in industries where purchases are infrequent or for new brands. Major brands – for example, The Body Shop, Haagen-Dazs and Swatch watches – were launched and developed largely through promotional activity. In the case of The Body Shop, it included the active engagement of customers in campaigning against animal testing. Haagen-Dazs used placements in leading restaurants and selective arts sponsorship. Swatch hung giant watches from buildings and early on built a customer club.[1] The 'Tango Bash' (Case Study 9) is also an example of this kind of promotion.

Crucial to such ideas is the understanding that people are selective in the attention they pay to advertising. There are more than 9500 brands in the UK that advertise enough for their advertising to be recorded by MEAL. How many can you name? Most people run out of names after a few hundred.[2] Promotional activity can cut through this selective attention.

8 Deflecting attention from price

An obsession with price on the part of your customers is dangerous. It can readily lead to price wars, which have a destructive effect on company profitability. Price wars are a form of mutual masochism into which many industries fall from time to time until, weary and impoverished, they find more sensible ways to compete with each other.

The purpose of a great deal of advertising is to replace price considerations with a focus on features such as quality, brand identity, performance and loyalty. That way companies can both compete effectively and achieve attractive margins.

Both price and value promotions are part of the armoury companies have at their disposal to do this. The key is to offer benefits that justify a higher price, and cost less than an equivalent price cut. If your product is priced at 10p more than your competitor's and that differential cannot be justified on intrinsic grounds, you can either discount by 10p to achieve price parity or offer an extra benefit that costs you 9p or less and looks at least as attractive.

A very wide range of sales promotional offers can achieve this objective. Among the main ones are:

- variations on price cuts, ranging from 'pence off next purchase' and 'buy three, get one free' to cash-back or cash share-out offers, that appear more valuable than a straight price cut

- making price comparisons less direct, by offering extra-fill packs or short-term multipacks or joint packs or by offering part of the product or service free for example

- long-term collector promotions, such as Shell's SMART card promotion (Case Study 13) or Green Shield stamps (Case Study 15), which can seem more interesting than price cuts.

SMP's promotion for Gale's Honey (Case Study 16) is a good example of deflecting attention away from the premium price of branded honey. It is a constant challenge for manufacturers of brands in markets in which retailers' own-label products have taken a significant share. Part of the success of Kleenex Facial Tissues in the last ten years has been the extent to which its active promotional campaigns have limited the market share of cheaper own-label tissues (Case Study 4).

9 Gaining intermediary support

Some products and services rely very heavily on the support of wholesalers, distributors, agents, retailers and other intermediaries. Others, sold directly to the end-user, rely less heavily on, but still benefit from, the support and recommendation of other businesses. And every business benefits from word-of-mouth recommendation from one satisfied customer to another.

All these people can be regarded as intermediaries. Gaining their support ranges from being absolutely critical to simply important, and there is a range of sales promotion techniques that businesses can use to this end. Among the key ones are:

- specific programmes directed at wholesalers, retailers, agents and distributors to gain distribution, display and cooperative advertising

- 'member get member' schemes, which reward customers for introducing new people to you

- promotional events aimed at the media and other influencers on decision making.

Gaining display is a central objective for promotions run by manufacturers who sell via retailers, wholesalers, distributors or other intermediaries. It is often the display that results in extra sales, but the promotion that secured the display in the first place.

Display can take many forms: extra shelf space, gondola end (the end of a shelving rack), a window bill, the display of door stickers, the use of point-of-sale material, the presence of leaflets, the installation of a dumpbin or special display rack. It is all about achieving extra prominence for your product or service.

A number of promotional offers are effective in achieving display:

- incentives directed at store managers and sales assistants

- price offers that enhance the margin to the intermediary

- the production of attractive, compelling offers of every kind that the intermediary believes will provide them with an advantage – tailor-made promotions, which run only in one store group, are particularly effective.

There is a close relationship between trade and consumer promotion in the retail trade. If a promotion succeeds with the trade, but lacks a strong consumer element, it may still succeed with the consumer – simply because of the display and volume support of the retailer. However, the reverse is not true: a promotion with a strong consumer element that does not appeal to the trade is unlikely to succeed with either.

Examples of effective promotions to intermediaries include Zantac 75 (Case Study 5) and the Electrolux campaign for the X8 (Case Study 20).

10 Discriminating among users

A large number of businesses – such as hotels, airlines, train companies and leisure facilities – face three unavoidable market factors. They have a high percentage of fixed costs in providing the service, which do not vary significantly with the number of people using it. Usage varies considerably from time to time. Also, different people are prepared to pay different amounts for the service and accept different levels of restriction.

This last factor enables businesses to manage fluctuations in demand. The price paid for an airline ticket varies depending on the time and day of the flight, the degree of flexibility allowed, how long in advance the ticket was booked, the type of seat purchased, the purchaser's participation in a loyalty scheme and the outlet where it was booked. The objective that airlines and similar businesses share is to maximize the revenue per seat – and that means avoiding giving better terms to those who do not need them at the same time as giving the optimum terms to those who do.

For these businesses, sales promotional thinking is at the heart of marketing strategy, and they use a number of mechanisms:

- customers who are motivated by price are self-selected – they book early or via particular outlets and so on – while those who are less motivated by price do not bother with these aspects

- the difference between business and leisure travel is marked by requirements to spend a Saturday night away to qualify for leisure pricing; business users are, in turn, given special discounts on leisure flights

- particular groups are given additional benefits not available to others – for example, families and the retired can buy train tickets at a price not available to a group of adults travelling together.

Pursued to its logical conclusion, discriminating among users allows companies to develop particular packages of product, price, distribution and promotion for different categories of user. The major challenge is to keep the boundaries between them clear, so that those prepared to pay higher prices do not take advantage of lower prices. This in turn means that offers are often deliberately short-term, focusing the benefits on those most motivated to take advantage of them.

PROMOTIONAL OBJECTIVES

At any given time, it will be possible to specify which of these ten objectives most coincides both with your overall business strategy and with the problems or opportunities you have selected as the task for the promotion. It is vital to be selective about this. Sales promotion agencies are sadly familiar with briefs that specify the objectives (often for a small-budget promotion) as 'to increase trial and repeat purchase, increase loyalty and increase trade distribution'. Desirable as it may be to do all these things, it is difficult to shoot at four goals at once.

If your business objective does not overlap with any of these ten, it may be that you do not have a promotional brief, but a brief for some other kind of marketing activity – or, indeed, for a rethink of your business as a whole.

Taking the objectives seriously means quantifying what the promotion is expected to achieve. For example, if the objective is increasing trial, it is important to specify how many trialists are sought, where they are to be found and the quantity of products or services they are expected to consume. Quantifying the objectives at the beginning enables you to measure and monitor the success of the promotion (a subject explored in Chapter 6).

It is now possible to ask the central promotional question: 'Who do I want to do what?' This is when you move from the business objective to the promotional objective. The transition comes when you start thinking about the people who will help you achieve your business objective and the things you want them to do so that you can achieve it.

Figure 4 shows the movement of a confectionery item from factory to end-user. Similar flow charts could be drawn up for the movement of any other product or service; some would be simpler, some more complicated. At each point on the flow chart, there is a number of people. These form the target for promotional activity.

In using the flow chart, it is important to ask yourself four questions.

Figure 4 *Flow chart of the journey of a confectionery item from factory to end-user*

■ Who holds the key to the business problem? Is it the end-user or the retailer? The buyer or the depot? Is it the consumer?

■ Who else on the chain has leverage? Is it a boss or other staff member? Is it children or friends? Who are they with when they are making the decision that I am interested in?

■ What are these people like? What other things do they do with their time? What are their motivations, interests and desires? What is holding them back from behaving as I would like them to behave?

■ What exactly do I want them to do? Buy one product or more? Use it more frequently or for the first time? Put it on display or tell their friends about it?

Achieving behavioural change requires a high level of focus on these questions. It is the point at which marketing thinking moves from the general to the particular. It is no longer a matter of market share, penetration, segmentation and the other abstract categories. It is now about Julie Smith and her son Wayne trying to get the shopping done on a busy Thursday afternoon in Tesco in Birmingham, and spending less than a minute passing the gondola on which your product is located. What will make her choose one brand of vinegar rather than another? Will it be a coupon sent door-to-door, a Tesco multibuy or an on-pack offer (if you can persuade Tesco to take it)? Sarson's vinegar found a particular solution to these questions with its 'Shake on the Sarson's' promotion (Case Study 22).

In the office stationery market, it is about the same Julie putting in an order for that week's needs for the small computer consultancy where she works part-time. What will make her choose one brand of sticky tape over another? Will it be an 'extra free' offer, a handy container, a straight discount or a personal benefit for her (if her employers will allow it)? Sellotape's 10,000 Lottery Chances (Case Study 14) provides one promotional solution.

In the pub market, it is about the same Julie and her friends having a night out in a large, modern suburban theme pub. What will encourage her to try out one brand of drink in preference to another? What will encourage her to try another within the limits of safe drinking? Colour by Smirnoff (Case Study 21) is an example of focusing on the particular characteristics of groups of young people in pubs.

In none of these cases is Julie alone. In the supermarket she is accompanied by Wayne. At work she is answerable to her boss. In the pub she is part of a group of friends. The social relationships of mother, employee and friend are very different and have different impacts on the way Julie will make her decision to choose one brand over another. Understanding the relationships and the contexts is crucial to finding the right means of encouraging Julie to do the thing you want her to do.

Thinking through Julie's needs and interests in relation to your business objectives is the key to promotional creativity, and is the subject of the next chapter.

PROMOTIONAL MECHANICS

Thinking about the variety of intermediaries and consumers you may want to influence, their relationships and lifestyles, creates a bewildering number of options. After all, people are varied. The other side of the coin is the distinctly limited number of mechanics that are available in sales promotion.

A 'mechanic' in sales promotion refers to the particular things that consumers have got to do – in other words, a competition is a mechanic and so is a free mail-in. There are surprisingly few mechanics available, and all promotions use one or more of them. In many parts of the EU, the number of mechanics available to you is further limited by law. Objecting to one of them on the grounds that it has been used before is like objecting to a newspaper ad because newspaper ads have been used before.

The creativity and interest of a promotion does not lie in the mechanic itself, but in its relevance to your promotional objectives and to your target market, in the way you tweak it and vary it, in the content of an offer, and in the way you put it across. For that reason, mechanics are discussed throughout the rest of the book in the context of actual offers.

Sales promotion has already been divided into price and value promotions. Mechanics can also be divided into those that impact immediately at the point of purchase and those that give a delayed benefit. Mechanics can then be classified as shown in Table 2.

Table 2 *Classification of promotion mechanics*

Promotional type	*Immediate*	*Delayed*
Value	Free in-pack Reusable container Instant win Home sampling Free on-pack	Free mail-in Competition Free draw Self-liquidator Charity promotion
Price	Pence off flash Buy one, get one free Extra-fill packs In-store coupon Finance offer	Next purchase coupon Cash refund Cash share-out Buy-back offer

Table 3 matches ten key mechanics to the ten objectives described in the previous section. The matching ranges from 0 (not well matched) to 10 (very well matched). The ratings can be used as a rough guide to suitability. Very often, it is the creative execution of a mechanic rather than the mechanic itself that is most effective at, for example, creating interest. Clearly, high-cost promotions like immediate free offers, are more effective on almost every criterion than low-cost promotions, such as self-liquidators.

If you have followed this process, you will have a clear promotional objective in mind, and you will have had an initial look at the mechanics that could meet it. Now it is time to look at matching the two together in an imaginative and effective way: it is time to see how to be creative.

CASE STUDIES

Every promotion in this book has something to say about the link between business objectives, promotional objectives and mechanics. Use the following questions to identify what it is in particular that these three case studies illuminate.

■ From the evidence presented, how successful were the three promotions in achieving their objectives?

■ What other mechanics could their agencies have considered to achieve those objectives?

Table 3 *Linking the objectives to the mechanics: how they match up*

	Mechanics								
Objectives	*Immediate free offers*	*Delayed free offers*	*Immediate price offers*	*Delayed price offers*	*Finance offers*	*Competitions*	*Games and draws*	*Charitable offers*	*Self-liquidators*
Increasing volume	9	7	9	7	5	1	3	5	2
Increasing trial	9	7	9	2	9	2	7	7	2
Increasing repeat purchase	2	9	2	9	5	3	2	7	3
Increasing loyalty	1	9	0	7	3	3	1	7	3
Widening usage	9	5	5	2	3	1	5	5	1
Creating interest	3	3	3	2	2	5	9	8	8
Creating awareness	3	3	3	1	1	5	9	8	8
Deflecting attention from price	9	7	0	7	7	3	5	5	2
Gaining intermediary support	9	5	9	5	9	3	7	5	1
Discriminating among users	1	9	1	9	9	3	3	5	1

Each number represents a rating from 0 (not well matched) to 10 (very well matched). Use it as a ready reckoner for linking your objective to the mechanics available.

CASE STUDY 4: KLEENEX FACIAL TISSUES

This case study covers seven years of the 'Hayfever survival' promotion, run since 1991 by Kimberly-Clark, manufacturers of the leading brand of tissues, Kleenex Facial Tissues. Created by The Blue-Chip Marketing Consultancy, it is a rare story of consistent promotional development.

The original brief was simple and focused: to build a strategic platform to sell Kleenex tissues in the summer. Why hayfever? About 10 per cent of the population suffer from it, concentrated in particular geographical areas and on particular days when the pollen count is high. They are heavy users of tissues, but responsible for a small percentage of volume. Focusing on hayfever gave Kleenex tissues a promotional theme in the summer that used the demands of extreme product usage as a metaphor for best quality, softness and strength. While focusing on the hayfever sufferer, the offer had to appeal to all buyers of tissues.

The promotional offer in 1991 was for a free hayfever 'survival kit' in return for three proofs of purchase. It comprised a toiletries bag containing an Optrex eye-mask, Merethol Lozenge pack, travel pack of Kleenex tissues, money off coupons for sunglasses and a room ionizer, and a 20-page hayfever guide from the National Pollen and Hay Fever Bureau. It was a partnership promotion, in which Optrex and Merethol provided their samples free. Why should they do so? Because Kleenex tissues could sample the hayfever sufferer in a way that no other brand could. Run on 900,000 packs, the promotion produced a 7.7 per cent response.

The 1997 promotion bore a strong similarity to the 1991 promotion, though now running on nearly five million packs and developed to include 'natural remedies'. In return for five proofs of purchase and 50p towards postage, the consumer received a toiletries bag containing an Optrex eye-mask, tube of Halls Mentholyptus, travel pack of Kleenex tissues and a hayfever guide from the renamed National Pollen Centre.

What happened in the intervening five years? It's a fascinating story of how promotions adapt to new needs and new opportunities – and how they can also lose their way.

In 1992, the recession forced a drop in the promotional budget. The toiletries bag was now unaffordable, and consumers were asked for 40p as a contribution towards postage. The contents remained the same, but, to pick up on interest in that year in Europe, the guide became a European hayfever guide, with handy tips for travellers. There was also a new opportunity. Vauxhall had just launched the first family-priced car with a pollen filter, the Corsa. One was made available as the prize in a free draw. Despite this addition, the offer was objectively less valuable to the consumer than in 1991, and redemptions dropped to 3.9 per cent.

Kleenex tissues tried a new tack in 1993 – a two-level offer. A new hayfever guide was available for one proof of purchase, and a set of samples for three proofs of purchase and 40p. A strong profile was given to an 0891 (premium rate) 'pollen line'. The creative treatment also changed. From focusing on 'hayfever survival', it now focused on 'those critical days' when the pollen count is at its highest. Extended to four million packs, the two-level offer was not a success. Redemption dropped to 0.3 per cent for the guide only, and 1.3 per cent for the sample kit.

This caused a rethink for the 1994 promotion. Providing a clear and uncomplicated incentive to trial and repeat purchase became the priority. The 0891 number was dropped in favour of a link with the *Daily Mail* and Classic FM. The sample pack was slimmed to a new hayfever guide and three samples – Kleenex tissues, Optrex and Strepsils. The central offer was a high-quality AM/FM radio consumers could use to find out the pollen count. It could all be obtained for £3.50 plus five proofs of purchase. The 'hayfever survival' theme was prominently back. Response increased to 1.7 per cent, despite the higher requirement made on the consumer for both proofs of purchase and cash contribution.

This was not to last. In 1995, the focus of the offer changed significantly. The central offer was a 'pollen filter' Vauxhall Corsa to be won each week for the ten weeks of the 'pollen season' in a free draw. The runners up – 10,000 of them – received hayfever survival kits that included a new hayfever guide. The pollen count information was still there, but reduced in profile. In 1996, the free draw mechanic stayed the same, but 10 'hayfever-free' family holidays replaced the Vauxhalls as the prizes in the free draw. Redemptions were 9.5 per cent in 1995 and 6.4 per cent in 1996. Unlike previous years, they included the option of 'plain paper' entries and did not require even one proof of purchase.

Then, in 1997, the wheel turned full circle. The promotion was a virtual remake of 1991, heavily focused on hayfever survival, offering high-quality samples in a high-quality bag in return for a significant number of proofs of purchase. The major addition was strongly featured pollen count information in partnership with the *Daily Express* and Talk Radio.

What has happened to the brand in this seven-year period? Its share of the branded tissue sector has increased from 50 per cent in 1990 to over 70 per cent in 1996, recording increases every year. Its share of the total market increased to over 40 per cent. Critical to this has been the brand's success in attracting extra volume from the 50 per cent of consumers who buy both Kleenex tissues and own-label tissues. Other factors are undoubtedly present, including product quality and product innovation – notably the launch of Kleenex Ultra tissues in 1995. However, sales promotion has been one of the key marketing weapons throughout this period and must take a major share of the credit.

Did the promotions lose their way in 1995 and 1996, when the mail-in was replaced by a free draw? On the surface, it looks like it, but it is hard to see that a single mechanic could have been maintained without declining returns. A single mechanic would also have been unlikely to have achieved the scale of media coverage the campaign has enjoyed, extending to over 100 publications a year. Operating on-pack, at point of sale, in the media and with third-party endorsers, it has been a thoroughly integrated promotion. The challenge for the future will be to keep the hayfever theme consistently fresh and relevant to both the brand and its consumers.

Three factors that stand out in this case study will undoubtedly help: the ability to seize new opportunities, such as the launch of the Corsa; the proactive relationship with third parties, including pharmaceutical and media partners; and the close partnership that Kimberly-Clark has formed with The Blue-Chip Marketing Consultancy. Unsurprisingly, it is the UK's most acclaimed promotion, winning 11 awards, including an ISP Grand Prix and two on a European level. It is a fine example of sales promotion in action.

- What changed and what remained constant in the business object-ives behind the 'Hayfever Survival' promotions?

- How many mechanics did Kimberly-Clark use over the seven years, and why were they used?

CASE STUDY 5: ZANTAC 75

Zantac 75 is a remedy for indigestion and heartburn that was launched in 1994 as an over-the-counter (OTC) version of Zantac, the leading prescription medicine. OTC products are medicines that the consumer buys without a prescription, but not on open shelves. The consumer must ask the pharmacist or pharmacy assistant for them, and will often seek their advice.

The difficulty Zantac 75 faced was that the product story was com-plicated. There were seven training manuals for sales reps to read. Unless reps could talk knowledgeably about the product to pharmacists, there was little chance that they would stock or display it, let alone recommend it to consumers.

The promotional objective was simple: to ensure that reps were fully educated about Zantac 75 and able to present it effectively to pharm-acists.

The Promotional Campaigns Group's solution was an e-mail game that took the theme of Zantac 75's world leadership in the prescription market.

Each rep chose a world leader from a list that included Margaret Thatcher, Boris Yeltsin and Nelson Mandela. This identity was flashed on their laptop computers every day. Every three days, a new episode of an amusing story about world leaders was sent by e-mail. The script was tailored to each rep's personality to increase involvement. Product learning was reinforced by questions from an imaginary Home Office, Treasury and Foreign Office.

All the reps participated, scoring an average of 90 per cent correct answers. Within four months, Zantac 75 had achieved 100 per cent distribution in independent pharmacists, and within six months it was the second most recommended brand of indigestion remedy in the UK.

Boring people into learning is hard work for learner and teacher alike. This promotion used a novel technique to make learning fun. It focused on product knowledge as the critical issue for the brand at that point in its life, and delivered the goods. Pensions companies that are counting the cost of poorly trained reps could well learn from this case.

- How had the manufacturers of Zantac 75 answered the 'Who do I want to do what?' question, and with what result?

- How many categories of intermediary were involved in selling Zantac 75 to the consumer, and how did the promotion relate to their different needs?

CASE STUDY 6: MUSIC FOR SCHOOLS

In 1996/7, schools were offered two entirely unconnected opportunities to build their collection of musical instruments. Both picked up on research evidence that schools were short of musical instruments and valued them highly. The promotions from Jacob's Club and the Co-op offer a contrast in objectives and execution round an identical theme.

Jacob's Club is the third biggest chocolate biscuit brand with a 6 per cent market share. It is constantly faced with the challenge of larger brands and new entrants into a highly competitive market. Half its volume is purchased for use in lunchboxes.

Its promotional objectives included achieving a sales uplift of 25 per cent, increasing consumption in lunchboxes, and reinforcing its family/caring image. The promotion devised by Clarke Hooper – printed on 150 million packs – invited consumers to take the wrappers to school. The school could in turn redeem them for musical instruments. Direct mail to 25,500 schools resulted in 30 per cent of them registering. Telephone follow-up increased that to 90 per cent.

The promotion ran from August 1996 to May 1997. Nearly 14,000 schools claimed a total of 36,000 instruments worth over £800,000 at retail price. The entry point was low – a descant recorder worth £6.99 could be obtained for 295 wrappers, a spend of £29. Brand volume rose by 52 per cent during the promotional period, and household penetration rose by two-thirds.

The Co-operative Retail Trading Group (CRTG), which provides buying and promotional support for leading Co-ops, faces a squeeze from more powerful multiple retailers. It has the particular problems that its coverage is not universal (not all Co-ops belong to CRTG) and that its sales immediately before Christmas decline as shoppers go to larger superstores. Its objectives were to retain family shoppers and to reinforce its historically close links with the community.

The Continuity Company's promotion for CRTG was targeted at 16,000 schools near to the 1300 participating Co-op stores. Recruitment was by direct mail, followed up by postal reminders. A total of 9000 schools registered. The mail-out to schools included posters, wallcharts and A5 leaflets to send home with each child. Co-op shoppers obtained one voucher with every £10 spent, which schools could redeem for instruments. There was a low starting point – just 35 vouchers entitled a school to a £5.99 descant recorder, representing an expenditure of £350.

The Co-op promotion stabilized sales in the period up to Christmas. It also resulted in 190,000 instruments being claimed by schools.

Both promotions were welcomed by schools – 91 per cent told Jacob's that they would participate again, and 98 per cent said the same to the Co-op. Both have a number of factors in common: not being market leaders; appealing to families; having a broadly sharing/community image; and facing intense market competition. It is not surprising that their promotional analysis led them to very similar promotions. Both succeeded against their objectives, and both attracted considerable PR coverage.

There are a number of details that are different, however:

- Jacob's backed the promotion with TV, the Co-op with press
- Jacob's used telephone follow-up, which the Co-op did not
- Jacob's enlisted the support of the Music Industries Association, while the Co-op used the endorsement of celebrities the likes of Richard Baker and Phil Collins
- basically similar descant recorders required £29 to be spent on Jacob's Club, or £350 in Co-op stores.

Does it matter that these very similar promotions ran at the same time? It would have done if they had been run by KitKat and Club or the Co-op and Asda, but Club and the Co-op are in different sectors. Analysis of similar promotional objectives can lead to similar solutions. The executional differences give a good example of how the way in which a promotion is carried out gives the promoter a range of options once the main approach has been decided.

- To what extent were the objectives and business context of Jacob's Bakery and CRTG different in the 'Music for Schools' promotions?

- How did the 'Music for Schools' promotions address the needs of different influencers on the purchase decision?

SUMMARY

Setting out the brief clearly and concisely is an essential first stage in devising a promotion. If the brief is not clear, your promotion will be built on sand. It is easy to miss out this stage if you are devising a promotion yourself, but it is a mistake. A good brief saves time, and well-defined objectives make the selection of mechanics straight-forward.

The business objectives and ten mechanics identified in this chapter do not constitute a rigid grid, but they provide a good checklist for you to develop and apply. The rest of the brief will help you to organize the promotion in detail.

To think through the next chapters, try this exercise. Set out a sample brief for a product you know, and use it as a yardstick to judge the promotions discussed in them.

3

HOW TO BE CREATIVE

What makes an ordinary promotion outstanding? How do you go about the process of translating promotional objectives into an idea that will achieve behavioural change? This is the art of creativity – the subject of this chapter.

TYPES OF CREATIVITY

Creativity is a much misunderstood word. For some people, creativity is the opposite of order and structure. It is thought of as the free expression of feeling, of your deepest self. Some talk about creativity as if it is only found in the visual or dramatic arts, such as painting or dance. They have difficulty thinking of the creativity of the engineer or physicist, let alone of the businessperson. In business, 'creativity' can be understood to mean bending the rules. For example, the 'creative accountant' is a dodgy accountant, not an imaginative and effective accountant.

Advertising people have added to this confusion. 'Creatives' in many agencies are distinguished from the businesspeople, the 'suits'. The background of creatives is normally in visual design, and their hearts may still be there. Awards for creativity given by the Design and Art Direction Association (D&AD) often put a premium on the clever, off-the-wall and fashionable. Every two years, the Institute of Practitioners in Advertising (IPA) runs Advertising Effectiveness Awards.[1] These reward campaigns that achieve the greatest results for sales and profits. Some – but far from all – also win 'creative' awards.

In sales promotion, creativity does not mean free expression, exciting pictures, clever copy or off-the-wall concepts. It certainly does not mean dodgy practices. It means generating the most effective concept possible. In this, it goes back to the original meaning of creation or creativity. Chaucer writes in *The Canterbury Tales* of 'All things as God created, all things in right order'. Bringing into being the wonders of the world out of nothing was what Chaucer had in mind. On a smaller scale, generating something new where nothing was before is at the heart of creativity. It applies as much to the engineer as to the musician. Order, structure and fitness for purpose are not enemies of creativity, but part of it.

Sales promotion, and indeed advertising and PR, communicate with one person at a time, usually the reader of a leaflet, poster, mailshot or press or TV advertisement. But they are not atomized individuals: they are people who build their understanding by means of their interactions with friends, colleagues, families and communities. The more specifically you can define your target audience in both individual and group terms, the more precise will be your creative approach and the more effective your promotion.

If you are going to be responsible for creating a truly effective promotion, you must be really clear about what it is you need to achieve and be capable of imaginative, lateral thinking. If others are to create the promotion for you, then this chapter will help you provide them with the best brief possible.

It is a sad fact of life that as people grow older, fewer and fewer show signs of creative ability. Research has shown that 95 per cent of children show strong creative tendencies, while only 5 per cent of adults show the same traits. We simply become less good at inventing and developing new and original ideas.

This is partly because creativity is the one life skill that has seldom been taught at school or university and partly because our elders and peers stamp it out of us. Remember when you were caught jumping on the settee and told off for doing so? Your mother just saw her child damaging the furniture. You were riding a horse, escaping from the Indians – exercising your creativity.

To create promotions, you do not need to jump up and down on your office chair, however much you might feel like doing so some-times. You do need to suspend belief and really and truly imagine. Experience shows that the latent creative ability can be liberated in most people. There are many exercises and procedures that can help you become more creative, and later in this chapter we shall look at some techniques that will be helpful in a business context. They will help you structure your creative planning to enable you to create a truly great promotion rather than an imitation of someone else's idea.

CREATIVE PROMOTIONS

Truly great ideas stand the test of time. A memorable promotion from nearly 30 years ago was the Osram 'Cash box and key'. This promotion deservedly won an ISP Grand Prix Award in the early 1970s.

Osram had produced a new lightbulb that lasted four times as long as a normal one but cost only twice as much. It was ideal for use in industry where bulbs are often changed all at once, towards the end of their life. Not only would the bulbs be cheaper over a period of time, there would also be considerable savings in labour costs. However, industry was not buying them.

Research indicated that this was because the maintenance department purchased bulbs and were usually instructed by finance departments as to the maximum amount they could pay. Maintenance staff were not allowed to suddenly spend twice as much as normal.

The 'Who do I want to do what?' question led to the answer. Maintenance and financial staff could only agree to buy Osram if they did so together. The solution was to send the chief accountant a cash box and explain that there was information inside the box on how to save more than 50 per cent on bulb replacement. The key was sent to the head of maintenance and this fact was also communicated to the financial officer.

To read the information inside the box, both the financial and maintenance representative had to meet, and they were then in a position to have a short discussion. Was it successful? Of course it was. A neat, elegant solution far more likely to succeed than a simple brochure mailing or trade press campaign.

Another elegant solution involved, of all unlikely things, a wellington boot. Sheraton Securities wanted to attract commercial property agents to visit their greenfield development site. These agents are inundated with similar requests, and are regularly sent brochures and inducements. Sheraton chose to deliver personally one left wellington boot to 50 selected agents. They then advertised in the trade press 'What possible use is one wellie?', stating that the other boot was to be found on their development site. This humorous and off-beat approach succeeded in bringing the agents along.

Ramada opened a new hotel in Manchester in the mid 1980s, shortly after the opening of a major competitor. There are many established hotels in Manchester and the Ramada was just not reaching its targets.

There are innumerable ways of promoting hotels, but one of the best of them is to encourage positive recommendations from existing guests. How, though, can you do that? The bizarre solution was to put a plastic duck in each bathroom and tell the guests, by means of a tent card, that they could keep the duck. Alternatively, if they wished, they could have it sent anywhere in the world in its own special crate for only £2.50 plus postage.

This promotion not only succeeded, it made a profit. The cost of the duck and crate were far less than £2.50 and hundreds were sold to intrigued guests. This promotion also won a European sales promotion Gold Award.

How would you go about sampling thousands of consumers with a new shoe-cleaning pad? Cherry Blossom must have considered door-to-door sample drops, banded offers and all the other techniques. The one they used, however, was to link with the Boy Scouts who, at that time, cleaned people's shoes outside supermarkets during Bob-a-Job week. Simple, cheap and a winner of several awards.

Many people still remember Shell's 'Make Money' promotion in the 1960s in which customers collected halves of banknotes. They could redeem them for their face value if they collected both matching halves. Obtaining that elusive matching £10,000 banknote half became compulsive, driving out any thought of visiting a competing petrol station. This promotion has been run several times in the UK and throughout the world. It works – it works again and again, and it has been copied over and over. It must be a great promotion.

All these promotions have a number of things in common. They are engaging. It is not immediately obvious what they are trying to achieve (the objectives are not showing). They were original when they were first implemented. They are very carefully targeted. The promotions' creators all clearly identified 'Who it was that they wanted to do what'.

The cash box promotion clearly identified that the company wanted the accountants and the maintenance people to meet and discuss the benefits of the new bulb. The developers wanted agents to come to their site. Ramada wanted people to tell their friends and business acquaintances about the new hotel. Cherry Blossom wanted people to try the new product and feel warmly about the company. Shell wanted people to come back to their petrol stations rather than visit those of their competitors.

It is this clarity of thought and clarity of definition of the target audience or, to put it another way, clarity of the promotional objective, that they all have in common. Once that is in place, humour, excitement, style, graphics and copy can be introduced in an appropriate way to enhance the overall offering to the customer. Indeed, it will be easier.

What has clarity of promotional objectives got to do with creativity? Essentially, it is the key to success!

Briefs often state that the objective is to increase sales by X or to increase distribution by Y. As discussed in Chapter 2, these are marketing objectives, not promotional objectives. A promotional objective is the answer to 'Who do I want to do what?' Remember that promotions are about changing behaviour. Setting the right objectives is often truly creative.

THINKING CREATIVELY

Very often, a marketing objective will turn into a number of different promotional objectives as you ask the question 'Who do I want to do what?' This is not a problem unless you try to achieve them all by the same promotion. Note that we are talking here about a promotion and not a promotional theme. You may decide on a theme that has several different promotions targeted at different audiences. Different people in the distribution chain will be motivated in different ways. The wholesaler, the retailer and the consumer all need to be attended to. Also, the same theme can be worked through different promotions over a period of time.

Let's take a typical brief, one that is often proposed by brand managers of lager beer. 'We want to generate sales of X cans during Y period. Our target market is C1/C2 men and women between the ages of 18 and 25.'

Have you ever met a C1/C2, or indeed anyone aged 18 to 25? The group contains postgraduate students, marketing managers, soldiers, lathe operators, nurses, car mechanics, musicians performing classical and heavy metal music, teachers, truck drivers, jockeys, farm workers, photographic models and so on. How can you possibly attract all members of such a diverse group? The only thing they have in common is that they visit pubs and off licences and like to drink lager. Think of them as a sociological category and you will end up with a bland promotion. Alternatively, although not a bad promotion by any means, you will focus on the single thing they have in common, giving away lager as an incentive – 10 per cent extra free, buy five, get one free are standard promotions in this market. But is that the best that you can do?

Before you go any further, have you spotted the flaw in the description I have given? I made an assumption, and this is always a very great mistake. I assumed that the 'Who?' was existing lager drinkers. Perhaps the promotion might target non-drinkers or wine drinkers. These approaches could be worth examining!

Never assume anything. In the case of Ramada, the normal action would have been to advertise to people who book hotels. The problem in that case is that these people are all over the world and do not see the same media. It would have been a possible but impossibly expensive strategy.

The first task is to answer the 'Who?' part of the question. In our lager example we can list:

- existing drinkers of the brand
- lager drinkers who buy other brands
- ale drinkers
- wine drinkers
- people who vary what they drink
- home drinkers
- pub drinkers.

However, this list only describes them in relation to their drinking. They have many other characteristics. They may be further categorized into:

- amateur pop singers
- fashion followers
- tennis players
- golfers
- classical music devotees

and many others.

Once we have decided the 'Who?' we must define 'What we want them to do'. Perhaps the list might be as follows:

- existing drinkers of the brand: suggest it to friends
- lager drinkers who buy other brands: switch brands
- ale drinkers: switch to lager, our brand
- wine drinkers: try lager when it's hot
- people who vary what they drink: be consistent, drink our brand
- home drinkers: go to the pub
- pub drinkers: take some home.

It is possible that some groups will have exactly or nearly the same 'What?' as others, so it might be possible to use the same promotion. For example, the same mechanic may well work with ale drinkers and drinkers of other brands. Already we can see the opportunity for creatively engaging these different sorts of people in different ways. Now we have the 'Who?' and the 'What?', it's time for the real creativity.

Let's study the second list of amateur pop singers, fashion followers, tennis players and the like. Remember that any one of the people in these categories may also be in one of the other categories. We have, therefore, the grounds for 35 possible promotional objectives, and the lists are by no means exhaustive. Let us take just one example: tennis players who vary their drinks. We can now start to build a picture of real people and work out how to motivate them. We know they are under 25. We know they drink a variety of things. We know they play tennis and are likely to visit the club bar. The answer to the question 'Who do we want to do what?' is therefore:

'we want tennis players who are not consistent in their choice of drinks to try our lager once a week in their club after their game.'

Now we can begin to devise a worthwhile promotion for these persons. We can imagine them as flesh and blood, coming in from the game, looking for a drink. We can imagine the place, the time of day. We can picture their friends, the things they will be talking about. It is far more real, far more focused than trying to attract that sociological category, the C1/C2 person between 18 and 25.

A number of ideas immediately present themselves for encouraging tennis players who are not consistent in their choice of drinks to take a lager once a week after their game. A chance to play tennis with a celebrity? A discount on tennis kit? The chance to collect something for the club?

However, tennis players are just one of our groups. A similar process will lead to similar thoughts about the classical music devotee who never drinks at home and the amateur pop singer who normally drinks beer.

Having categorized the consumers, it is worth looking at the inter-mediaries – at the publicans, managers of off licences and supermarkets, cash and carry buyers and the rest. Like the consumers, they are immensely varied.

Let's assume that the tennis club idea proved a basis for a promotion themed on sport and leisure, and designed to offer a range of celebrity sports opportunities. We can now go back to our tennis club and develop the trade dimension of the promotion. We must consider the bar steward. He will now become the 'Who?' The 'What?' might be

'To suggest a cooling lager is best after a game.' It being a club, we may also have another 'Who?': the committee, which might have to give permission to allow the promotion to run. Should the club be given the opportunity to host the celebrity events or another incentive?

If you follow this method of identifying 'Who?' and 'What?', you will quickly devise hundreds of different promotional objectives. This is delightful but you are unlikely to have the time to work them all up into full promotions – and you could not afford to run them all anyway. You need only work through those promotional objectives that are most likely to achieve the marketing objective. To do this requires careful assessment of the extent to which your promotional objectives will grip the underlying marketing objective.

There are a number of questions to ask about each of your promotional objectives and the initial promotional ideas that go with them.

- Is the particular audience a reasonable proportion of the total or can the idea at least be attractive to a wider group of people?

- Is it likely to be achievable within the budgetary, legal, timing and other constraints that you face?

- Does it lend itself to simple, clear expression to the trade and to consumers?

In this case, we may conclude that these tennis players form too small a group to be significant, but that there is an opportunity if we add them to a range of other active club sports.

The process of devising a promotion is far from over when you have a flip chart covered with possible promotions. However, to try to be creative without attempting to answer the question of 'Who?' and 'What?' will usually result in promotions that are less effective than they could be.

In the case of the Ramada promotion, long before ducks or anything else was considered, it was realized that, mainly due to budget limitations, the 'Who?' would be the guests and the 'What?' would be telling their contacts about the hotel. It was as simple as that. The statement of the promotional objective in that case and in many others is creative in itself.

In this case, the creative process then had to find a way of getting guests to talk about the hotel. A business hotel is not something one normally talks about – except in negative terms – as they are fundamentally similar across the globe. A true creative leap was required. It was realized that one thing all guests do when they are in a business hotel room is to grab some relaxation time, often by taking a bath or a shower. We should catch them while they relaxed and are likely to be receptive.

Brainstorming was useful. Could we put a waterproof joke book by the bath? A bathroom karaoke kit? Something useful? Humour seemed appropriate and, eventually, along with boats came that deeply loved creature of children's baths, the duck. Brainstorming was not the only technique used. To devise good promotions, you need to use a range of creative techniques.

CREATIVE TECHNIQUES

Here are five creative techniques that are particularly useful in moving from 'Who do I want to do what?' to an effective promotion.

Listing

As we have already seen, making lists is a very useful technique. It was a straightforward process to list all the different types of young lager drinkers, for example.

Lists help you order your thoughts and show up any gaps. They do have one disadvantage, which is that it is often difficult to see the connections between items on a list and particularly on several different lists. One way round this is to use the largest sheet of paper you can find and draw lines to show these connections. For example, you could link rugby players and golfers as people who would be members of a club, and therefore involved with bar stewards.

Another way of showing connections is not to write a list, but to draw a 'mind map'.

Mind maps

This is a formalized way of connecting ideas. Take a sheet of paper and start with one idea. It could be anything related to the subject – for example, 'wine drinker'. Then, draw a line from it. Along that line write connected ideas – for example, 'sophisticated', 'educated' and 'travelled'. From each of these words draw other lines, and write the words that occur to you. For example, from 'travelled' you might write 'airline tickets', 'currency', 'passport' and 'duty free'. Keep on doing this and the interconnected ideas stay together. Connections also appear that will not at first have struck you. For example, 'duty free' brings you back to 'wine drinker'. Is there a promotional idea in that?

Brainstorming

Once you have really defined your chosen, practical promotional objectives, you may then decide to brainstorm. Brainstorming is not meant to be a woolly general discussion. Set the objective for the session very clearly and ensure everyone understands it. For the Ramada promotion, it was 'What can we put in a bathroom, in a business hotel, that will amuse the guests and encourage them to mention how good the hotel is to the person who booked it and to colleagues?', and the related one 'Is it also possible to provide something that would act as a constant reminder to the guest?'

It is useful to spend just a few moments on a warm-up exercise to get people into the right frame of mind. Perhaps you could examine where else the session could have been held that would increase the creativity level. The best hotel in the world? The most beautiful? Then imagine you are there.

There are no right or wrong answers in a brainstorming exercise. It is important that people are not allowed to feel foolish or they will cease to contribute. They may have that brilliant idea lurking in their heads just waiting to pop out. Use affirmative expressions such as 'yes, and . . .' rather than 'yes, but . . .', let alone 'no, because . . .'.

The village

A very useful technique is to define all the types of 'Who?' and, in your imagination, people a village with them. Imagine the houses they would live in, the places they would meet, the resources they would need, where they would go for fun, where they would shop. Then, aim your promotion to appeal to the village. Think how they would react to it, how it would come up in their conversation. If it does not appeal to most of the villagers, you probably need to redefine your objectives or run more than one promotion.

Being someone else

If you feel you are not capable of solving the problem creatively, imagine someone you think could. Imagine a great artist – say, Picasso – or think about the most imaginative person you have met in your own life. Then, in your mind ask them what they would come up with.

A variation of this is to mentally take six people out to dinner and ask them what suggestions they have. Imagine a series of different people, the different perspectives they would have on the question and how they would discuss it among themselves. Why not even imagine one of the 'villagers' and ask them?

Practice makes perfect

Thinking about promotions can be turned into a party game, perhaps for use on long car journeys. Think of a product category known to you and list all the brands in it. Then assume an objective and a set of mechanics and match the two together. Examine the following list of confectionery brands and promotional offers.

After Eight	Free Levi's jeans to be won
Yorkie	Win a racehorse
Jellytots	Free Mother's Day lunch to be won
Dairy Box	Win a holiday in LA
Toffee Crisp	Win a visit to Legoland
Drifter	Win a chopper bike
Lion Bar	Win a day out in a tank

Are they well matched? No. Why not give them a better matching, and then see if you can think of even better promotions to encourage repeat purchase for each of these brands?

MAKING THE MOST OF YOUR IDEA

Deciding on your mechanic and theme as the answer to the 'Who is it we want to do what?' question is an important step. Now you must make it work well.

There may be some pitfalls you need to identify. In the case of the Ramada duck it was recognized that if it was left in the bathroom with no explanation it might look as though the room had not been cleaned properly. People who took the duck, something the Ramada wanted them to do as a reminder of the hotel, might feel guilty. If they did so, they would be unlikely to carry the message about the benefits of the Ramada hotel in Manchester.

The problem was solved by printing a small tent card that introduced the duck and explained that it could be taken home or posted anywhere. The duck was also given a distinctive personality and distinctive packaging. Named 'Reggie', he was supplied with a specially constructed cardboard 'crate'.

In the case of Sheraton Securities' wellies, the different sizes of feet had to be taken into consideration.

It is essential to identify problems and practical difficulties – such as ensuring that a sales representative's car can carry sufficient quantities of your latest creative brainwave. More positively, you also have the ability to polish and extend the creative idea. However, be careful of so extending the idea that it becomes impossibly complicated.

Mazda ran a competition in 1994 that offered the chance to win a holiday.[2] The stages involved required some imagination. Consumers were enticed by teaser ads in a newspaper, and directed to another and bigger ad; there they were asked to identify an island; then they had to go to their local Mazda dealer and identify three other photographs; identify another 'special photograph'; complete an entry form; and, should they so wish, phone a London telephone number for a clue. The persistent motorist would, however, have noticed that nowhere did a Mazda car appear, and at no stage did the Mazda dealer play a part in the promotion. Creativity? Not of a sales promotional kind.

The golden rule is to keep it simple and keep it relevant. The duck crate is an example of a simple extension that enhanced the promotion, yet the promotion would still have worked without it. That promotion was later extended further by putting the duck on Christmas cards and providing star staff with duck merit badges.

When you devise a promotion, be aware of what is current. You can often create far more interest about the activity at little extra cost. Linking in with a current fad can work. Golden Wonder crisps once offered embroidered jeans patches showing the Wombles. This was just as the characters became famous and as jeans patches became fashionable. It seemed that everyone was eating crisps all day judging by the response.

Be especially careful if you promote overseas. It is vital to know the traditions and expectations of your foreign consumers. In developing countries, cigarettes are often sold singly as 'sticks'. Thus, any promotion using packet tops in such countries will only benefit the retailer.

When you find a promotion that can be extended in many different ways, you know you have a winner. It is always worth polishing and extending an idea until you have bled it dry.

Once you have your promotional concept, there is a lot of work to be done to turn it into an effective operational plan. For this you need suppliers (the subject of Chapter 4) and an effective implementation strategy (the subject of Chapter 5). In doing so, though, never forget the importance of the original idea. One that can extend and extend. One that is elegant and simple. One that you are really proud of. You will hear a voice in your head asking why no one has done it before.

You will begin to worry that there must be something wrong. Don't worry. If you have followed the steps above you will have created a memorable promotion that will succeed. Congratulate yourself.

CASE STUDIES

This chapter has been full of examples of creative promotions. Many are from high-profile consumer fields. The two case studies that follow demonstrate that promotional creativity can be found on fairly sticky wickets – in promoting intellectual property law and an ageing motor car.

CASE STUDY 7: EVERSHEDS

Intellectual property is a dry, complicated but increasingly important, branch of law. Most companies – not least sales promotion agencies – need to think very carefully about who owns the ideas, trade marks, designs and copy that their staff and subcontractors create. The trouble is, drawing up the necessary contracts is something that can always be put off until tomorrow.

The leading legal firm Eversheds wanted to promote its 'Intellectual Property Health Check' in 1996. An ordinary brochure would not have broken through the apathy. Instead, they sent a simple letter accompanied by a piece of wood with a hole drilled through it, marked with the Eversheds logo. They offered a prize for the best answer to two questions. What is it? And what intellectual property rights apply?

The engagement of leading businesspeople in the questions was enormous. So, too, was the response. The object (which turned out to be a wine bottle holder) was genuinely intriguing. The follow-up letter contained winning solutions, an analysis of no fewer than five intellectual property rights that could apply to it and an invitation to arrange a 'Health Check'.

Eversheds deserved to succeed with this promotion. Simple and to the point, it showed that even lawyers could be creative!

■ How exactly did Eversheds answer the 'Who do I want to do what?' question?

■ What other promotional solution could you devise that would be as good or better?

CASE STUDY 8: ROVER GROUP

To understand this promotion by the agency Ammirati Puris Lintas, point your browser (Internet explorer or Netscape) at http://www.mini.co.uk Such is the nature of Internet sites that what is true in late 1997 may not be true forever. . . but this is the story so far.

In 1996, Rover was faced with the question of what to do to stimulate sales of the ageing and much-loved Mini. Sales were to long-established customers, who were declining in number. Could the Mini appeal to a younger generation who may not know it is even available? Potential customers needed to be made aware that they could still buy one, and that Rover's enormous range of options meant that they could virtually design their own.

The solution was found in an interactive Internet site with a monthly competition to design your own Mini with real and fantasy features. Designs are entered on a gallery, where visitors to the site vote for the best design. The winner is rewarded with Mini merchandise, and winning designs are posted on a special page. Everyone wins the chance to turn their design into a game and download it as a screensaver.

Like any good web site, it is constantly changing. Developments include a walkround film and a concept car section. These have helped it to be one of the top ten UK sites and to be voted Microsoft's site of the month. As well as an ISP Award, it was voted commercial web site of the year in the UK Yell Awards and best automotive site by *New Media Age*.

In its first four months, the site received three million hits, 5 per cent of them turning into brochure requests. Will it convert into sales? The jury is out on this, but the commercial logic is far stronger than on many other sites. The promotional mechanic of a design competition is proving effective in engaging people with the Mini, and with the differential advantage it has over far newer cars: the capacity to design your own.

- Think about the 'village' of visitors to this web site. What other products and services featured on the Internet would they like?

- What promotions could you devise to encourage them to visit your own company's web site (or, if you don't have one yet, a site you know)?

SUMMARY

Creativity is about finding effective solutions. It requires the ability to think laterally and imaginatively, which can be developed with practise.

There are several techniques that can be used, including mind maps and brainstorming.

Creative promotions arise out of close attention to the question 'Who do I want to do what?' Once the process of answering this question is begun, hundreds of possible promotional objectives emerge. A really good idea can be versioned and developed in many ways.

4

HOW TO USE SUPPLIERS

All promotions need suppliers. Even the simple offers run by my local chippie in Leeds need suppliers of sign-written posters and *Jurassic Park* dinosaurs. Complicated national promotions require an army of suppliers: promotional and design agencies, premium sourcing specialists, printers, point-of-purchase manufacturers, handling houses and telephone response companies. Many of these will, in turn, have suppliers that are critical to the success of the promotion. This chapter deals with how to select and use them.

Sales promotion can present a particular difficulty in this respect. A company will normally have a wealth of experience of component suppliers and subcontractors for its core products and services. There will often be long-term supply agreements and careful supplier assessment in accordance with established quality criteria. In sales promotion, the picture is different – discontinuity is the rule. Promotions are different from one to the other so each promotion often needs different suppliers from the last one. Yet, the same requirements of quality assessment and value for money apply. For this reason, many firms try, where possible, to build long-term partnerships.

There are two models of supplier relationship:

- the 'quotation model' assumes that you know what you want and can obtain the lowest price and best terms from a range of suppliers by setting out your specification as an invitation to quote

- the 'partnership model' assumes that you will obtain the best solution by working with a chosen supplier from the earliest stage, incorporating the supplier's skills into the specification. This second model is often called 'partnership sourcing'.

Some organizations – particularly in the public sector – have rules that require them to obtain three quotations for every piece of work. Others believe that the constant use of tenders and quotations keep suppliers on their toes. The risk in sales promotion is that you never use exactly the same product or service often enough to be able to specify what you want without the help of a supplier. That supplier is most likely to help if you build up a long-term relationship, and bring them into the planning of a promotion from the earliest stage.

SALES PROMOTION AGENCIES

Who they are

Most sales promotions are conducted by people who are not sales promotions specialists – by marketing managers, sales managers, managers of small businesses and by executives in general advertising agencies. In a number of large consumer goods companies, promotions are under the aegis of a sales promotion manager, but even then implementation is often the responsibility of non-specialist sales and marketing executives.

Many of the biggest and most high-profile promotions are developed and implemented by specialist sales promotion agencies. They are often called 'consultancies' because, unlike insurance or advertising agencies, they derive much of their income from fees rather than commission. However, sales promotion firms also derive a proportion of their income from selling artwork, merchandise, print and other services, which is not normal practice among consultancies. The word 'agency' is used here as the description commonly applied to firms engaged in providing marketing advice, consultancy and implementation.

There are over 200 firms listed in the ISP's 1997 *Directory of Sales Promotion Agencies*. Some 60 firms belong to the Sales Promotion Consultants Association (SPCA), an association formed to represent the leading agencies. In the main, they are on the ISP list, too. Outside these two lists, there is a wide variety of agencies that include the words 'sales promotion' in their list of services. Some are advertising agencies, which may or may not employ dedicated sales promotion specialists. Some are purveyors of particular sales promotional vehicles, such as travel or merchandise, that may be very competent, but are not necessarily impartial about the types of sales promotion they recommend. And some are newer agencies, which may be extremely good, but have yet to qualify for SPCA membership.

Sales promotion agencies arrived in Britain in the 1960s, at a time when many companies were adopting the American approach to marketing. They swiftly outgrew their American parentage and, by the 1980s, British sales promotion agencies were actively buying up their American counterparts. During the 1980s, a number of leading agencies became public companies, but the volatility of the agency world meant that this situation did not last. In 1995/6 there was only 1 sales promotion agency with a turnover of over £50 million, 5 more with over £20 million, and a further 7 with over £10 million.[1] Even among the 60 SPCA members there are many quite small businesses.

How they work

There are many different ways that sales promotion agencies originate, and this is reflected in their continuing diversity of structure. Some began as spin-offs of sales promotion specialists working in advertising agencies; others as the breakaways of advertising agency sales promotion departments; others from a base in supplying print, merchandise or incentives; and yet others (and this is increasingly the case) as green field start-ups that are meeting the growing demand for specialist sales promotion services.

Despite the variety in their size and structure, sales promotion agencies have a number of features in common.

- They charge for creative and conceptual work on a fee basis that reflects their time input. This method of working – comparable to that of solicitors and accountants – means that it can be possible to use them simply for creative thinking and to do the organization and implementation of a promotion yourself.

- They are normally equipped to supply design, artwork, premium sourcing and a host of other services that are needed to make promotions happen. Sometimes these services are supplied in-house, sometimes by subsidiary or associated companies and sometimes they are subcontracted. Agencies will always make a margin on these services, but their prices benefit from economies of scale and can be highly competitive.

- They work on an *ad hoc* or continuing basis. It is conventional for advertising and PR agencies to work with clients on a continuing, contractual basis. Sales promotion agencies like to do this, and increasingly do so, being paid a retainer rather than one-off fees. However, many clients still use them on an *ad hoc* basis, briefing them for particular promotions as and when required.

- They are increasingly involved in a broad range of marketing services. We discussed in the Introduction the reasons for the growth of sales promotion. Most of these apply also to the use of an integrated mix of sales promotion, direct mail, PR and other tools assembled to meet particular needs. The disciplines of sales promotion agencies provide a good basis for providing these integrated marketing services, and many have taken up the challenge.

- Account handlers are heavily involved in the creative process. There is a tradition in advertising agencies for account handlers – the people who meet the clients – to be largely excluded from the creative process. In sales promotion agencies this is not the case. The creation of effective promotions is an interdisciplinary, brainstorming affair, simultaneously conceptual and practical, and the person you meet will play a central role in that process.

- They tend to be of moderate size. This partly reflects the relative newness of the industry and partly their low start-up costs. New agencies tend to be tightly run, enthusiastic and entrepreneurial and almost always run by the people who set them up.

- They are able to give impartial advice on the type of sales promotion that will most meet your particular needs. This is perhaps the most important benefit of their fee basis of payment. They have no particular axe to grind over whether or not the promotion is a competition, an on-pack or a mail-in or uses travel, clothing or cash. In a world where there are many axes ground, that is a bonus in itself.

Sales promotion agencies earn their living from a combination of fees for time spent and mark-ups on goods supplied. The balance between the two will vary, but most commonly includes a fee for time spent, normally calculated at £60–£120 per hour (1998 rates), depending on the seniority of the staff involved, and a mark-up on goods supplied (print, artwork, premiums and so on) of 15 to 20 per cent. These two combine to give an overall margin of 25 to 30 per cent (lower for bigger jobs and higher for smaller jobs).

Some agencies have dropped the words 'sales promotion' as the description of their business in favour of 'integrated marketing', 'below-the-line marketing', 'promotional communications' or any combination of these. They describe the increasingly integrated nature of sales promotion and the business that agencies do rather better. The trouble is that client firms do not always understand them. 'Sales promotion' remains a broad description that people understand – as long as you recognize that it includes a great deal else besides.

What to look out for

Choosing the right agency is a difficult process. The SPCA offers a useful service of putting together a portfolio of the work of ten or so agencies from among its members that can be reviewed at its London offices. Both the ISP and SPCA publish annual Awards brochures, detailing the best promotions of the previous year. Also, there is regular coverage of leading agencies in the three specialist sales promotion magazines – *Incentive Today*, *Promotions & Incentives* and *Sales Promotion*. All these offer a good starting point for drawing up a short list.

A relationship with a sales promotion agency normally starts with a pitch. The SPCA and the Incorporated Society of British Advertisers (ISBA) have devised a set of guidance notes for them. They provide a good basis for the often vexed process of competitive pitches, and are obtainable from either the ISBA or SPCA (see the Useful addresses list at the back of the book for details). The principles are to treat each other with fairness:

- prepare the background information properly
- don't ask more than three agencies to pitch
- write a proper brief and allow time for it to be responded to
- decide quickly and objectively
- give the losers the chance to learn how they could have done better.

Fees for pitches are a subject of regular dispute. The SPCA's Code of Conduct discourages its members from making speculative pitches. The reason is that promotions are devised for a particular brief and so have no salvage value. Some companies pay agencies a briefing fee, sometimes known as a pitch or rejection fee, but a survey by *Promotions & Incentives* in 1996 found that 78 per cent of firms never do.[2] Nevertheless, if an agency produces acceptable work, but the promotion is not run for reasons outside its control (for example, you have changed your own plans), it is only right that it should be paid for its work.

It is an open question as to whether or not agencies should be paid briefing fees for competitive pitches. Agreeing to pay them intimates that it is recognized that each concept is tailor-made for each brief and has no salvage value. Equally, it is always possible to find smaller, hungrier agencies who will pitch for nothing.

In practice, most agencies are happy to compete against a reasonable number of others for a real piece of business, and all of them are happy to compete for ongoing business. The distinction is one of common sense. If you repeatedly brief half a dozen agencies for single promotions that may not even materialize, they are unlikely to find it profitable to respond. Conversely, if you brief a limited number for promotions that do materialize – and particularly with a view to establishing a long-term relationship – most agencies will respond professionally and effectively.

There are five key attributes that companies normally look for in their sales promotion agencies, and which form a handy checklist for selection.

- **Creativity** The capacity to produce promotions that are more imaginative, more effective and more eye-catching than you could do yourself are the fundamental reasons for using an agency. Creativity should stand out in an agency's presentation of its work.

- **Communication skills** Promotions are produced to meet specific marketing objectives. In the way it presents its work, an agency should be able to demonstrate an understanding of a range of different marketing situations and of the techniques appropriate to communicating effective solutions.

- **Budget control** Implementing promotions requires a range of design, artwork, premium, handling and other resources. It is not important that these should all be in-house, but an agency should be able to demonstrate that they are to hand and that they can control them within your budget.

- **Good service** A successful promotional relationship requires client and agency to be on the same wavelength. It is important to meet the people you will actually work with – not necessarily the same people as those who make the new business presentation – and get on well with them.

- **Good track record** The evidence from awards brochures and from the trade press is critical here – and a call to existing clients can also tell you about qualities of service and budget control that might not be obvious from published work.

Having applied these criteria, you may end up with three agencies you feel you could work with. It is then common practice to put a brief to all three, and to make a judgement on the basis of their response.

Once you have run a promotion with a particular agency, you will be able to judge its performance in practice. There are broadly three ways you can work in the longer term.

- **Occasional supplier** This is an arm's length approach – the agency is given the minimum information necessary for the job, is always in competition with others and is briefed only when the need arises.

- **Rota member** This is a compromise approach, where two or three agencies are put on a rota of agencies used by the client. Rather more information is given and some or all briefs will only be given to one of the agencies on the rota.

- **Business partner** Here, a single agency is appointed to work as an extension of the client's marketing department. Marketing plans are discussed jointly from an early stage, and a renewable contract establishes an ongoing partnership.

Agencies understandably dislike the first approach. It makes planning their own business difficult and results in a high percentage of wasted and unprofitable work. Clients that insist on 'occasional supplier' relationships can find that they are presented with off-the-shelf promotions, dusted down and rejigged without too much thought and effort, generally from second-rate agencies.

Clients are understandably wary of the third approach. It does involve putting all their eggs in one basket, and can lead to complacency and staleness on the part of the agency. Retainer fees, paid on a regular monthly basis, are liked by agencies as they provide a regular income. However, they only make sense when there is a steady, predictable flow of work.

For these reasons the second approach is often where client and agency find themselves in mutual agreement. It gives the client flexibility and it gives the agency a reasonable basis for predicting the amount of business it will get. Variants on this approach include using one core agency most of the time, but trying out others for particular briefs or in particular areas where the core agency may lack specialist expertise.

Is it worth letting between a quarter and a third of your budget go to the sales promotion agency? If the agency is any good, the answer is 'yes', and for three good reasons:

- part of the agency's margin will be covered by buying promotion items effectively and by its ability to produce promotions cost-effectively

- part will be covered by saving your time in devising, planning and executing the promotion
- most importantly, a good agency will produce a promotion that is measurably more effective.

HANDLING HOUSES

Who they are

Handling houses originated in the need for premiums items to be warehoused, customer applications to be received and processed, and for goods to be dispatched. From this basis, handling houses have grown into sophisticated businesses that offer data capture, database building, in-bound and out-bound telephone call centres, barcode scanning, downloading of e-mail sites and a range of customer interface operations. Gathered together in the Promotional Handling Association since 1984, handling houses joined with the Direct Marketing Association to form the Response Council in 1996.

How they work

Poor handling can destroy consumer confidence in a promotion and the brand behind it, as well as create considerable work for you as you try to limit the damage. Conversely, good handling can create added value in the information collected about participants in promotions and build consumer confidence through the promptness and accuracy of your response to them. The following 20-point checklist, developed from that given by the Promotional Handling Association, identifies the details to be included in briefing a handling house.

- **The promotion** incentive offered, instructions to applicant, any restrictions on entry.
- **Handling requirement** how it should be done, turnaround time.
- **Duration** start date, close date.
- **Response forecast** anticipated volume, variation over time.
- **Promotion media** on-pack, press, TV, direct mail.
- **Application format** coupons, leaflets, plain paper, telephone.

- **Point of purchase requirements** number, type, tolerances, count procedure.

- **Payment requirements** amount, coins, cheques, postal orders, credit cards, charge cards, tolerances, need to await cheque clearance.

- **Bank account** client's, handling house's, responsibility for charges.

- **Postage and dispatch** first class, second class, discounts for bulk mailings, recorded delivery, registered, carrier, cash floats for postage.

- **Packing** pre-packed, envelope, padded bag, carton.

- **Goods storage** quantities, period, special security.

- **Insurance** client's, handling house's.

- **Application details** captured manually, computerized, fields required, deduplication, selections, sort criteria.

- **Reports** type, frequency, period covered, analysis headings.

- **Consumer relations** incorrect applications, correspondence, complaints, returns, exchanges, refunds.

- **Audit** retention of applications, record of dispatch dates.

- **Stock control** re-order levels, returns, final disposal.

- **Goods inwards** delivery dates, counting-in, quality checks, receipts.

- **Security/confidentiality** expectations, special requirements.

Thinking through what you need under these headings will ensure that both you and your handling house know what is expected. You can also obtain an accurate quotation for the job. Clearly, these vary depending on the amount of work involved. A typical cost might be 80p for receiving and checking three proofs of purchase and dispatching a model car. For setting up an in-bound telephone call number, receiving calls for a brochure, data capturing and posting the brochure, you might pay £1.86 (both 1998 rates).

What to look out for

If you brief your needs early enough, handling houses are an ally. The main decision you face is one of cost and sophistication. If all you need is the receipt of applications and the mailing of items, there are local facilities in most parts of the country that will do the job for a low cost. However, this is probably missing an opportunity, both in terms of data capture and customer relations. More sophisticated operations cost more.

Points to look for include the audit trails a handling house offers for goods and cash, the scale of their computer operations, the training they give to telephone staff, the efficiency and security of their warehousing and the nature and timeliness of their reports. All these mark out the sophisticated from the low-cost operation. Whatever type of handling house you use, make sure you have a good contract (see Chapter 5 for further details).

If you are running promotions regularly, it makes sense to build a long-term relationship with a handling house that becomes an extension of the company for both you and your customers.

POINT OF PURCHASE MANUFACTURERS

Who they are

Drawn from a background in shopfitting or design, manufacturers of units for use at the point of purchase (POP) have become an industry in their own right. The activity used to be referred to as point of sale (POS), but the initials created a confusion with electronic point of sale (EPOS). POP is clearer, but watch for the fact that POP is also the acronym for proof of purchase.

The leading firms are members of the Point of Purchase Advertising Institute (POPAI), set up in America in 1936, in Paris in 1989 and in the UK in 1992. The industry was estimated by research firm Nielson to be worth £332 million in the UK in 1994 – ahead of the amount spent on posters, radio or cinema. In 1998, the value was probably closer to £500 million.

Why the interest in point of purchase? Research for POPAI North America by the Myers Research Corporation in 1995, mirroring other research in the field, identified that just 30 per cent of purchases are specifically planned. A further 10 per cent are generally planned and a massive 60 per cent are unplanned. In some categories, spontaneous purchases account for 90 per cent of all purchase decisions. Point of purchase manufacturers enable promoters to attract attention, communicate offers and brand image, and increase impulse sales at the point at which the great majority of purchase decisions are made.

How they work

The incorporation of sound, light, movement and promotional offers in a single unit has moved POP well beyond its origin in cardboard dumpbins or PVC shelf-barkers. Recent examples show the inventiveness and scope of POP.

- Cadbury's Creme Eggs enjoy a short but intense season between January and Easter. Advertising is wasted unless there is adequate display. In 1997, Cadbury introduced a dumpbin flashed with a question that echoed the advertising: 'How will you eat yours?' Consumers pressed a button on the dumpbin to release a flashing roulette sequence of lights that stopped at one of five suggested ways to eat your egg. A total of 50,000 outlets were visited by the company, 30,000 dumpbins placed, and display in targeted stores jumped from 60 per cent the previous year to 90 per cent.

- Shortly after the UK introduction of Canadian Moosehead lager to the UK in 1993, the brand faced the challenge of increasing distribution in larger outlets. Standard POP material tends to get lost in them. The solution was an eight-foot relief map of Canada that featured a barcode reader. Consumers received a swipe card with every Moosehead purchase. When swiped through the reader on the map, it set off a swirl of LED lights that ended up in a different destination in Canada each time and a different prize to be claimed from behind the bar.

- Spillers Petfoods developed a 'shelf purrer' to launch its cat food brand Purrfect Selection in 1995. The battery-operated device sensed customers within a 12 feet radius and set off a voice message 'Indulge your loved one with a can of new Spillers Purrfect'.

The primary applications of POP are in sectors that sell via retailers. Leisure outlets such as hotels, pubs and sports clubs are also important. However, POP is increasingly used to communicate brands well away from their normal sales outlets. Interactive displays in shopping centres, airports or anywhere else people gather can sell almost anything. Increasingly, the use of smart-card technology and interactive video enables promoters to target particular offers to particular people, capture data about them and communicate product benefits and promotional offers wherever people have the time and propensity to respond.

What to look out for

Sales promotion is about influencing behaviour. Consumer behaviour at the point of purchase is the behaviour that matters most. This leads Alan Toop, who has written on sales promotion and run promotional agencies for 30 years, to argue that marketing thinking should begin at the point of purchase. The experience is often the reverse. The enormous point of purchase operation to introduce the UK National Lottery was implemented in less than four months, long after other elements of the mix had been put together.

Critical points to look out for in using point of purchase are:

- think early about POP needs and integrate them into your advertising and promotional planning

- use it to gain exposure in non-standard outlets; there are often great opportunities for joint promotions based on a POP unit

- make the best use of increasing opportunities for light, sound and movement; there are real benefits to being an innovator in POP

- think hard about the operational issues, especially who will distribute, site and install the units and (if high-tech) keep them running.

The leading manufacturers in the field are increasingly able to offer an all-in design-to-upkeep service. For details of them, contact POPAI (the address can be found in the Useful addresses list at the back of the book).

PROMOTIONAL INSURERS

Who they are

Any promotion carries an element of risk. Specialist insurance brokers, among whom the market leader is PIMS, exist to limit that risk. There are four main promotional risks that can be insured.

- The offer can be so appealing that consumer redemptions vastly exceed your expectations, playing havoc with your budget. This is dealt with by over-redemption insurance.

- A promotional premium can have met all relevant consumer legislation, and still be faulty. In the worst case, you may need to recall all the premiums in the market and cancel the promotion. You need product liability and recall insurance for this.

- You can have carefully calculated the number of winners in a prize scheme, only to find that, as a result of a printer's error, you have vastly more winners than you expected. Printers' errors and omissions insurance will take care of it.

- As promotions increasingly involve events, you will need insurance for the jugglers, fire-eaters and dancers that accompany them.

How they work

Whether you are offering a free mail-in item in return for a number of proofs of purchase, issuing a coupon in the press, sending out direct mail offering a brochure or offering retailers a reward for display, you need to calculate the likely number of redemptions. Only then can you calculate how many mail-in items to buy, how much money to set aside for coupons, how many brochures to print and how many retailer prizes to organize. The calculation is simple.

$$\text{Opportunities} \times \text{Redemption Rate} = \text{Redemptions}$$

Most promoters will have experience of the likely redemption rates on promotions they regularly run on their own brands, but what if you are wrong? What if you are running a promotion that is new to you or in a product category that is unfamiliar to you? PIMS has a database of more than 5000 promotions built up over the last 10 years that analyses redemption rates by brand, product category, commun-ication mechanism, reward and promotional technique.

PIMS can first of all advise you of the likely redemption rate – which may vary from 2 per cent to 30 per cent or more. It can then insure against redemption that is higher than this. If the likely redemption rate is 10 per cent, it will typically insure redemption of between 10 per cent and 15 per cent at a cost of 17.5 per cent of the amount you want to insure. It is possible to insure 100 per cent of the risk, but most contracts specify that you carry the risk if redemption is more than twice the expected level.

How do you know what amount to insure? It is very much up to you. If you are running a free mail-in for a model car with a cost of £1, you are most likely to want to insure for the cost of the car and the cost of postage and handling. A typical calculation would look like this.

Offer Free model car with two proofs of purchase.

Opportunities Offer printed on 200,000 packs, so, as 2 proofs of purchase are required, that gives 100,000 opportunities.

Redemption rate 10 per cent.

Redemptions 10,000 (100,000 × 10 per cent)

Cost per redemption £1.80 (£1 for the model car, plus 80p handling and postage).

Over-redemption insurance requirement 10 to 15 per cent.

Number of redemptions covered 5000 (15,000 – 10,000).

Sum insured £9000 (£1.80 × 5000).

Premium payable £1575 (7000 × 17.5 per cent).

It is worth noting that, at present, insurance premiums are not subject to VAT, though they are subject to Insurance Premium Tax (IPT), which, in 1997, stood at 4 per cent.

Is it worth it? It all depends on how confident you are that you have estimated the redemption rate correctly, and how capable you feel of carrying the cost of over-redemption. A management benefit is that you can calculate the budget for all your promotions for the year and be confident that you have covered all eventualities. Unsurprisingly, insurance is most often taken out on promotions that are new to the promoter or their agency.

Product liability/recall and printers' errors and omissions insurance can apply either to single promotions or (more economically) to all the promotions you run in a year. For many manufacturers, it can be an extension of existing product liability insurance. The particularities of sales promotion mean it is often best to deal with it separately from the very specific product liability insurance a company will have negotiated for its own products.

Is it a good idea to have this kind of insurance? The tendency for consumers to prosecute companies for things that go wrong is increasing all the time. Many promoters now believe that insuring against it has become a cost of doing business and a cost of sleeping easily at night.

What to look out for

There are three things that companies need to do when thinking about the risks involved in promotions.

■ Be absolutely clear about the scale of your risk. Look at existing data on redemptions, look at case studies of promotions that have gone wrong and understand consumer protection legislation. Only then can you can make a decision about what to insure and what risk to take yourself.

■ If you are thinking of using an insurer, talk to them early on. Their experience of redemption rates can help in your budgeting, and sometimes show that particular offers are not affordable. They can also help ensure that your contracts with suppliers are as watertight as possible.

■ If you do insure a promotion, make sure you stick to the number of opportunities you have declared. Insuring on the basis of 200,000 packs and then printing 250,000 could invalidate the insurance.

If you do decide to carry the risk yourself, remember that there is a real cost involved. Set aside part of your annual budget to cover the minority of promotions that will, for all your planning, over-redeem or go wrong in some other way.

SPECIALIST PRINTERS

Who they are

Many promotions use standard leaflet, brochure and packaging printers. If you are intending to run an instant win promotion or to use games or scratchcards, you need to enlist the services of a specialist printer. Other printers specialize in the short runs that are sometimes needed for display material or individual-outlet promotions. Others specialize in label leaflets (those that carry a large amount of information in a concertina leaflet the size of a sticker).

How they work

If you are running a game or instant win promotion, you need to know that the right number of winning cards have been printed, that they are evenly distributed, that there can be no leakage of cards from the printers or distributors, that they cannot be counterfeited and that you can verify the winners. This is a tall order and leads to constant innovation in the technologies involved.

Part of the development is in the inks used. Latex overprints are the standard format for game cards. Developments include heat-sensitive inks that reveal a message on being touched, cold-sensitive inks that respond to a cold drink being put on them and microwave inks, which respond in a microwave. Case Study 22 discusses an imaginative promotion for Sarson's vinegar – it used an ink that responded to vinegar. Another development is to replace hidden messages with a crack-open card that reveals another card inside. Special inks can increasingly be used on ceramics, plastics and textiles.

Avoiding counterfeiting has led to the development of computer systems for verifying winning tickets. One process is to mark winning tickets with a security number that, when entered into a database, shows the exact layout of the card. Another is to print winning tickets with codes that only show in ultraviolet light or that can be read only when matched exactly to a template. Holograms and three-dimensional technology are also used – and the best techniques, naturally enough, are not even disclosed to promoters.

What to look out for

Make sure you use a printer who really understands this business: winding up, as one retailer did, with 27 winners of its top prize in the first week of a promotion is a cost you cannot afford. Ensure, also, that your printer has errors and omissions insurance that specifically covers games.

Once the material has been printed, look closely at the procedures for packing and distributing winning tickets. If you are including an instant win inside a product (for example, underneath the cap of a bottle), make sure it is safe against tampering, both by retail staff and consumers. Keep up with evolutions in game technology. Games succeed as much by novelty as by the scale of the prizes being offered. It is well worth using a specialist printer's knowledge to be the first in your field to use a particular ink or game device.

FIELD MARKETING AGENCIES

Who they are

Field marketing agencies offer a large number of mainly part-time staff as a long-term extension to your own company's staff or to undertake one-off projects. The Field Marketing Association, which represents the leading firms, estimates that there are 35,000–40,000 people employed part-time in the business. A large firm may have as many as 15,000 people on its books.

The major firms are increasingly moving towards full-time staff working on long-term contracts for major promoters. They also overlap with handling houses in offering database, storage and dispatch services as well as staff. You can expect a competent agency to provide not just the personnel, but also to plan geographic coverage, create briefing materials, dispatch and control the items needed in the field, monitor and control the staff, analyse the results and even design and produce special uniforms for them.

How they work

Field marketing personnel can be employed to do almost anything that needs people out in the marketplace, they can act as a salesforce to smaller outlets, install promotional material, distribute leaflets and coupons, hand out samples, collect consumer data, undertake mystery shopper calls, staff exhibition stands, sell directly to consumers, provide information in shopping centres and airports, and carry out blind product tests. Their application in promotional campaigns is huge.

Prices vary depending on the nature of the work to be done, but are typically based on a personnel cost of £6 per hour (1998 rate). A typical brief may be to call on independent retailers with promotional material and stock. Taking planning, travel, briefing and supervision into account, you could expect to pay £12 per outlet visited for this service (1998 rates).

What to look out for

The critical point to remember is that field staff are part of your firm as far as the people they meet are concerned. There is a balance to be struck between the cost a firm charges and the level of briefing, training and supervision that staff receive. Increasingly, the emphasis is on higher quality, and rightly so. Effective use of field marketing agencies depends, as with every other promotional supplier, on clear briefing and a clear understanding of what you are wanting to achieve.

PREMIUM SOURCING HOUSES

Who they are

Open any of the three promotional magazines and you are confronted by page after page of advertisements for clocks, sweatshirts, electronics, model cars, crockery, books, pens . . . you name it, it's there. The British Premium Merchandise Association (BPMA) acts as the trade association for manufacturers of premiums, and its magazine is an effective advertising feature for its members' products. For any given product area, there are also endless sources of manufacturer information in trade directories and, increasingly, on the Internet.

Why not go direct to these companies to buy the premiums you need? For small quantities, and for standard items, it often makes sense. However, for large quantities, special products and products made in the Far East, it can make most sense to go to a company that is set up to design, source and ship promotional premiums to your specific requirements. These are the premium sourcing houses.

These businesses are not large – few have a turnover of more than £10 million. They typically have extensive contacts in the Far East, a direct or indirect base in Hong Kong, design facilities in the UK, processes for quality checking in the country of origin and other developed countries and extensive knowledge of international customs regulations, product safety legislation, shipping arrangements and trade finance.

How they work

Premium sourcing houses ensure that promotional items are created, manufactured and delivered to the specific needs of a promotional campaign. Recent examples show the nature of their work.

■ Nestlé has a continuing requirement for products that give 'playground cred' to Smarties among 7–9-year-olds. The right premium ensures that Smarties remains an attractive product for this age group, and not just something that your kid sister eats. Developments in low-cost consumer electronics meant that it became possible to create the Zapper. This is a Smartie-shaped widget with eight coloured buttons that emits noises of sirens, machine guns and the like, and is cheap enough to offer with five proofs of purchase. The electronics were manufactured in one country, the plastic casing in another. It has been supplied to Nestlé subsidiaries throughout the world.

- Mugs are a promotional evergreen, used by coffee, tea and confectionery manufacturers among others. Traditionally, they have
been sourced in the UK, but UK prices are not competitive in world
terms. There are numbers of low-cost producers, but their quality
has often been inadequate. There are also increasing regulations
governing the toxicity of printing inks. Long-term collaboration
between a sourcing house in the UK and a Far East factory led to
the development of the right mug for KitKat at the right price.

- Another high-profile promotion run by Nestlé in 1996 was themed
on magic tricks. The company had identified a series of injection-
moulded magic tricks that it could obtain from China, but was
forestalled by quota restrictions on imports from China imposed
by the EU. Its premium sourcing house was able to identify a
manufacturer in India and help the factory meet unfamiliar quality
requirements.

What to look out for

You can expect a premium sourcing house to have extensive contacts
with manufacturers throughout the world, and to have a track record
in creating and manufacturing products and shipping them across the
globe. Pay particular attention to their quality systems. If you value
brand reputation, it is not worth skimping on the quality process.
Premium sourcing houses registered to ISO9001 will have demon-
strated the capability of their systems. It is seldom worth the risk of
dealing with an intermediary company offering products at knock-
down prices that cannot demonstrate quality systems.

It is worth bringing premium sourcing into an early stage of the
discussion of promotions. In a number of markets – children's products
in particular – the choice of premium may be critical to the success of
a promotion. A good premium sourcing house will understand
marketing as well as premiums. If you form a long-term relationship
with a sourcing house, you will often be the first to hear of innovative
products that are right for your market.

SUMMARY

Sales promotion agencies, handling houses, POP manufacturers,
promotional insurers, specialist printers, field marketing agencies and
premium sourcing houses form an infrastructure of businesses with
one common thread: making promotions work. There are others, too

– including the companies that supply off-the-shelf promotions (discussed in Chapter 7). The trade press regularly reports on them, not least because they provide a substantial amount of advertising, and that makes much of the reporting uncritical. You need to use the trade press and exhibitions such as Incentive World. You also need to do your own supplier qualification.

If you do any amount of promoting, you are likely to need all of them at some time. It pays to identify a company in each sector with a solid financial basis, to consult with them at an early stage of promotional development and to build up a long-term relationship. No promoter can hope to develop specialist expertise in each of these fields. It makes sense to use them for their skills. If you decide to put all your promotions to a sales promotion agency, it still makes sense to know who they are using for specialist services. One weak link in the promotional chain – whether it be handling, premium sourcing or field marketing – is enough to destroy a promotion.

5

HOW TO IMPLEMENT A PROMOTION

If you've followed the process so far, you will understand the crucial ingredients in devising a promotion. You'll be clear that for your product or service:

■ there's a business task to be fulfilled for which you can specify a concrete objective, such as increasing volume or gaining trial

■ you know the strategic nature of the brand, its values and customers

■ sales promotion, as the part of marketing that focuses on behaviour, is the right answer to your business need

■ you know how to convert the business objective into a promotional objective by answering the question 'Who do I want to do what?'

■ the processes of brainstorming, list making and mind maps have been used to enable you to think imaginatively about promotional solutions

■ you have in mind the suppliers you can use, and the ways in which they can help you devise and implement an effective promotion.

Now it is time to look at the nuts and bolts of implementing a promotion. This chapter looks at five components of implementation: budget, timings, communication, logistics and legalities. It then sets out a simple cycle to take you from initial idea to completed promotion.

BUDGET

In many cases, particularly if you are working in an agency, the budget is given and you simply have to work within it. Will you be able to achieve all you want within the available budget? Are you sure? If not, go back to the beginning and start again. It is best not to try to cut corners as it is usually more expensive in the long run.

What, though, if you have the freedom to set the budget? Money for promotions comes from the same budget as money for every other part of the promotional mix. Money for price promotions may be accounted differently (this is discussed in Chapter 9). There are four ways in which companies set their promotional budgets.[1] They set the figure as:

- what they spent last year, plus a little bit more for inflation and any expected market growth

- a fixed percentage of turnover, established over time for the company and industry

- the same as, or in ratio to, what major competitors spend

- the amount needed to achieve particular defined marketing objectives.

Marketing academics recommend the last method. In principle, it is the right way to do it. The only justification for spending money on promotional activity is that it will achieve marketing objectives that contribute to long-term growth in profits. Relying on what your competitors are doing or on budgets fixed by someone else in the past are excuses for not thinking through the business objectives that face you today.

Starting with a blank piece of paper each year is a difficult task and, in practice, companies use one of the first three methods or a combination of them. However, for sales promotion, there is a particular reason for using the last method. Promotions can be costed as a separate and specific intervention in the market. The cost of making the offer and the margin it generates can be compared to the margin you would expect to make if you did not make the offer.

There is a simple piece of arithmetic that is basic to sales promotion and deals with the relationship between promotional packs, proofs of purchase, opportunities to apply (OTA), redemption rate and cost. In this example, assume you are offering consumers the opportunity to mail in for a free model car on a packaged grocery product. The sequence is as follows.

1   Your first decision is how many labels to print the offer onto. Assume you want the promotion to last for a month. Take a month's volume, add 10 per cent for extra uptake, and you can calculate the number of promotional packs required as being 250,000.
2   Next, you decide how many proofs of purchase you will ask consumers to send in. Set it too low and your regular consumers have no incentive to buy more. Set it too high and your less regular consumers have no chance of participating. A good rule of thumb is to set it at the average level of purchase of the category (not your brand) in the promotional period – in this case, a month. Assume, on this basis, you decide on five proofs of purchase.
3   Now you can calculate the opportunities to apply (OTA). This is the number of promotional packs divided by the proofs of purchase. It is impossible for there to be more redemptions than this. In this case the OTA is 250,000 ÷ 5 = 50,000.
4   Now you must estimate the likely redemption level. This depends on the attractiveness of the premium, the ratio between proofs of purchase and purchase frequency, the amount of support you give to the offer, the strength of your brand and a host of other factors. Assume in this case a 6 per cent redemption rate. The calculation is then the OTA multiplied by the redemption rate. In this case it is 50,000 × 6 per cent = 3000.
5   Now you can bring in the cost of providing the model car and receiving and handling applications. In the discussion on handling houses in Chapter 4, there was an estimate for handling a model car of 80p. Assume the car costs you £1.20. The total cost per redemption is thus £2.
6   Now you know the cost of this part of the promotion. It is redemptions multiplied by the cost per redemption, in this case 3000 × £2 = 6000. You can add to this the cost of artwork, special printing and other support for the promotion. Assume this is a further £6000, giving a total of £12,000.
7   Finally, you can express this figure as a cost per promoted pack by dividing it by the number of promoted packs. In this case it is £12,000 ÷ 250,000 = 4.8p.

This last is a very useful figure. You can use it to compare the costs of different promotions on a like-for-like basis. You can use it to calculate how many extra packs you need to sell for the promotion to break even. If the cost is too high, you can also use it to go back to your calculations and try to find savings – for example, by asking consumers to contribute to the cost of postage or finding a cheaper model car or increasing the number of proofs of purchase.

If you are running a coupon (see Chapter 9 for details), the same calculation applies. Remember that the OTA are not calculated on the readership of a newspaper, but on its circulation. Those with a higher number of readers per copy may have a higher redemption rate, but a coupon can only be cut out once.

You will also need to keep a careful watch on VAT. Customs and Excise produces a series of booklets dealing specifically with promotions, business gifts and retail promotional schemes.[2] They are, of course, subject to change, so you should make sure you have up-to-date copies to hand.

TIMINGS

Sales promotions are often run to meet short-term market needs. They must also work with the lead times of intermediaries and suppliers. This makes timing a critical issue, and one about which there is often conflict. It is important to be clear from the beginning about the following time constraints:

- when the promotion is needed to impact on the consumer
- how long it will last for
- how that relates to the purchase frequency of your product or service
- what lead times intermediaries require
- how long you have for print and merchandise delivery
- when you need your promotional concepts ready.

The time available at each stage strongly affects what can and cannot be achieved. Managing this can be significantly helped by the use of simple project management charts.[3]

COMMUNICATION

Every promotion is communicated in or on material of some kind. The options include:

- the wrapping of the product
- leaflets in or with the product or service

- leaflets separate from the product or service

- advertisements in press, on radio, TV or posters

- sponsored shows or events

- posters, stickers and other support material

- sales aids

- mailshots.

At an early stage, you need to identify ballpark costs for what you want to do. You can firm them up later, but you need to know that the promotion is, in principle, affordable. To do this you need to:

- select the appropriate communication media

- estimate the quantities needed

- estimate the specifications (colour, weight, frequency and so on)

- estimate artwork, photography and other design requirements

- obtain ballpark costs at first, detailed costs later.

This can involve a great deal of phoning to print, media and other suppliers. A useful short cut is to obtain one of the published guides to print and media prices, and base your estimates on that. Another is to keep a file of all promotions that you have costed, and cannibalize the prices. Sales promotion agencies tend to be particularly good and quick at this, as they have a wealth of experience to draw on.

While the nuts and bolts are being developed, time can be spent drafting the words that will be used to communicate the promotion. There are always two parts to the verbal presentation of any promotion: the up-front claim and the technical details, rules, instructions and other essential, but secondary, information.

It is common for agencies to present concepts showing what the printed material and advertisements will look like. This has one major danger: until the copy or scripts are written it is impossible to know how big the printed material will need to be. Often the concepts are presented and the budgets agreed but later someone has to ask for an increase in budget because the leaflet needs an extra page.

Write the copy or script first, even if only roughly. This will guide the designers and enable them to create a far better visual concept. Experience shows that the tighter the brief given to designers and copywriters, the better the results and the greater control you have over costs.

Keep the creative approach simple. You have very little time to communicate your concept to the consumer. It is better to have a 'Win a holiday' headline than 'Bloggins summer spectacular'. The first communicates the benefits, the second nothing to those not directly associated with Bloggins.

You'll also need to consider how the offer will be presented graphically. Whether it is communicated by leaflets, advertisements or in a small space on a pack, some form of graphics is needed. Even if you are doing the promotion yourself, some help will be needed here. It is important to reflect the style and feel of the offer in your graphic design and (if possible) enhance the underlying values of your product or service.

LOGISTICS

Every promotion requires something to be given away – whether it be a prize, a coupon, a free mail-in premium or a charity donation. Having isolated what the offer consists of (win a holiday, send in for a kitchen knife, redeem a 10p coupon) it is possible to do the following:

- draw up a specification for the items involved

- estimate the quantity needed

- obtain at least ballpark costs.

Again, it is helpful to have reference books to hand to short-cut the process of phoning or writing for samples and prices. You can then turn to the operational characteristics of the promotion – how the promotion will actually work.

- Who will do what?

- Where will items be stored?

- How will they be distributed?

- What resources are needed at each stage?

What comes into this depends very much on the scale of the promotion and on your own resources. For a simple retail promotion, it may be no more complicated than arranging the printing and distribution of POP material. Other promotions can be very much more complicated, and can involve marshalling half a dozen different organizations, a dozen types of printed material and offer materials of many kinds.

You'll need to ask yourself how feasible your promotion is. A brand manager once bought some excellent deck chairs at an extraordinarily good price for use as a dealer loader (these are gifts given to retailers – see Chapter 10). It meant that his dealer loader offer would be far better than usual and far superior to those of his competitors. Unfortunately he forgot that most of the sales representatives were on the road for 3 days at a time making 15 calls a day. The brand manager had forgotten to consider how to fit 45 deck chairs into a Ford Escort. However, before you decide it is not feasible, ask yourself how it can be done rather than accept that it cannot. Be positive. Only when every option has proved impossible should you give up. After all, your great idea deserves to see the light of day.

LEGALITIES

The legal and self-regulatory controls on sales promotion are discussed in Chapter 13, but it is worth discussing the subject briefly here.

It's best to start with the positive values that exist in your brand and in your relationship with your customers. Creative promotions have their origins in the values of a brand, in a shaft of lateral thinking that captures the imagination and fits the brief like a glove. However, sometimes, you can get carried away with enthusiasm.

Ask yourself does the activity conform with the various codes of practice and the law? If it does not, then the worst thing you can do is to try to bend the promotion to fit. This usually ends up by emasculating the promotion and making it too complicated.

Remember also to check how the activity will reflect on the promoter. Short-term gains that are achieved by an unfulfilled expectation on the part of the consumer will damage the company's reputation in the longer term. If something looks too good to be true, it probably is. Remember how the Hoover flights promotion (Case Study 11) almost killed the company.

A very simple rule to follow is to put yourself in the position of the consumer and think how you would feel about being made this offer. If you would be unhappy, then so will your targets. You may also think again of your imaginary village and see how its inhabitants would react. 'Do unto others as you would be done to' is as applicable to promotions as the rest of life. Think highly of consumers – they are neither stupid or gullible.

A STRUCTURED PROCESS

Managing the implementation of a promotion is no easy task. It helps if you divide the work into three stages from brief to implementation, each separated by evaluation and decision phases, and resist the temptation to go straight to the detailed development of the first concept that comes to mind.

- **Stage 1** Think through the possible solutions to the promotional brief.

- **Stage 2** Develop your leading concepts in outline form.

- **Stage 3** Develop the top concept into an operational plan.

Below, we shall look at each of these three stages in turn, focusing on the work to be done at each stage – possible solutions, outline development and detailed development. It is essential to keep the stages separate.

Stage 1: possible solutions

A list of possible concepts is a rough working document. Each concept will be described in a dozen or so words, often with further possibilities in brackets. A concept could be described as 'Competition – spot the ball (try a variant?) – holiday prize (Tenerife? Florida?) – plus vouchers for everyone who enters (if they cost less than £500)'. Another may be even less specific about mechanics, but focus more on a theme: 'Win a holiday – competition or free draw – total prize pot £5000'.

Now you have to apply a rough filter to the ideas you have developed. Figure 5 shows how it looks in flow chart form.

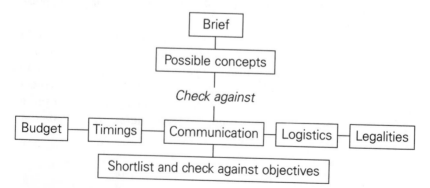

Figure 5   *Stage 1 – how possible ideas are tested for feasibility*

In the shortlisting phase you will need to go back to the marketing objective and see whether or not your brilliant idea is likely to achieve the objective. To continue with the lager example from Chapter 3, will promoting it in tennis clubs really achieve a sufficient increase in sales? If it will not, you will have to start again. Be particularly careful of the promotion that grips the consumer, but not the objective. Sales promotion is there to do a business task, not simply to engage the consumer.

Depending on the brief, you will end up with as few as one or two possible solutions or as many as half a dozen. You can take these forward to outline development. Typically, a sales promotion agency brings these items together on a 'concept board'. This is a rough illustration with the key message on it that instantly communicates the offer, backed up by one or two sheets of A4 on which is set out how the promotion will work and what it will cost. If you are doing it yourself, you will still need to see what the offer will look like and note down its key costs and operational characteristics.

Stage 2: outline development

The task now is to flesh out the details of your shortlisted concepts and to establish whether or not they will actually work in practice. This process is as shown in Figure 6.

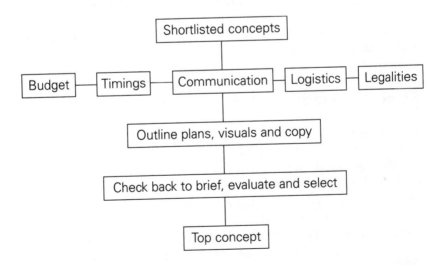

Figure 6   *Stage 2 – the process of checking shortlisted concepts are capable of being taken further*

Working up the shortlisted concepts is not a matter of doing different things to the first stage – it is doing the same things in more detail. So, for example, you will work out the detailed print specification and start writing the body copy. This process will narrow down the candidate concepts. You know that the concepts you are left with will work, and how they will work. These are the concepts to choose from. Now is the time to go back to the brief, and critically examine each candidate concept against it. Which really fits the best? Which has strengths in one area, but loses out in another? Which really meets the core objectives? Which gives the most added value? And which will turn on your target audience the most?

For a big promotion, formal research is often advisable at this point, but research of some kind can be done for every promotion – simply by asking people you know. Friends, colleagues at work, customers – all can be subjected to what is often (unfairly) called 'the idiot test'. Simply line up the concept boards, ask them to think themselves into the position of the target audience and rate your concepts on three criteria: clarity, attractiveness and accessibility.

It is surprising (and mortifying) how often your favourite concept will leave other people cold. You are often too close to it to be objective yourself. And even if the concept is clear enough, there will be points where it can be improved and ideas for these tweaks will come from the most unlikely sources.

At the end of this process, you are in a position to select the top concept. If it fits the brief like a glove and excites the people you show it to, you know you have a winner on your hands. At the very least, you will have a sound, workable promotion that meets the brief you set. Now it must be turned into physical items, such as leaflets, posters and the like.

Stage 3: operational plan

This stage takes your top concept through to implementation. The elements of this stage are shown in Figure 7.

This is the stage at which to finalize and check all the secondary copy for the promotion – entry instructions, rules, descriptions of the prizes and so forth. It is imperative to follow the Code of Sales Promotion Practice in so doing. The rough visual also needs to be turned into artwork for all the various printed items needed for the promotion. Outside help will almost always be needed here.

The materials necessary to the promotion can now be obtained. It is normally possible at this stage to beat the ballpark prices obtained

Figure 7   *Stage 3 – the actions involved in implementing the chosen concept*

earlier because you now have a firm intention to proceed, so it is worth shopping around for better prices.

It is particularly important to pay attention to the operational plan. Many promotions fail despite excellent concepts, superb designs and exciting offers because a simple error has been made in the administration system. It is vital to go through this in the finest detail, and to ensure that every aspect of delivery, handling and distribution is fully organized. Handling houses, and other suppliers described in Chapter 4, are crucial at this stage. A detailed operational plan sets out exactly what will happen when, by whom and how. A really tight plan leaves no room for error or misunderstanding, and saves a great deal of time in the long run. After a while, the framework of a good promotional operational plan for your own company will become established, and so the process of drawing it up will become quicker as time goes on.

The operational plan must include contracts with third parties. They are of particular importance where the operation of a promotion depends critically on another company performing functions delegated to it. Contracts should always be drawn up for the following.

- **Joint promotions** These are a disaster if the relationship turns sour, and one of the most effective ways of promoting if the relationship flourishes. A contract not only establishes the ground rules, but obliges each party to think through all the eventualities before committing to a promotion.

- **Agency relationships** A relationship with a sales promotion agency should always be governed by a contract setting out mutual responsibilities.

- **Premium supply** Contracts beyond normal purchasing conditions are not generally necessary if you are making a one-off purchase of premium items. They are necessary if, for example, you are seeking to call off items for a promotion in the future or if a special item is being made.

- **Support services** Contracts are advisable with handling houses, auxiliary sales forces, telesales operators and other specialists.

The formats of contracts vary enormously. Some companies write special contracts, others use long and complicated standard contracts. Many find that an exchange of letters backed by a set of standard conditions of trade provides the best balance. As promotional redemption rates are not always predictable, it is important to allow for changes in requirements in your contracts, and to know on what basis the cost of any extra work is calculated.

Finally, you should establish the evaluation systems. It is too late to think about how to evaluate a promotion after it has been run, when it will be too late to record much of the information. The time to do this is beforehand. There are various key measures that will flow from your objectives (this is discussed further in Chapter 6).

Now it is time to run the promotion. A promotion set up along the lines of the processes described here should run without a hitch, but it is always important to monitor its progress and be prepared to react to unforeseen developments. Redemption rates, in particular, should always be monitored closely against the expected rate. Remember, too, a promotion ends when you have analysed all the available information to establish whether or not it achieved the objectives set for it and to draw out whatever lessons can be learnt. This is the subject of the next chapter.

SUMMARY

Implementing a promotion is a logical three-stage process. It is a mistake to try to short cut it. The process can take a short time – just a week if necessary. The benefit of a system is that it takes you logically through all the stages and avoids costly mistakes. Following the system will not guarantee world-beating promotions, but it will ensure practical, workable promotions that achieve your objectives. It is vitally important to attend to issues of budget, timing, communication, logistics and legalities in turning a promotional idea into a fully fledged promotion.

6

HOW TO RESEARCH AND EVALUATE

Sales promotions are undertaken to achieve specific business objectives. They are undertaken in preference to other forms of marketing
expenditure because they are thought to be the most effective way to
achieve the task in hand. To be effective, they must offer real benefits,
and that normally costs money. So, it is absolutely critical that you
ensure your promotions are researched and evaluated, otherwise they
will not be as effective as they possibly can be.

Far less research is undertaken in sales promotion than in other
fields of marketing. The reasons for this are various:

- individual promotions seldom have the budgets that justify an
  additional research budget

- promotions can, in many respects, be measured by sales results

- there is often not the time to design and implement research before
  the next promotion is due.

Most books on the application of research techniques do not mention
sales promotion research – itself a measure of the limited demand for
it.[1]

However, those who do research their promotions know the benefits
it brings – and there is every reason to undertake evaluation that can
be carried out from your desk at nil or notional cost. This chapter
looks at the ways in which you can research and evaluate your promotions both before and after undertaking any particular piece of
activity. However, it cannot take the place of specialist books on

research. Although there is little written about promotional research as such, the techniques used in other fields of marketing research can be applied to it.[2]

RESEARCH OBJECTIVES

Like a lamppost, research should be used to shed light, not to lean on. It cannot make decisions for you, but it can narrow the areas of uncertainty and limit the possibility of error. There are three main areas of promotional research:

- **planning research** to segment your market into particular groups that will be susceptible to particular types of promotional activity

- **pre-testing research** to identify the particular promotional concepts that will meet the objectives you have

- **evaluative research** to measure the effect and impact of promotions you have undertaken and to feed into the planning of future promotions.

Each of these areas can be addressed by the three methods of desk research, field research and market testing discussed later in this chapter.

Planning research

Planning research is an input into strategic questions such as how to split your marketing budget between advertising, sales promotion, direct marketing and publicity, and the formation of a strategic plan for sales promotional activity over a number of years.[3]
It can be used to address the following type of questions.

- How do particular groups of intermediaries and potential customers respond to sales promotional offers?

- What kind of promotional offer do they find most compelling?

- What other products and services would they link your own product or service to for the purposes of joint promotions?

- How do they react to different kinds of charity offer?

- What frequency of purchase is it sensible to aim at in constructing proof of purchase requirements?

This kind of research is done far too seldom and, as a result, companies find themselves relying on hunch and tradition in how they answer these questions. If sales promotion is taking a significant share of your marketing expenditure, it is worth getting the basis right by undertaking some planning research, either on its own or as part of a wider marketing research programme.

The greatest advances in this area have been made in promotions to children and young people, where changing fashions have made it critical to understand the issues that motivate them. On a larger scale, it is too much for one brand. There is immense scope for it in alliances such as that announced in 1997 between Cadbury Schweppes, Bass, Kimberly-Clark and Unilever to pool research and database information.

Pre-testing research

This research comes in when you have clearly established objectives for a particular promotion and a series of alternative promotional concepts that meet those objectives.

The research itself also needs clear objectives; overarching questions such as 'Is this a good promotion?' are unlikely to generate dependable responses.

There are several questions that research can be used to answer and that can have a vital bearing on the selection of the promotional concept:

- the level of response you can expect from a particular offer with particular entry requirements

- the effect on response rates of changing a particular element in the promotion; for example, the number of proofs of purchase required or the nature of the premium item

- the clarity of communication in the particular way the offer is themed and expressed

- the effect on the image and value of your product or service made by a particular promotional offer

- the level of spontaneous interest in, and therefore the attractiveness of, different promotional concepts.

It is important to be clear about which of these questions actually have a bearing on your choice between a number of competing promotional concepts. In many cases, all the concepts will have a similar effect on the image and value of your product or service and it will be pointless to explore the matter further. Equally, you may feel that the clarity of communication of the offer is best judged by yourself – and be proved wrong by consumer response.

The most sensitive issue is always the response rate. For a free mail-in this can vary from 3 to 15 per cent or more. On-pack coupons can be redeemed at rates of anything between 5 and 25 per cent. This variance has enormous implications for your budget, so reducing the area of uncertainty is crucial.

Evaluative research

The straightforward in-house part of evaluative research is collecting together all the factual data on response rates, sales patterns, consumer complaints and other readily measurable variables. This type of evaluation should be standard operating practice and is covered in the final section of this chapter.

The other type of evaluative research focuses on tangibles such as the impact of a promotion on brand values and on the reaction to the promotion by those who did and those who did not take up your offer.

All mail-in promotions produce a list of people who took up the offer. These form an excellent list for running a simple postal questionnaire. Getting to those who did not take up your offer requires rather more effort in list building, but it is important to obtain proper comparisons. More in-depth research into consumer reaction to promotions can be obtained via group discussions.

DOING THE RESEARCH

There are various ways in which you can go about doing promotional research.

- **Doing it yourself** This is the only way to undertake factual evaluative research on sales patterns, as only you will have access to the data. Because resources are normally limited, the more you can do the other types of research yourself, the more likely it is to be done.

- **Using specialist researchers** Most market research companies will undertake promotional research, and a number have developed specialist methodologies in the field.

■ **Including it in an agency brief** Sales promotion agencies now have longer-term relationships with clients, and often have in-house resources in market research. It can make sense to build a research element into every brief if you use an agency.

Whichever way you go, it is important to be clear that research is designed to produce actionable answers to specific questions that significantly affect the decisions you have to make. If the answers are not actionable, or their impact is insignificant, nothing will have been achieved. This applies to all three types of research discussed below.

DESK RESEARCH

Desk research has the major advantage that it can be done by yourself, at your desk and at nil or low cost. If you can answer the questions – or at least narrow the amount of uncertainty – by means of desk research, it is always best to do so.

There are three main data sources for desk research, and they can be built up over time to provide you with the material you need to evaluate competing promotional concepts.

Your own promotions

Details of your own past promotions are the best and the first form of research data. An evaluation system is recommended on pages 107–110, which should be used after every promotion.

Using this data for research purposes means identifying similarities and differences between past promotions and your promotional concepts, and intelligently estimating from there. The data can also be used to identify the promotions that will work with particular target groups and to achieve particular objectives.

Competitors' promotions

It is possible to build up a fair amount of market intelligence about the promotions run by your competitors, their likely cost and their likely effectiveness.

It should be standard practice to buy every promotional pack and collect every promotional leaflet issued by your main competitors. From these you can list the nature of the offer, the entry requirements and the theme used.

Rather more detective work is required to gain an estimate of costs, response rates and effectiveness.

■ For a prize promotion, simply cost the prizes on offer. For a premium promotion, obtain and cost the premium on offer. Make an estimate of the quantity of leaflets and other support material, and cost these, too. This should give a rough indication of budget.

■ Use your own sales data, and continuous market research data if you subscribe to it, to establish whether or not any discernible sales effect has been achieved by your competitors' promotions. Other tracking studies can measure their impact on awareness, distribution and other variables.

■ Make your own subjective assessment on the clarity of communication of the offer, and on its impact on brand values, awareness and other less quantifiable measures.

None of this is an exact science, but the information will provide you with the best available guide to what your competitors have found effective.

Wider promotional activity

There are various sources of information about sales promotions in a wider sense. These include:

■ the trade magazines *Incentive Today*, *Promotions & Incentives* and *Sales Promotion*

■ regular features on sales promotions carried in the weekly advertising and marketing press, in particular *Marketing*, *Marketing Week* and *Campaign*

■ publications from the ISP and, in particular, the annual brochure describing winning promotions entered for the ISP Awards

■ occasional research reports published by a variety of business information and research organizations, including Euromonitor and Mintel

■ conferences on sales promotional issues, normally in London, at which leading practitioners describe and discuss promotions they have undertaken and trends in the industry.

Those few companies that employ an in-house sales promotion manager benefit particularly from the build-up of expertise in this area, and it is also a particular strength of sales promotion agencies. However, anyone spending any significant sum on sales promotion should make it their business to monitor and evaluate wider sales promotional activity and learn from it.

FIELD RESEARCH

Field research involves collecting information directly from the market by way of a sample designed to be representative of your target market. There are four main methods that can be used for promotional research.

- **Street interviews**, which provide quantitative responses to a relatively simple set of questions. As a means of testing the response to promotions immediately after purchase, interviews outside superstores can be particularly effective.

- **Hall tests** (where consumers are invited into a nearby church hall or similar venue), which also provide quantitative responses, but allow more opportunity for detail. This can extend to creating a simulated buying situation and comparing consumer behaviour.

- **Group discussions or focus groups**, which provide considerable qualitative information on consumer attitudes, and are often used before quantitative testing. Of all the methods, these are most likely to provide individual and social feedback on promotional ideas.

- **Postal and telephone questionnaires**, which have major cost savings over face-to-face interviews. Because of the need to see promotional offers, their use in promotional research is really restricted to planning and evaluative research.

The use and implementation of all these types of field research is a science in itself, and, as such, is outside the scope of this book. However, there is a view that field research should be treated with more caution in promotion than in other areas of marketing.

The reason for this relates to the gap between what people say they do and what they actually do. It is well known that consumers understate their expenditure on socially disapproved activities such as smoking and drinking. In the same way, they understate their enthusiasm for sales promotional offers. Field research can be misleading if it takes at face value what people say rather than what they do.

MARKET TESTING

Market testing overcomes the gap between what people say they do and what they actually do: it measures actual behaviours in the marketplace.

This technique is prohibitively expensive for most applications of market research because it involves placing a product or service out in the market and producing it in uneconomic production runs. However, for sales promotional research, it is much more feasible. It is often quite possible to sticker a small quantity of a production run with a particular offer and use it as a door-drop sample. In the retail food trade, it is no longer possible to test a promotional offer in a particular store or area and measure the response, but it remains possible to do so in the leisure trade. For service companies, the exercise is even simpler – just produce a short run of the leaflets or other material communicating the offer and try it out in one part of your market.

Clearly, there are logistical and planning aspects to take into account, of which the most important is the time required to organize and evaluate the test. Some promoters believe that the danger of good ideas being seen and adopted by competitors makes field testing impossible. Others believe that lack of field testing means that really innovative ideas are held back, as promoters do not have the faith to take a risk. Back in the 1960s, it was standard practice for Procter & Gamble to field test promotions and develop innovative concepts (see Case Study 18). One of the major advantages of a strategic approach to sales promotions is that the time for proper market testing can be built in.

EVALUATION SYSTEMS

What they are

A good evaluation system is used by all those in the organization who run promotions, is consistently applied and makes the results available to everyone who needs to know now and in the future. It is a key to collective learning in any company or agency and, over time, becomes a valuable asset.

The challenge in setting up an in-house evaluation system is knowing what you need to record and what you can reasonably discard. The challenge in operating it is finding the time to do the recording while the evidence is still available, and knowing what to circulate, what to put on your database and what to keep in manual files. Make the system too complicated and you run the risk that it will not be used. Make it too simple, and you will not have the information you need next time round.

In sales promotion, this challenge is tougher than it is in many other areas of business because promotions are so varied and so often conducted by staff who move on to other jobs. Many agencies have built a spreadsheet of response rates to different coupons, free mail-ins and other offers. These are invaluable, but are at the pinnacle of a good system. The place to start is recording the basic data for each promotion you run.

How they work

The most practical approach is to produce a document wallet containing all the key information about a promotion. You can organize your data under the following four headings.

Under the first three, you can either write an appropriate paragraph or include a piece of paper in your file. The last one requires you to stand back from the evidence and think.

Background and objectives

List here the products on which the promotion ran, the quantities involved and the name of the promotion. Also record the three key points that led you to undertake the promotion: the business task, the promotional objectives and the answer you gave to the question 'Who do I want to do what?' Including the business task ('we faced a major challenge from a new competitor') locates the promotion in a context that may be forgotten in a year's time.

Description

This is a detailed description of what the promotion involved. You may simply be able to include your operational plan – but, before you file it, make sure you update it to show what actually happened, not what you planned to happen. Make sure you included:

- the offer made to the consumer
- mechanic (including detailed rules and entry requirements)
- operational structure (who did what, agencies and suppliers used)
- communication materials (type and quantity)

- media support
- timings
- trade/intermediary support
- salesforce activity (if relevant)
- copies of all relevant printed or video material
- suppliers and contacts.

What happened

There are three primary measures of the results of a promotion, and they relate, respectively, to promotional response, sales and finance. In many cases, it is simplest to include the evidence in your document wallet rather than to spend time entering it into another document. For example, if your handling house gives you an analysis of applications for a free mail-in, simply include that piece of paper. Make sure you cover

- **promotional response** consumer uptake of the promotion, trade participation, the results of any market research or surveys undertaken, a note of any consumer, trade or salesforce comments
- **sales** sales figures for the periods before, during and after the promotion, the results of any continuous surveys of market share, distribution and penetration, relevant figures for competitors' products
- **finance** the cost of all material produced for the promotion, any trade discounts, fees and other costs, and any calculations that you make about the profit contribution the promotion made.

Sales and finance data will, in most cases, be information generated by other parts of the company. Make sure you include information that helps in promotional evaluation, not just because it is there.

Analysis

Did the promotion work? How you answer this question depends on the culture of the company. To listen to some brand managers and agency personnel, there's never been a promotion that didn't transform the fortunes of the promoted product. For the analysis to be useful, however, you must be as honest as possible. You should include:

- **statistics** how the promotion performed against quantitative objectives set for participation, sales, penetration and market share; how it performed against the operational plans you set, the budget and timings

- **comments** an assessment of the lessons learnt from it – particularly, what you would do differently next time, the points learnt from it and the experience it has given you of suppliers, trade partners and internal departments.

The analysis section is not just a matter of reporting that sales increased by 11 per cent against a target of 10 per cent. If a major competitor suffered a production blip at the same time, you need to record it. Analysis is about why a promotion performed as it did. The answers are not always easy to find, but repeated and honest analysis makes the process easier.

What to look out for

Putting a promotion finally to bed with a document wallet containing the information and analysis listed above is the basic building block of an evaluation system. Before you put it away though, you need to make sure that:

- the wallet is indexed and accessible so others can find it

- any basic data that can be held on a central database – for example, response levels – is transferred

- there is a debrief meeting so that experience is shared.

The enemy of good evaluation is the next job, but resist the temptation to switch to it. Taking these steps would, in most companies, transform the quality of promotional evaluation. It would even give you the information you need to enter your promotions for, and maybe win, an ISP Award.

SUMMARY

Proper research and evaluation make sure that you are getting your money's worth from your promotional expenditure, and that you are spending it on the right things. There is no excuse for failing to evaluate every promotion, nor for failing to do the basic desk research beforehand. This should be planned into every piece of promotional activity.

Use of field research and market testing depends on your budgets, but can only help to reduce uncertainty. In the end, however, research cannot make the decisions for you, particularly in such a fluid and fast-moving field as sales promotion.

Part 2

Techniques

7

OFF-THE-SHELF OFFERS

For all the variety of promotional objectives, there are some offers that come up again and again – because they work again and again. An industry has grown up that creates and supplies these offers to promoters. Many of them revolve around travel, hotels, theme parks, films and insurance. They often offer a benefit out of all proportion to the cost to the promoter – such as something worth £50 to your customers that only costs you £1.

Of course, the £49 has to come from somewhere. An immense amount of ingenuity is put into devising offers of this kind and most of them are largely funded by a third party. There are some very good offers as well as some distinctly dodgy ones. Before using any of them, it is essential to understand how they work, what the people supplying them are getting out of them, and what conditions apply to their use.

This chapter describes the leading off-the-shelf offers that businesses can use, what to look out for and the questions to ask anyone selling you the latest unmissable offer. By following the rules, you can snap up excellent deals and avoid leaving behind you a trail of disappointed and angry customers.

Remember, sales promotion is constantly changing, so you should make your own enquiries before using any particular offer. (The addresses of leading suppliers are given in the Useful addresses list at the back of the book.)

FREE ACCOMMODATION

The offer

Free hotel room offers date back to 1971, and have been going strong ever since. The concept is simple. You purchase a number of free room vouchers from a specialist operator. These can be used by your customers to obtain free accommodation at a specified range of hotels. The stipulations vary. During the 1980s, the standard requirement was that consumers bought their meals (breakfast and dinner) at the hotel. This would cost them £10–£20 per person per night. Over time, people became wary of over-priced hotel meals. The offer now tends to be 'two nights for the price of one'.

How it works

The logic of this offer is strong. Hotels have a high level of fixed costs. However high or low their occupancy rate, they still have to pay their capital costs and most of their staff. An empty room is revenue lost forever. The 'free room' concept meets the needs of hotels to fill rooms rather than leave them empty. Satisfied guests can also be expected to return at a later date, paying the full rate.

Hotels participating in such offers are generally privately owned and smaller: the big chains are able to devise and advertise their own 'bargain break' discounted weekends, which (in terms of the discount being offered) can come to the same thing.

Of course, if a hotel offered deals of this kind to everyone, it would soon go out of business. So the offer must be restricted to people who would not otherwise come, those who genuinely are 'extra customers'. Free room deals are therefore communicated by companies that put together a list of hotels on a national basis, and make the offer available as a promotional tool.

What to look out for

A large number of companies supply free room offers. Some are better than others, and the concept is still getting a bad name as a result of some cowboy operators. Customers can ring a hotel to book a room and find that it no longer participates or that rooms are only available in the middle of February. Sometimes they will find that the requirement to buy meals or pay for one of the two nights has not been made clear, that prices are different from those quoted, that they are accommodated in a second-rate annexe instead of in the main building or that the price of the night they have to pay for is the same as the cost of a weekend break.

All this rubs off on the companies that use such a promotion as a sales tool. They are blamed – and rightly so. Giving your customers a duff promotion is bad business and ignorance is no excuse. Sadly, some very big companies (and very big advertising agencies) are still making this mistake.

The answer is to select a reputable company that has been operating free rooms for some years, has a well-controlled and regularly inspected hotel network and adopts a long-term and professional approach. There are several of these companies; they are not much more expensive than the cowboys, but they are infinitely better.

The characteristics that distinguish a good operator from a bad one are straightforward. You can use these questions to sort out the professionals from the cowboys.

- Do they operate a central reservations system?

- Do they ensure that bargain breaks offered by their hotels outside the free room service do not devalue that offer?

- Do they recommend (and insist on) a description of your promotion that accords with the Code of Sales Promotion Practice?

- Do they provide evidence that the list of hotels is regularly inspected and updated?

You can expect to pay £3 to offer your customers 3 nights' free accommodation for 2, £6.50 for 7 nights and £10 for 14 nights (1998 rates). Three-night offers are typically valid in 150 hotels, longer breaks in 300 hotels. Some operators also offer a 'club membership', which costs around £20 (1998 rate) for any number of three-night breaks in a 12-month period. Others offer a 'holiday bond' which gives £500- or £1000-worth of accommodation costs and amounts to much the same over an extended period. Costs to the promoter for all these offers are substantially discounted for large quantities.

Free rooms have deservedly been working successfully for a quarter of a century and have been used to enormous effect by companies from banks to motor manufacturers. Barclaycard, for example, issued 500,000 over a two-year period to new users of the Visa card, with a very high level of customer satisfaction. Usage of the vouchers is often as high as 30 per cent, which indicates the high regard consumers have for them. There's no harm in running an offer that's been used

10,000 times before – after all, straight cash discounts have been used millions of times. The secret of successfully using this offer, and most of the others in this chapter, is an accurate match to promotional objectives.

HOLIDAY VOUCHERS

The offer

Holiday vouchers give customers a saving of around 8 per cent when they book almost any package holiday, but with some operators the saving can be as high as 11 per cent. The saving can be given in a variety of ways – as a cash discount, traveller's cheques, a duty free shopping voucher, free luggage or any other item of equivalent value. The most popular are foreign currency and cash discounts.

The size of the saving is also variable. It can be geared to the price of the holiday booked. For example, £20 off a holiday costing £200–£300, £30 off a holiday costing £300-£400. It can be a flat sum (typically £50, £100 or £200) with certain conditions. For example, that the holiday booked be for two adults for a minimum of two weeks, or on higher-value savings, that it is spent on long-haul flights and holidays.

How it works

Customers achieve the savings by mailing their holiday vouchers to a nominated specialist travel agent, together with the completed booking form from the back of a tour company's brochure. The travel agent deducts the value of the vouchers from the cost of the holiday – or gives it in traveller's cheques, duty free vouchers or any other product of equivalent value.

The price you pay to offer this deal varies enormously. In reasonable volume, you could expect to pay around 75p for a £50 saving on a European holiday, and around £1 for a £100 saving on a long-haul holiday (1998 rates).

The key to this offer is the discount allowed by package tour companies to travel agents. This is normally 10 per cent, though some companies also offer overriding volume discounts of 2–3 per cent. This discount more than covers the cost of making the booking and processing the travel documents. It is needed, however, to cover the high overhead costs of running a high street shop, staffing it through the week and providing the advice that some customers require prior to booking.

If the job of a travel agency can be reduced simply to making the booking and processing the travel documents, the cost of handling each booking falls radically. This is what the specialists who provide holiday voucher offers have done, and it is what enables them to offer savings of around £50 on a standard family holiday.

What to look out for

There are very few drawbacks to this offer. Most people are quite capable of collecting their holiday brochures, making their choice of holiday and completing the operator's form at the back. Perhaps unfairly, they can even seek their local travel agent's advice first!

More than a dozen firms now offer holiday vouchers. Travel agent chains such as Going Places offer them, too. Using a high street chain makes booking easy for customers, but the savings tend to be lower than when using a firm that operates by post. There are six main things to look out for in these firms.

- Are they ABTA, IATA and ATOL bonded to act as travel agents?

- Have they experience of running this offer? It is very easy for an inexperienced firm to get its margins wrong and end up going out of business, leaving your customers high and dry.

- Is it the best deal available? Working this out requires some simple calculation to establish the level of discount being offered. If it is not a very good deal, it is not likely to motivate your customers.

- Are the conditions realistic? Some operators insist on at least two adults booking. This may be restrictive if you are selling to single people. Others insist that people take out holiday insurance; you should check that their price for insurance is reasonable.

- What up-front price are you paying to participate? This varies greatly and should be in proportion to the value of the saving to your customer. The nearer a holiday voucher operator gets to rebating the whole discount, the more it is reasonable to charge you. Some will, of course, try to charge you at a high level as well as hanging on to a large chunk of the discount.

- Are all the relevant operators' brochures included? Almost everyone includes the main Thomson and Airtours brochures, but if your market is young people, for example, you should check that specialist brochures directed at them are also included.

DISCOUNT COUPONS

The offer

Several firms create and promote books of coupons that give savings on a range of theme parks, family days out, restaurants, cinemas and services such as dry cleaning and film processing. Some of them are off-the-shelf. For example, Entertainment International publishes 165 different 'city books' for cities around the world. They also produce a 'premier dining' directory, complete with membership card, offering savings at 400 UK restaurants. You would expect to pay £17 per book for quantities of fewer than 1000, and £6 for quantities over 10,000 (1998 rates). It becomes economic to overprint a standard product with your own brand name and message in quantities of over 1000.

The form of the saving varies greatly within each book. The main variants are a 10 per cent discount, a £3 cash saving, children free with adults, one admission free with a full-price admission or one free course in a meal for two people. They vary as widely as this because each participating outlet determines the deal it wants to offer.

Most of these discount books or cards are themed on entertainment and leisure. For large quantities, specials can be constructed. For example, in 1996 Barclays Bank wanted a reward for 16–18-year-olds opening a bank account. Entitled 'student cash code', it offered savings with Red or Dead, Fosters, WH Smith, the Youth Hostel Association, Pilot Fashion, Sony Music, Deep Pan Pizza, Warner Bros cinemas and others. A 24-voucher version of this would cost £1.72 for 10,000 and just 47p for quantities of over 250,000 (1998 rates). On the theme of 'get to/gether with your mates', Ruddles inserted a 12-voucher book offering over £200 in savings in 4-packs sold in the off licence trade. The vouchers were redeemable in places including the SnowDome, London Dungeon and the American Adventure Theme Park. The unit cost to the promoter was about 20p.

At a different end of the market, the *Financial Times* ran a promotion early in 1994 offering 'lunch for a fiver' and featuring a range of leading restaurants. It followed it up with a 'gourmet breaks in France' offer. This required readers to collect 12 tokens published in the paper over a fortnight and send in £10. In return, they received a directory of French hotels and a further offer for P&O ferries. Altogether, 8.7 per cent of *Financial Times* readers responded, and sales increased by 6 per cent on weekdays and 4.5 per cent on Saturday. Fundamentally the same offer, targeted at totally different lifestyles, is as effective at the top and the bottom of the market.

How it works

These are very much two-way promotional tools. Participation is sold to those offering the discounts on the basis that it will bring in extra custom from those to whom you have given the vouchers.

If a holiday-maker seeks out a restaurant or museum on the basis of possessing a discount voucher, then that is certainly true. Everyone is happy – the participating outlet that gets the extra business, the customer who makes the saving and you (the promoter) who have paid very little to give the books of coupons in the first place.

What to look out for

The drawbacks arise with the small print. A big directory can turn out to include only a few restaurants or parks near where any single customer lives; there may be limitations on the days of the week when the offer is valid; the location may offer its own superior offers, which make yours look second-rate; and there may be tiresome restrictions, such as on the use of credit cards. And, of course, not everyone wants to plan their leisure time round a set of discount offers.

Consumers can see these offers as a substantial and attractive bargain, but they can also be devalued by offers that seem too good to be true and end up being a con. An offer of '£100 of savings' that turns out to be £90 off a £1000 cruise plus a host of 10p coupons would certainly be misleading. It is important to ensure that any discount coupon offer really does offer genuine savings, and that it is not talked up beyond what it really offers.

TWO FOR ONE FLIGHTS

The offer

These offers work on the simple proposition that one flight is free when a second flight is paid for at the normal rate. There are numerous variants on the theme. In 1996, Guinness offered instant win prizes of free flights on its draught bitter, plus the opportunity for all purchasers to obtain half-price flights with British Midland to Paris, Amsterdam and Brussels in return for four ring tabs. Barclays Bank offered the chance to 'Fly free with Virgin Atlantic' to those opening new savings accounts.

How it works

Airlines face the same situation as hotels: an empty seat is revenue lost forever. They thus make blocks of seats available at less popular travelling times for use in sales promotions. On a typical London to Paris flight, the return flight may cost £120. The consumer buys one return flight for £120, and gets the other free. A travel promotion specialist, such as Brevis Marketing Services, would pay the airline about £65 for each seat. The balance of the cost – perhaps £10 – is the cost the promoter pays for the voucher (all 1998 rates).

What to look out for

The same considerations apply to your choice of operator as apply to free accommodation offers. However, there are some additional points to check.

Air fares are highly varied and there are many ways in which airlines offload surplus seats. It is important to make sure that your offer is at least as good as the standard discounts offered in the travel sections of the weekend newspapers. Finally, be warned by the ghost of Hoover (Case Study 11). Hoover's flight promotion was so attractive that people bought the product simply to obtain the offer – and nearly destroyed the company.

HIGH STREET VOUCHERS

The offer

More than 160 retailers and other suppliers produce vouchers for gift and promotional use. The concept started in 1932 with the launch of book tokens, swiftly followed by record tokens. Since the 1970s, it has become a branded business: books and gardens are the only remaining generic vouchers. According to the Voucher Industry Forum, voucher use is worth £400 million a year, and is growing twice as fast as retail sales as a whole.

Discounts for vouchers are very low – nil on small quantities, and up to 5 per cent on quantities of over £50,000. The choice is between a single-store voucher (Marks & Spencer and Boots are the most popular) and one that can be used in a wide variety of stores (the Bonusbond, produced since 1971, can be used in 25,000 stores, including many leading chains).

How it works

Vouchers are off-the-shelf products, but cost the promoter their face value or close to it. In this they differ radically from the other promotions discussed in this chapter. So why use them? The reason is that they carry with them the brand values of the retailer. If £10 in cash were given, it may be used to pay a bill. However, a £10 voucher redeemable at a leading store brings with it the anticipation of a pleasurable shopping trip and a purchase that might not otherwise be made.

What to look out for

Vouchers are cash alternatives. The main point to watch is that they need careful administration. They can be bought direct from suppliers, from producers such as Bonusbreaks, or from firms that act as clearing houses for a wide range of retailers' vouchers.

INSURANCE OFFERS

The offer

Every car owner or mortgage holder is obliged to hold third-party motor insurance, house building insurance and life insurance respectively. Insurances of these kinds are therefore widespread. Take-up of other insurance products – for house contents, legal expenses, personal accident, travel and so on – varies enormously and is very much lower. Every type of insurance can be used as a promotional premium, but the less widespread products are particularly attractive.

An insurance principle also lies behind assistance and helpline telephone services, whether for legal advice, pet care, travel or household maintenance. In all these cases, the cost of providing the advice (normally by means of a dedicated telephone line) depends on the proportion of those entitled to use the advice line who actually do so. Advice lines can be offered in exactly the same way as insurance. A breakfast cereal, for example, may want to offer a benefit that is attractive to pet owners. Free pet health insurance or a free advice line on caring for your pet could both be provided on an insurance principle.

How it works

Specialist brokers – among whom PIMS is the market leader – have put together insurance products in a number of areas that (in volume) are far cheaper than the policies that consumers can buy from their brokers or insurance companies, thus offering consumers high perceived value.

For example, insurance for a £1000 camcorder could cost the consumer £80 if bought from a broker. Its cost to a promoter is much less, and reflects five areas of cost-saving that the promoter can offer the insurer.

- Take out the selling costs of the broker and the administration and marketing costs of the insurance company, and the actual insurance cost is just £30.

- Part of the cost of insurance reflects the fact that it is often only taken out by those with a higher than average risk. Offer an insurance to everyone, and the average cost reduces to reflect low- as well as high-risk customers.

- You could also give the insurer the opportunity of a bounce-back offer – a second offer sent to those who respond to the first offer. The bounce-back offer will give the insurer the potential for new business.

- Offer publicity for the insurance firm on your product or in your advertising and they may subsidize the offer from their own advertising budget.

- Write the policy in such a way that claims are settled with a new camcorder and not cash and you reduce the level of fraudulent claims.

All these measures can mean that, in bulk, an insurance worth £80 to the consumer can cost the promoter less than £10. It's then a real possibility to offer 'free insurance' as an attractive and low-cost incentive.

Sometimes, a trial period of insurance can be offered without cost to the promoter. In 1990, the *Daily Mail* offered three months' free pet health insurance in return for a number of proofs of purchase. About 30,000 people responded – and the insurer took the cost of the claims that resulted. It also converted 7500 people into regular customers, clawing back its costs and making a profit over time.

Insurance products can be varied to suit a range of products and services. In 1993, Lloyds Bank offered insurance-based benefits free to those who took out loans for cars and house improvements. For cars, the benefit included road assistance; for house improvements, it included home repair assistance.

What to look out for

Like any insurance policy, these specialist policies need to be examined closely for exclusions that limit their real effectiveness. It is essential to use a specialist broker that understands both insurance and marketing, and to make sure that there is a genuine consumer benefit in the offer. The best of them are as good as any policy bought in the normal way, and very much cheaper. This is because they pass on real economies.

- There are economies of scale for an insurance company in providing 10,000 policies in one go, especially for low-cost policies.

- Those who have received free insurance make a good mailing list for insurance companies to sell the same or related products to, and insurance companies make an allowance for this.

- One-off policies with fairly low insurance ceilings distributed widely across the population tend not to be abused by customers making false claims, and the insurance cost can be averaged across high- and low-risk consumers.

- Insurance companies like to achieve retail visibility and be associated with leading brand names.

Because insurance companies are looking for volume, this promotion is more suited to larger than to smaller businesses, although there is no reason small businesses should not get together to make the offer. Insurance promotions have been used extensively with electrical goods, in the motor trade, with mobile phones, credit cards and leisure products, such as bicycles. They could be used more widely.

PACKAGED SCHEMES

The offer

Take free accommodation, two for one flights, discounts on cinema tickets, half-price entrance to theme parks, a restaurant privilege card, 50 per cent off household insurance and £200 off selected holidays and what do you get? You get the kind of package that is offered by Safeway as part of its ABC loyalty card, by Barclays Bank as part of its Barclayloan Lifestyles scheme and by Toyota as part of its Club Toyota owners' incentive.

These particular packages were put together by Brevis Marketing Services, one of the leaders in the customer loyalty market, and there are several other suppliers. A promoter could also construct them individually, but there are evident savings in using schemes that have already been negotiated.

How it works

A packaged scheme marks the point at which sales promotional devices become part of a long-term loyalty scheme. The emphasis shifts from providing a short-term reason for buying to providing a basis for building relationships over the long term. The contents of the package can be accurately targeted by selecting the particular balance of offers that suits the lifestyle and aspirations of the customers you are wanting to attract. And the benefits to the hotels, airlines, theme parks and restaurants included in the package can correspondingly become more long term. The lifestyle package becomes a platform on which different companies can reach each others' customers and strengthen their identification with them to their mutual benefit.

A particular packaged scheme in wide distribution is Air Miles. It currently claims 1.5 million collectors and an 89 per cent awareness level. Owned by British Airways, its basic offer is flights, but Air Miles can also be used for cruises, ferry crossings, action weekends, theme parks and cinemas. Providers in 1997 included Sainsbury's (1 point for every £1 spent: 250 points convert to 40 miles); NatWest credit cards (1 mile for every £10 spent); and Vodafone (1 mile for every £10 spent). Consumer rewards can be claimed from as little as 100 miles, though most flights require very many more.

Air Miles are used for consumer promotions, trade promotions and staff incentives. Smaller companies, and those wanting to use them in low volumes, can buy them at 20p each for a minimum quantity of 25,000 miles for employee and sometimes business-to-business use. In moderate quantities, the price drops to 15p each, and downwards from there for large-scale sector-exclusive offers (1998 rates).

What to look out for

Building a long-term incentive scheme is a major investment. A major scheme may cost as much as 3 per cent of turnover. It is not worth doing unless you are clear that your target audience is going to be more substantially attracted by it than by the lower prices your competitors may offer. The issues involved are discussed in Chapter 8 and in Case Study 13 on the different approaches to the petrol market taken by Shell and Esso.

FREE FILM PROMOTIONS

The offer

A long-running off-the-shelf promotion is the offer of free film processing. These offers are normally made available to promoters for a fixed fee that includes handling and redemption. Fotorama, the leaders in the free film market, also offer fixed-fee promotions that do not involve films. A common one is an offer of a free model van, but the same principles apply.

How it works

A typical free film promotion would offer a colour film worth £3.50 in the shops in return for 5 proofs of purchase of a 60p product and 20p for postage. This promotion would run on a million packs and would be supplied to you for a fixed fee of just £12,000 by a specialist film processing company. Across the million packs, the fixed fee would amount to just 1.2p per pack (all 1998 rates). This enables you to compare the cost to other offers (see under Budget, Chapter 5, for how to do this). There are four distinct stages involved in the processing company's ability to arrive at this cost.

■ First, the OTA figure is calculated. This is arrived at by dividing the number of packs on which the offer is communicated by the number of proofs of purchase required to participate. In this example, there are a million packs and five proofs of purchase. So, a maximum of 200,000 films worth £700,000 at retail price could be redeemed.

■ Second, the predicted redemption rate is calculated. This is the estimate of the number of people who will actually take up the offer. It varies widely, but, in the absence of specific information, it is fair to assume 5 per cent. This reduces the likely number of films that will be redeemed to 10,000 with a retail value of £35,000.

- Third, the offer is linked in with a 'bounce-back' offer – a second offer is made to those who respond to the first offer. Those who receive their film will also receive a letter from the processing company offering discount mail-order film processing. The money made on the film processing allows the company to subsidize the first offer of the free film.

- Fourth, the processing company will add in its administrative and handling costs to arrive at a fixed cost for providing the promotion as a whole. This will be expressed to the promoter in pence per OTA. In this case, the offer will be quoted at £12,000 or 6p per OTA on 200,000 OTAs. This can in turn be expressed as a cost per promoted pack – in this case 1.2p per pack (all 1998 rates).

Once the promoter has accepted this quotation, there is nothing more to worry about. The processing company will supply the film, receive the applications, send out the films and take care of all related handling issues. The company will also bear any fluctuations in redemption. Whether 500 or 15,000 people send in for films, the price to the promoter remains the same.

What to look out for

This is a promotion that gives a fixed, all-in cost and brings to bear the interest that film processing companies have in recruiting new users to reduce the cost to the promoter. It is a promotional evergreen because film processing is a large and varied market.

This example has focused on free film as a fixed-price promotion. Some companies also offer free processing, free cameras, free sunglasses, free tights, free model vans, or any other item, on the same principle. The common factor in all cases is the bounce-back letter – in the case of model vans, it is often an opportunity to collect more model vans.

When the offer is film-related, and the bounce-back is film-related, it is easy to see the commercial benefit for the film processing company and how this enables it to subsidize the promotional cost. The same applies to collectibles, such as model vans. The picture is rather different when the commercial benefit in the bounce-back becomes tenuous – for example, when a film processing bounce-back is included with a pair of sunglasses.

Fixed-fee promotions then become a version of promotional risk insurance, which was discussed in Chapter 4. It can be very useful for a promoter to insure a promotion against an unexpectedly high redemption rate. There can also be good arguments for paying a company to take on the whole promotion for a fixed fee, particularly if you lack the time to organize the premiums and handling yourself. Fixed-fee operators offer that service. However, it may cost more than if you organize the premium and the handling yourself and take out promotional risk insurance. The commercial logic of fixed-fee promotions depends on the degree of subsidy the operator can give the promotion on the strength of the bounce-back.

CASE STUDIES

The case studies that follow offer two successful examples of the use of travel and activity promotions and a disastrous one. They provide a graphic illustration of the issues discussed in this chapter. As you are reading them, ask yourself the questions that follow each case study.

CASE STUDY 9: TANGO

In the last ten years, Tango has grown to be the most successful, imaginative and stylish youth-focused soft drink. It dominates the fruit carbonates market, not least as a result of a radical approach to advertising, packaging and PR.

The brand sets serious objectives for its promotional work. In 1994, these included increasing the frequency of purchase, encouraging purchase of larger sizes, appealing to all trade sectors and creating ownership of a unique event.

This led to Tequila Option One's two-stage promotion. The first asked consumers to collect 16 points from Tango packs to claim a 'free go's' directory. This offered a free go at three of 30 activities, ranging from bungee-jumping to windsurfing to music workshops to go-karting. It featured on all pack formats, with varying points being required to obtain the directory depending on the size of the pack. Sales increased by 20 per cent during the promotion.

The second stage was a series of three one-day events in August in Scotland, Nottingham and London. Named the 'Tango Bash', each of these was held in conjunction with a local radio station, with tickets available at HMV stores for £6 plus one proof of purchase. Proceeds were donated to the Prince's Trust. They featured high-profile groups and fashion gurus, music and activities, and attracted more than 30,000 participants.

This promotion involved thinking big and building partnerships. The 'free go's' directory is a version of the event and activity booklets featured in this chapter. The 'Tango Bash' events were organized in conjunction with local radio stations, giving substantial free coverage. Donating proceeds to the Prince's Trust opened doors to celebrities and media coverage. Tango created something unique to itself, but it did so by orchestrating existing networks and resources.

In communications terms, every possible media type was used: regional TV, press advertorials, point-of-sale material, PR, in-store videos in a sports chain, radio, advertising on the tube in London, a roadshow. The events also provided a setting for trade and press hospitality. It is a good example of sales promotion creating brand properties, and doing a job well beyond traditional definitions of sales promotion.

- Why was a package of activity events particularly appropriate for Tango?

- What logic can you see in Tango's decision to have a two-tier promotion, with both an activity directory and a series of outdoor events?

CASE STUDY 10: *THE SUN*

January is a key time for switching newspapers or switching off them altogether. It is also a key time for booking holidays.

The Sun addressed the challenge of locking in existing readers in January 1995 with a promotion that succeeded on a colossal scale.

The paper optioned all low- and mid-season capacity in 140 UK holiday parks. It produced a 12-page pull-out brochure in the paper and backed it up with a £220,000 TV campaign. Readers were asked to collect six tokens on six consecutive days and mail them in with £8.50 per person per four-day holiday.

Around 1.1 million passenger holidays were redeemed – making *The Sun* the country's biggest UK tour operator. The paper sold 180,000 (3 per cent) more copies during the promotional week. It won an ISP Gold Award and an award for outstanding contribution to British tourism. Unsurprisingly, the promotion has been repeated in subsequent years.

This is sales promotion on a massive scale – an option not open to many brands. However, at the heart of it is a simple deal. It sold off-season breaks for the holiday camps and newspapers for *The Sun* by virtue of a compelling customer benefit that also benefited all concerned.

- What package of activities other than discounted UK breaks would have been suitable for *The Sun*'s readers?

- If you ran a holiday park, what steps would you take to gain the maximum benefit from *The Sun*'s promotion?

CASE STUDY 11: HOOVER

In autumn 1992, Hoover needed a promotion to pull itself out of the doldrums. Hoover Europe, owned by the American Maytag Corporation, had made a £10 million loss in the first nine months of the year. It launched an offer of two free flights to America for £100 or more spent on any Hoover product. The promotion was to dog the company for the next five years.

Within weeks, retailers were reporting that Hoover products were walking out of the door. People were buying two vacuum cleaners at a time to take advantage of the offer. The travel agency handling the promotion reported 100,000 responses by the end of 1992, twice what they had expected. The downside of the promotion was also becoming clear. Consumers were reporting unexpected delays and difficulties in obtaining flights. Industry experts were asking how Hoover could possibly fund two free flights to America from the profit on a £100 sale.

In March 1993, an investigator for BBC TV's *Watchdog* programme took a job in the travel agency's telesales department. The trick, it appeared, was to use the small print of the offer to put off those who wanted to book their free flights – unless they also booked accommodation, car hire and insurance worth at least £300. Some consumers persisted in trying to take up the offer, and took Hoover to court. In 1997, Hoover was still paying out to those who took their cases against Hoover to the county courts.

Meanwhile, Maytag had sold the company and provided £20 million for the cost of picking up the pieces of an offer that should never have been made. It was foolish in many ways. The economics of the promotion never made sense. The estimates of redemption were unrealistically low. The procedures for handling were inadequate. Also, when the scale of the disaster became apparent, Hoover did too little, too late to put it right.

- What would you do to avoid getting into the mess that Hoover did?

- What effect do you think the Hoover experience has had on public confidence in sales promotion?

SUMMARY

The offers featured in this chapter can strike consumers and promoters alike in two ways: it can seem a piece of magic that something worth £50 can only cost £1; it can also seem a sleight-of-hand in which someone must be losing out somewhere. The truth is more ordinary. Offers that sound great but cost little work on the basis of a number of related factors.

- They bring to bear the commercial interests of a third party – whether this be a hotelier seeking to fill empty rooms or a film processing company wanting new customers.

- They use the discount structure available in certain industries (particularly travel and insurance) to create savings opportunities that customers could not otherwise obtain.

- They are created and marketed by specialist companies with immense experience in the field that are constantly seeking to devise new offers; the best of them have been around for 25 years or more.

Avoiding the dodgy schemes and securing the opportunities that the good schemes create depends on promoters keeping their eyes open, asking hard business questions and not being mesmerized by seemingly unmissable offers. It is simply not worth degrading your business reputation by using a dubious offer any more than it is worth tarring all these offers with the same brush. If any of the offers in this chapter strike you as unmissable, be cautious. Remember not to take an offer and find a use for it; always start with your promotional objectives.

8

JOINT PROMOTIONS

Most promotions involve giving away some of your own margin in the form of discounts, cheap interest rates, competition prizes or premiums. Extra business should more than pay for this, but there's no getting around the initial investment. Joint promotions involve sharing that cost with someone else. No company or charity wants to do this for you without getting something in return. The secret of joint promotions is establishing a mutually beneficial partnership.

Joint promotions are defined by two fundamental factors:

- they bring together organizations in different markets that share a common set of customers
- they give participants a real commercial benefit that each side is anxious to realize for the other.

This chapter shows how businesses should go about setting up and running joint promotions. Any business can do it, and it is one of the fastest-growing and most beneficial forms of promotion. This chapter looks first at the planning principles and then at four main types of joint promotion – sampling, referral coupons, charities and loyalty schemes. Finally there is the phantom partnership – using an event in the public domain without a formal partnership agreement.

PLANNING PRINCIPLES

Most companies spend time thinking about their own market and their own customers. Naturally enough, they think about them from their own business viewpoint, and in relation to their own competitors. So, for example, a pub will think about the drinkers in the area, what they look for from pubs, what interest they have in food and related services and how the market splits between young and old, male and female, and lunch and evening trade. Equally, a detergent manufacturer will think about customers as people with clothes that need washing, their expectations, the washing machines they use, the family units they belong to and so forth.

Identifying a joint market involves thinking about your customers in broader terms, both in relation to other people who are trying to sell to them and in relation to people you are trying to reach who are already customers of someone else. The key to planning a joint promotion is an accurate profile of your existing customers. The key elements in this profile are:

- demographic data – age, sex, social class, geographical distribution

- their relationship to you – how often they buy, at what price level, with what degree of loyalty

- their needs, interests and aspirations – other things they buy, what they want from life.

This third level is increasingly the key determinant for joint promotions. Credit card companies were among the first to spot it with the development of affinity cards in the 1980s. Now virtually every major charity and interest group from the Royal British Legion to the Liberal Democrats has its branded credit card, typically rebating the organization concerned 1 per cent of the value of credit card spending.

What, though, of those who have no such affinity or only a weak one? Barclaycard offers the equivalent of the rebate in the form of points that can be collected for catalogue items in its Profiles scheme. That is fine as far as it goes, but the benefits are limited to the items in the catalogue. HFC Bank took this thinking a step further in 1997 with the launch of the Goldfish card. This works on the basis of a partnership with British Gas (which offers up to £75 off certain gas bills), ASDA (which offers discounts on shopping) and Boots (which offers discounts at Boots and its other outlets, including Do It All and Halfords).

What distinguishes those attracted by a British Legion card, Barclaycard and Goldfish card? The fundamental product is the same, though interest rates and conditions vary, and they can be used interchangeably in almost any outlet that accepts credit cards. The distinction is the affinity that their possession indicates – to a particular charity, to assembling catalogue points or to mid market shopping discounts.

Plate 1
*Kleenex Facial Tissues: the first Hayfever
Survival promotion in 1991 (CASE STUDY 4)*

Plate 2

Kleenex Facial Tissues: the 1997 Hayfever Survival promotion (CASE STUDY 4)

Plate 3

Music for Schools: the Jacob's Club promotion (CASE STUDY 6)

Plate 4
Gales Honey (CASE STUDY 16)

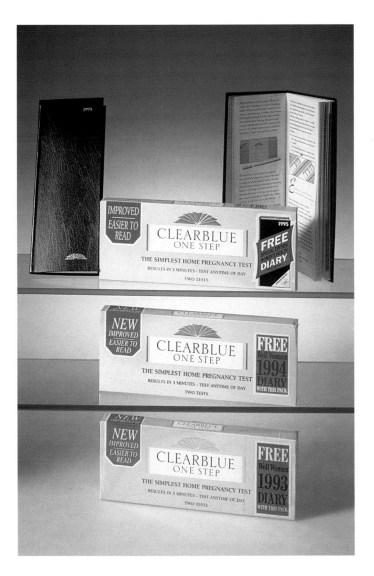

Plate 5
Clearblue One step: the well-woman diary
(CASE STUDY 19)

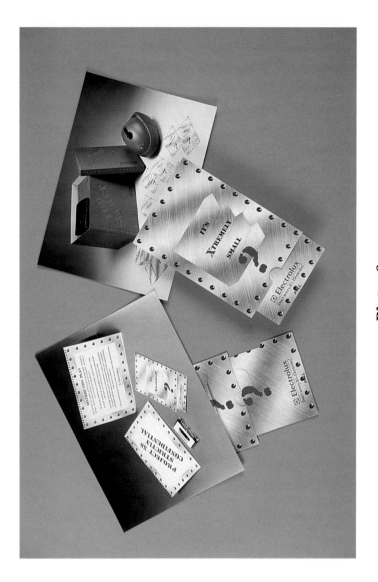

Plate 6

Electrolux's promotion for the XS (CASE STUDY 20)

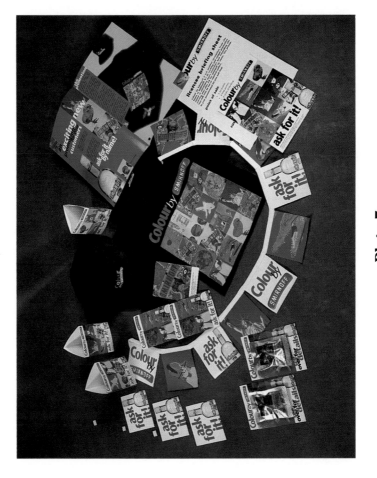

Plate 7

Colour by Smirnoff (CASE STUDY 21)

Plate 8
Tony Stone Images (CASE STUDY 24)

There is only a limited correlation between demographics and affinity. The critical point is that people have different affinities.

Many joint promotions are short term, designed to achieve trial or sampling objectives. Others are developed on the basis that there is a long-term customer overlap between non-competing brands. They reflect the development of the idea of 'tribal marketing'. The idea is that we are forming modern tribes, characterized by our purchasing habits. Those who belong to English Heritage, support charities and go to bookshops form a different tribe to those who do DIY, enjoy home entertainment and join discount clubs. It is possible to conduct research to define these tribes, but they prove difficult to pin down. It is more effective to develop promotional offerings that enable people to define their own tribal affiliations, and to use the increasingly extensive lifestyle databases to attract more of the same.

The process has also developed in business-to-business markets. It is important to profile the size and type of industry, the number of employees and the level of person you deal with. But that is only the start. People in business belong to different tribes as much as consumers. Some feel an affinity to golf, some to charitable work, some to business benefits. Identifying these affinities enables you to seek out partners who are not competitive to you with whom you can run a joint promotion.

Once you have created this profile, the next stage is to establish which other companies share the same customer profile. The more thoroughly this profiling is done, the more likely it is that a joint promotion will be successful, as the closer the fit, the better it is for both sides.

The biggest obstacles to successful joint promotions lie in the process of making them work. The major culprits are greed, misunderstanding and suspicion. However well the customer profiles fit, if your intended partner is not prepared to talk to you openly about their own customers, and is determined to get the maximum out of it without putting anything back in return, the result will be as disastrous as any other partnership erected on false foundations.

When you have identified likely partners with whom you have customer profiles in common, look for those with whom it is possible to establish agreement about each other's objectives and honesty about tackling present and possible difficulties. Even when there appears to be initial enthusiasm on both sides, a number of factors can emerge that can scupper the best-laid joint promotions. It is therefore vital to ensure the following.

- **Involve everyone** If the deal involves other people in your company communicating details of another manufacturer's products, they will only actually do so if the promotion is fully explained to them and they share your determination to make it work. Involvement of senior management in joint promotions is particularly important.

- **Make realistic promises** Everyone is inclined to talk up the number of customers and contacts they have. This can lead to considerable suspicion when it turns out not to be the case. It is best to be realistic at the start about what you can guarantee to deliver.

- **Avoid unplanned changes** Circumstances can change in a company for all kinds of reasons, which lead to a particular promotion being played down. This can be hard for partners to understand, particularly if they are fulfilling their side of the bargain. Management must undertake at the start to minimize this risk.

- **Build in good liaison** Once a deal is set up, it is tempting to get on with the next job. Good liaison is essential to successful joint promotions, and it must involve people at every level of the company throughout the life of the promotion. It is essential to set up the machinery for both liaison and resolving disputes.

- **Bargain realistically** Everyone wants to get the best deal, and negotiates accordingly. However, because joint promotions depend so heavily on goodwill, it is a mistake to bargain simply to minimize your costs and maximize your returns. Bargaining should be directed at maximizing mutual benefit at an agreed cost to both sides, and both sides must agree to this in their negotiations.

- **Be proactive** There is a tendency for the company that made the initial approach to be expected to make all the running and contribute most. This is a mistake. Once the promotion is conceived, it becomes a third entity, shared equally, in which both sides should be proactive.

The only way to establish whether or not likely partners will have the qualities needed for joint promotions is to talk to them. This can be often done via an intermediary, such as a sales promotion agency. The agency can oil the wheels to a considerable extent, and is likely to have met similar circumstances before. Alternatively, membership of the same Chamber of Commerce or business club can provide the basis for a fruitful business relationship. Whichever route is adopted, it is essential to keep your eyes open. If the goodwill and honesty are not there, it is a waste of time proceeding any further.

Once you have found a likely partner – one with a customer profile like yours and that you believe you can work with – it is possible to hammer out the needs you each have that can be met by a joint promotion. Normally, you will have this in mind at the beginning of the process of looking for a joint promotion partner.

The needs joint promotions can meet include the following:

- to gain trial for your product or service from among the customers of another product or service

- to associate your product or service with someone else's in the mind of your target audience

- to make a promotional offer that will attract your customers at low cost to yourself

- to explain to your customers new ways in which your product or service can be used

- to place your product in an environment where potential customers are likely to see it

- to reduce the cost of a planned piece of activity by sharing it with someone else.

Each side must be able to see the promotion fulfilling one or more of these needs. Normally, they are not identical. For example, company A will be seeking to generate trial, while company B will be seeking a low-cost promotional offer. This can lead to the partners in a joint promotion being categorized as the carrier (the product on which the offer is carried) and the carried (the benefit that is carried).

Building partnerships is no easy matter. In 1997, Shell's SMART card saw Ford, Sainsbury's and Allied Domecq disappear as partners, and Lloyds TSB, Hilton Hotels, Commercial Union and Vision Express join. Perhaps this represented a natural evolution of participants. It may also be that, in some cases, partnership principles had not been thought through as well as they could have been.[1]

SAMPLE PROMOTIONS

The offer

When people buy product A, they obtain a sample of product B. This is often something that they need to buy on a continuous basis to use product A or where there is a clear connection between the usage of the two products.

How they work

A long-established example of sample promotions is a free packet of washing powder in new washing machines. It carries with it the actual or implied approval of the washing machine manufacturer for the particular brand of detergent. The free sample is of real and significant value. Other examples include the banding of packs of Nescafé with packs of Hobnob biscuits – creating a clear link between the brands in a common usage occasion.

What to look out for

This is one of the most effective ways of gaining trial and, if the partner is selected well, it can be highly cost-effective, too, compared, for example, to a door-drop sample. However, the cost of giving away full samples is high, and it is normally necessary to include some repeat purchase incentive as well. Both the cost and the potential of this promotion make it one to test very carefully in advance.

REFERRAL COUPON PROMOTIONS

The offer

When people buy product A, they receive a coupon they can redeem against purchases of product B. These promotions are often called 'cross-ruff, or cross-rough, coupons' – a name that implies that they are a hit or miss affair. The name has stuck although there is nothing rough about them, and they are particularly common between non-competing brands owned by the same company.

How they work

An example is the book of holiday-related coupons given with purchases of Thomas Cook's traveller's cheques. Another is a 'kids eat free' promotion, first developed by Persil and Little Chef in the mid 1980s and now widely used by child-related household brands in partnership with family eating and leisure operations.

What to look out for

Referral coupons have the advantage of being far cheaper to run than sample promotions, but lack their level of trial-gaining impact. They have important benefits in that you can measure how many people have been enticed across, and that they do not require special packs. Run as a partnership between half a dozen or more companies selling complementary products, they can be particularly effective.

CHARITY PROMOTIONS

The offer

Charity promotions – or cause-related marketing – take many forms. At the heart of it is evidence that customers are more likely to buy from firms that are seen to contribute to social and environmental needs. Many of Britain's best-known charities go out of their way to meet both their own fundraising needs and the requirements of the firms they team up with. It is a commercial relationship, and all the better for it. Charities need funds, new supporters and wider publicity. Businesses need promotions that show their worth in extra profit and also link them to issues that matter to consumers.

NCH, the National Children's Home, one of the biggest partners in sales promotion, is very clear about this: 'Each promotion with a manufacturer or service company is tailor-made for maximum commercial effectiveness'. So runs the introduction to its publicity leaflet, aptly entitled 'Selling almost anything with NCH is kidstuff'.

Every non-commercial organization has a market it appeals to. It may be national and across the board, such as a major children's charity, or it may be local and quite specific, say, a local arts theatre or a regional sports organization. There needs to be a close fit between the image and values of the non-commercial organization and those you are seeking to put across for your company. There also needs to be a close fit between your target market and the market from which the non-commercial organization gains its support. Selecting the market thus involves a degree of lateral thinking about your customers.

- What sorts of charities and voluntary organizations appeal to them?

- What kinds of project would they like to be associated with?

- What sorts of charities and voluntary organizations connect with the usage area of your product or service?

■   What are the charitable and voluntary concerns that are likely to
    have the highest public exposure over the coming months?

From answering these questions, it is possible to draw up a list of
areas – sport, arts, children and so on – that look suitable. It is then
best to look through one of the charity reference books to find out
which organizations operate in the areas you have chosen. The
Charities Aid Foundation can be a good starting point for this.

How they work

There are various types of charity promotion. Among the longest
established are collector promotions, which require consumers to mail
in wrappers or coupons that are designated as being worth a certain
amount to the charity. The promoter counts the wrappers mailed in
and hands over the equivalent sum. Very often, charities will ask for a
guaranteed minimum to justify the use of their name and to reflect
the difficulty of estimating redemption levels. Collector promotions
run with charities can generate a huge response, particularly if schools
and youth organizations can be encouraged to collect the wrappers
or coupons.

For example, opticians Dollond & Aitchison teamed up with Barnardo's in the run up to Christmas 1996, a traditionally quiet time for
optical sales. Dollond & Aitchison pledged £5 for every pair of
spectacles sold, and raised £229,000. The offer was featured in 430
Dollond & Aitchison branches, 315 Barnardo's branches, in a London
media launch with Anthea Turner, and in regional media events with
celebrities from local pantomimes.

Charity links can be used effectively to achieve defined purposes.
BT wanted to remove the old, pre-microchip phone cards from
circulation during 1996. To do so, it offered a donation to Shelter when
the old phone cards were handed in, which both collected a large
number of phone cards and £100,000 for Shelter.

They can be equally effective as a long-term differentiator. HP Foods
relaunched its ketchup brand in November 1995 with a licence to print
the NSPCC 'Happy Kids' logo on the front of its bottles in return for
1p for every bottle sold. On Fathers' Day in 1996, it offered an 'I Love
My Daddy' mug as a self-liquidator, triggering a further 25p to the
NSPCC. Van den Burgh supported its London Marathon sponsorship
by offering a sports bag as a free mail-in item on Flora and promising
£1 to the British Heart Foundation for every bag claimed. The link
between the Marathon, Flora and the prevention of heart disease was
made in the minds of consumers as a result of this promotional activity.

Charity promotional events have taken a wide variety of forms, from the Oxo/Barnardo's Champion Children of the Year to the Jaguar/NCH Royal Gala Evening at the Albert Hall. These events are pegs on which to hang a host of other promotional activities. They can be particularly good for business entertaining and can give rise to free draws, mail-ins and other promotional activities. Events depend critically on your imagination in devising something that will stand out and then attaching the promotional mechanics to it.

What to look out for

The criteria that apply to charity promotions also apply to promotions with voluntary or community organizations, such as sports and arts associations, and are similar to those that apply to joint commercial promotions. There is the same need to be clear about what each party is in for, and to identify a common set of customers. There is the same need to ensure commitment on both sides, keep everyone involved and secure good liaison; and to be wary of the pitfalls of over-promising, being reactive, of over-bargaining and of unplanned changes on either side.

There are four additional factors that are particular to non-profit organizations, and which need to be taken into account in finding out what they want. Some of them do not apply to the very big national charities, which have their own sales promotion departments, but they are all-important in dealing with smaller organizations. They are as follows.

- **Locate the priority objectives** Most non-profit organizations have an almost limitless set of needs and wishes. Finding out the priority objectives that are within your means to realize takes time, patience and understanding.

- **Identify the decision makers** Non-profit organizations tend to be run by committees and have complicated and involved internal processes. It is essential to understand these processes, to know where the real decisions are made and under what constraints and influences the decision makers are working.

- **Establish trust** The ways of thinking in profit and non-profit organizations are not identical, and an element of initial suspicion and distrust is understandable. It is essential to think yourself into the values and aspirations that motivate those involved in a non-profit organization – whether they are helping the young or the old, organizing sports events or putting on plays. These are invariably centred far more on the thing itself than on the money that makes it possible. To establish trust, you must associate with these values.

- **Have respect** The implementation of any non-profit organization promotion must ensure respect for the recipients of the money raised. For example, people with disabilities find it offensive to be called 'the disabled' or to be described as 'sufferers' from a 'disease'. Considerable sensitivity is required to ensure that raising money is not done at the expense of self-respect.

Approached in this open way, it is possible for companies to sit down with charities and other non-profit organizations and hammer out a deal that meets the needs of both sides. However, remember that your commercial needs are fairly clear to the outside world; the onus is on you to find out the needs of your prospective non-profit partner.

LOYALTY SCHEMES

The offer

From petrol stations to airlines to supermarkets, loyalty schemes are near-universal. Large-scale schemes invariably involve joint promotions – there simply is not enough in any one company's product range to cover all the lifestyle needs that a loyalty scheme tries to meet. The offer to the consumer is both simple and endlessly varied: sign up for the scheme, provide purchasing and demographic data, obtain a card and start collecting. From the management viewpoint the concept is equally simple. Develop the version that suits your business, and you have a loyalty scheme. Or do you?

How they work

There is considerable dispute about how loyalty schemes work. Are they really about loyalty or are they just old fashioned 'points mean prizes' collector schemes dressed up with electronic cards and relationship language? Alternatively, are they a means of delivering highly sophisticated database marketing on a mass scale?

- Supporters of loyalty schemes point to the substantial increase in market share enjoyed by Tesco since it launched its Clubcard in 1995. There is an expectation, fostered by promoters of schemes such as Air Miles, that the present 140 schemes will coalesce into a series of consortia, each comprising a bank, supermarket, airline and utility, telecoms and leisure business.[5] On this reading, the operation of loyalty schemes becomes central to a firm's market positioning.

- Doubters accept that loyalty cannot be bought, but believe it is possible to use card-based schemes to target particular types of buyers and increase the amount and frequency of their purchases.[4] Effective management of data is critical to this, and the measure is whether or not the particular incentives you give create additional sales. Managers can cite examples of this happening and not happening – it is far from automatic.

- There are three radically different views among marketing people. The strongest critics of the schemes point to evidence that the more someone buys of a particular product category, the more products they will buy within it.[2] Thus, the more you travel by air, the more airlines you will use. The more supermarket shopping you do, the more supermarkets you will use. If there are loyalty schemes available, and you like participating in them, you will participate in them all.[3] Of course, market share can change, but that comes about because of an increase in both frequent and infrequent users. What does not change is the ratio between the frequent and infrequent users of your products or services. In fact, across dozens of markets, that ratio is found to be constant. Loyalty schemes are, according to this argument, a complete misnomer.

- So, the question remains open: what part did Tesco's loyalty scheme play in the bundle of characteristics (price, convenience, store layout, checkout speed and so on) that influence the consumer to choose one supermarket over another for a particular shopping trip? Proponents of loyalty schemes often neglect to recognize the progress made by Asda in the 1990s despite its lack of a loyalty card, and the continuing loss of market share by Sainsbury's both before and after its loyalty card launch.[6]

What to look out for

It is essential to recognize that 'loyalty' schemes are not about loyalty, but about providing repeated reasons for customers to use your product or service. They are a bundle of sales promotional techniques, of which the principle one is a long-term collector scheme. On the back of that, they can be used to convey short-term incentives of every kind and to engage the consumer in competitions, and special events. The downside of these schemes is their cost and complexity, and the danger that they can become a substitute for attending to product and service quality. It is best to measure them on a disaggregated basis – not the scheme as a whole, but each mailer, each subsidiary offer. The scheme works to the extent that its separate elements work.

My expectation is that loyalty schemes will come to an end in their present form in due course, just as Green Shield stamps did in the late 1970s. Their demise was predicted in the sales promotional press within months of the take-off of UK supermarket schemes.[7] It has not happened yet, but there is a cycle in sales promotion, well-illustrated in Case Study 15 on Tesco's experience over the last 20 years, and Case Study 18 on a classic Procter & Gamble promotion of the 1960s.

In the meantime, promoters should focus on the detail: if the individual elements are answering the question 'Who do I want to do what?', it does not matter whether they are dressed up as a loyalty scheme or not. If the individual elements are not persuasive reasons for the consumer to act, no 'loyalty' framework will make them effective. Long after the present wave of loyalty schemes have gone, these individual elements – 'buy one, get one free' (BOGOF) offers, special evenings, items to collect and the like – will still be going strong under another name.

PHANTOM PARTNERSHIPS

The offer

Not everyone can sign up the joint promotional partners they would like. When McDonald's signed up as Official Euro '96 sponsors, its competitors Burger King were left without a direct link to a theme dominating the public imagination – and smaller fast food outlets such as Long Row Fisheries were left completely in the cold. The 'phantom partnership' can come to your rescue in such circumstances.

How they work

Phantom partnerships are about making a connection with an event in the news without breaking copyright law. In summer 1996, McDonald's ran a 'game of two halves' promotion, offering football merchandise and match tickets. Burger King built on its sponsorship of the England, Scotland, Wales and Northern Ireland teams with an instant win promotion offering football merchandise and match tickets.

However, what if you don't have any agreement in the relevant field? Flymo didn't, and they gave away free branded footballs with selected mowers, produced POP material showing the cherub from their TV ad kicking it, and offered £50 cash back in the event of Scotland or England winning (which seemed more possible as the event progressed than it did at the beginning). Case Study 14 in this chapter describes a similar phantom partnership between Sellotape and the National Lottery.

What to look out for

Cross the line into implying a partnership and you will have the full weight of copyright lawyers on your head, and rightly so. Imply a partnership with a charity that you do not have, and the public reaction will be damaging. However, make a legal connection which does not infringe copyright with an event like Euro '96 and most people will applaud your imagination. It is an ideal field for enterprising and careful promoters looking to hook their brands onto whatever is uppermost in the public mind.

CASE STUDIES

The three case studies chosen here reflect three different types of joint promotions: a business-to-business promotion; a long-term loyalty scheme; and a phantom joint promotion. Other case studies in this book that are relevant here are the Bovril sampling campaign (Case Study 2), the Sainsbury's 'Schoolbags' collector promotion (Case Study 3) and the Jacob's Club and Co-op 'Music for Schools' promotion (Case Study 6).

CASE STUDY 12: NATWEST/BT

New small businesses are formed all the time. How do banks attract them as customers? In autumn 1993, The Communications Agency hit on a simple mechanic that picked up on a key concern of the start-up business: how to be connected to telephone and fax at the lowest cost.

NatWest teamed up with BT to offer three concrete telecommunications benefits. In return for opening a small business account, customers could obtain a free business telephone, £35 off a fax machine and 15 per cent off an answering machine.

Against its primary objective of driving recruitment of new accounts, the promotion worked well – new account openings were 52 per cent ahead of target. It also worked against its secondary objectives – showing that NatWest understood the needs of small business, and gave their salesforce a simple, clear offer to focus on. The promotion won an ISP Gold Award. It couldn't be simpler or more direct in concept and execution, and offered reciprocal benefits for BT.

■   What other partners could NatWest have sought who would have appealed to the start-up business?

■   What mechanisms for communicating this offer would you have recommended to NatWest?

CASE STUDY 13: SHELL

Petrol purchasers in 1997 were faced with a complicated choice. From the supermarkets, claiming a 21 per cent market share, there were low prices, but often inconvenient locations. From Esso, there was 'Price Watch' – the claim of petrol at supermarket prices right on main driving routes. From Shell, and most of the other forecourt businesses, there were various heavily promoted card-based schemes.

Shell's 'SMART card' was launched in 1994 as a five-year programme to take it to the millenium. The background to the promotion devised by Tequila Option One was clear: Shell was the market leader, but losing share in the absence of a long-term loyalty programme. It needed to build sales while maintaining premium pricing, and embrace all motorists while targetting high-mileage users. It needed a long-term scheme that still gave the opportunity for tactical promotions.

Shell's SMART card was set up with the participation of Air Miles, HMV record shops, UCI cinemas, TicketMaster and other third parties. It offers a choice of instant redemption and long-term saving, third-party purchases and catalogue purchases, charity donations and personal benefits. It was promoted via TV advertising, door to door, promotional assistants and POP on forecourts, local radio promotions, direct mail and inserts in charity magazines. The structure of the card offers both security for points and the capacity for detailed analysis of transaction history. Within a year, Shell had achieved the figure of three million cardholders.

Shell's SMART card won an ISP Gold Award and exceeded all its early targets. It has continued to develop, with partners changing to include

Dixons, Curry's and Victoria Wine. How will it look at the end of its life – particularly in relation to Esso's very different price promotion? That promotion is estimated to have increased Esso's market share to rival that of the supermarkets, at colossal cost to its margins. There are real questions about its sustainability.

The trade-off between market share and margins is a critical decision for any company. Petrol retailers face a particular challenge in relation to supermarkets: they have high fixed costs in refining and oil exploration, while supermarkets can buy on the 'spot market' without any such investment. Margin calculations are thus very different for supermarkets and petrol retailers.

Sales promoters can do very little about that. They can help target those for whom price is not the critical factor – and they tend to be mainly high-mileage drivers, often buying petrol at their company's expense. Shell's persistence with its SMART card and Esso's persistence with 'Price Watch' suggests that it is possible for collector and price promotions to run side by side in the petrol market, appealing to people with different priorities.

- Looking at the current range of Shell's partners, what do you think they have in common?

- Look around at the current range of petrol forecourt promotions. What do they say about each company's answer to the 'Who do I want to do what?' question?

CASE STUDY 14: SELLOTAPE

Sellotape is both the generic name in the sticky tape market and the premium-priced brand leader. It's not an exciting product, and the person buying it for office use is often not an end-user. How could Sellotape underline its brand leadership to these buyers?

Tequila Option One saw that an answer was offered in 1994 by the launch of the National Lottery. Sellotape formed a syndicate to buy 10,000 £1 tickets for an early Lottery draw on behalf of office users who submitted a proof of purchase. Entrants needed company permission and could devote their winnings to charity. This ensured the promotion was within Code guidelines. It also encouraged buyers to discuss with their managers the reason for preferring Sellotape to cheaper brands.

There was no major prize for the syndicate, but the promotion increased sales by 40 per cent in the 6-month period of its run. Could it be repeated? Perhaps not with the Lottery, but with any other major event that offers the opportunity for a low-cost promotional piggy-back.

- What current and forthcoming events do you think could provide the opportunity of a phantom partnership such as Sellotapes' with the National Lottery?

- Look at the case study from the ASA that covers a Lottery-related promotion run by *The Sun* at the end of Chapter 13. What did Sellotape have to do to ensure that the syndicate arrangement did not promise customers more than it could deliver?

SUMMARY

Joint promotions are the staple promotional vehicle of companies such as Procter & Gamble, Lever Brothers and Kellogg. There is every reason for companies of every size to emulate them. However, it is vital to remember that joint promotions are based on a mutual business-building partnership. The best test of success is if both partners want to run it again. If you have identified your market and identified likely partners with the necessary thoroughness, and you enter into the process with integrity on both sides, they will work a treat. If not, you are best keeping away from them.

Promotions with charities and other non-commercial organizations can have enormous publicity benefits, excite tremendous response and associate you with values that are important to your customers. They must be undertaken responsibly and with respect for the needs and feelings of the people you are helping, but they are rightly a commercial operation.

9

PRICE PROMOTIONS

Price is the only element in the marketing mix that produces revenue. All the others involve you in costs. Fixing the price is one of the most difficult and sensitive parts of marketing strategy. It is also a feature of relatively developed markets: in many parts of the world, price still means the point at which buyer and seller are finally in agreement.

Economists have a model of 'perfect competition' in which many suppliers face many buyers in a market with very little product differentiation. Much of the purpose of marketing is to remove the firm from dependency on perfect competition. That is why so much effort is spent creating superior-quality products, developing brand identities, building distribution strengths and establishing unique customer relationships.

Why throw this away by getting involved in price promotion? That is the argument of those who regard price promotion as a destroyer of brand identities. This chapter sets out the different ways that companies think about price promotion and the many techniques available. So much discussion of price promotion is hindered by different ways of thinking about price that the first two sections look at the principles of price setting and price segmentation respectively.

HOW PRICES ARE SET

Some companies have made the absence of price promotion a key part of their positioning. Woolworths and Marks & Spencer did so in the last century when they pioneered the idea of 'one price for all'. Daewoo did so when it launched its manufacturer-owned retail showrooms in the UK in 1995. In distinction to the rest of the motor trade, there is simply no discounting in a Daewoo showroom.

Why can't everyone be like Daewoo? The first reason is competition. It only needs one company to discount its prices for others to feel the need to respond. Companies would, in general, prefer that this did not happen. That is why, in most countries, there are laws that prevent manufacturers fixing prices between them. Until 1962, resale price maintenance (the ability of manufacturers to fix retail prices) was the norm in the UK. When the book market was opened to price competition in 1996, it was of one of its last bastions.[1]

The second reason is that companies have different costs of supply. By reducing cost by means of superior productivity, firms can achieve the profits they seek and still charge lower prices than their competitors. Being the lowest-cost supplier is one of the main strategies for achieving competitive differentiation.

The third reason is the variation in demand. Some people are more sensitive to price than others. Most people travelling between Leeds and London may prefer to take an early morning train. Rail companies have long recognized that over-full morning trains and empty mid morning trains neither satisfy customers nor maximize revenue. It therefore costs more than twice as much to travel before 9am than it does after 9am. That divides travellers into those who are prepared to put time before cost, and those who are not or cannot.

These three elements – competition, supply and demand – contribute to an individual firm's pricing decisions. Setting the price of a product or service is not a primary concern of sales promotion. The normal selling price to final users and intermediaries will be a factor to take into account in planning a promotion, as are the product's packaging and distribution. Sales promoters are not normally asked to review pricing strategy, any more than they are asked to review brand positioning. However, just as sales promotion alters the product, packaging and distribution in the interests of short-term advantage, so it gets involved in altering the price.

The approach your company takes to pricing strategy determines, to a large extent, how price promotion can be used and how the firm accounts for the difference between normal and promotion prices. Much of the disagreement about the use of price promotion arises from people not understanding the difference between two fundamental pricing strategies.

The first is the 'target mark-up'. In this process, the company decides the margin or profit it wants to make, and adds that to the product or service cost. Sometimes this margin is calculated from the return on capital the company wants to make. Sometimes it is the standard level of return in the industry. For many years, advertising agencies marked up goods and services by 1.1765 to give a return of 15 per cent. The professional body for architects recommends a scale of fees for marking up building costs. This method starts with supply as the primary factor in setting the price.

The second simple method is the 'going rate'. This starts with competition rather than costs. The price is set by reference to what other people are charging. Builders, printers and designers will all look at the going rate for particular jobs at particular times. They then work back to the costs that they will incur, and see how much margin they can make. They start with competition rather than costs because they know that if they don't get the job, there's no margin anyway. This method is often used alongside a target mark-up, at least as a point of reference. If they did not have a mark-up in mind, they would not be able to tell whether a particular job would be profitable or not.

These two simple methods lead to very different views of promotional pricing. Those who work on the basis of target mark-up will always think that a discount equals money given away, but does it? Only if they would have been given the order at the higher price. Those who work on a going rate basis are always engaged in promotional pricing, but it tends to be unstructured. Every quotation is its own price promotion. It is difficult to make sure that they are not giving money away unnecessarily.

How do you resolve this dilemma? More sophisticated companies balance a concern with competition and cost with an emphasis on the third element in pricing strategy – demand. This leads to three different pricing policies.

- **Psychological pricing** works on the basis that we often think a high-priced product must be better than one costing less. Firms will set a high price and defend it. Perfume companies try to stop discounters selling their products because the cost of perfume is part of its specialness. Those who go for psychological pricing will often aim at a small section of the market that is looking for the very best and is not sensitive to price. They will regard price promotions as totally unsuitable for them – and they will be right.

- **Value pricing** is based on the idea that top quality and low prices can go together. This works for a company if it can achieve a volume big enough to give it the lowest production costs in the market. The aim is to set a consistently low price and maximize volume. Among retailers this strategy is reflected in the 'everyday low prices' (EDLP) claim made by Wal-Mart in the USA and Asda in the UK. Price promotions can be part of this, but not a central part.

- **Segment pricing** is the pricing strategy in which price promotions really come into their own. It starts with the idea that people are different. Some are sensitive to price and some are not. Some will shop around and others will not. Some will wait to enjoy a service or receive a product and others will not. The argument is that prices should be determined in accordance with the demands of each segment of the market.[2]

Until chains of shops began setting 'one price for all' in the nineteenth century, the price was always negotiated between buyer and seller. In some markets (for example, the price of shares on the Stock Exchange or commodities on commodity exchanges) it still is. Segment pricing is a sophisticated and modern way of managing individual negotiation on a mass scale. The next section looks at this approach in more detail.

SEGMENT PRICING

What makes a segment? Marketing people talk about segments of the market in a variety of ways. There are occupation and income classifications that enable them to distinguish ABs from C1s and C2s. They also talk about them in lifestyle terms. Aspiring young professionals may be of similar age and income to lager and football fans, but spend their time and money very differently. People can also be segmented by their stage in the lifecycle, from dependency to pre-family and post-family.

Segmentation is a delightful game, and marketing magazines are full of new ways of doing it. The practical problem comes when you try to design versions of a product to meet the needs of the segments you have identified. This is the process of 'versioning' a product. The theory is that for each segment of the market there should be a version of your product that fits it like a glove. Unfortunately, this is very difficult to do.

When Midland Bank launched a series of bank accounts for different segments of the market in 1987, it did so in these terms. Their 'Orchard' account was aimed at older, more settled people, the 'Vector' at the young and mobile. Unfortunately, these segments did not exist in the way they thought. Customers became confused about the segment they were supposed to be in, and unsure why different charging and service arrangements applied to them. In 1996, Orchard and Vector were replaced with the Midland Bank Account – a single product that could be varied in its details to suit individual needs, but was not versioned by segment.

If you peel an orange, the segments are immediately obvious. If you peel an apple, they are not. You can chop it up into segments if you want to, but they are your creation – they are not inherent in the apple. Midland's Vector and Orchard accounts failed because the Bank did not understand that difference.

For promotional pricing to be effective, segments have to be real. Business travellers will pay more to travel at a convenient hour than leisure travellers. That is a real segment for ticket sales. However, do business travellers want something different to leisure travellers from the catering facilities at a station? One study suggests that for catering services there are two rather different segments: those in a hurry and those not in a hurry. These cut right across the business and leisure segmentation.

There are three rules of thumb for telling whether or not a segment is real enough for segmented pricing to work:

- people in each segment must have different sensitivities to price – that is, they must be prepared to pay different amounts for the same service or product[2]

- there must be some physical, structural or time separation between the higher- and lower-priced segments, preventing those in the higher-priced segment deciding to buy at the lower price

- the segments must be real enough for consumers not to feel dissatisfied and resentful, and for the cost of operating segmented pricing to be worth while.

The most common segments are formed on these principles as follows.

- **Time** Travelling or telephoning at busy times of the day costs more than at quiet times. Buying toys before Christmas costs more than after Christmas. A video costs more when it is first released than later on.

- **Location** Conveniently located shops, hotels and restaurants charge more than less conveniently located ones. Products and services brought to you cost more than those you have to fetch.

- **Conditions** Buying in volume costs less than buying in small units. A year's subscription costs less than an individual theatre ticket or copy of a magazine. Tickets bought in advance will cost less than tickets bought on the day.

- **Version** Superior service costs more than the standard. Peace of mind can be bought, but at a price. Fundamentally, the same product or service can be versioned or packaged at different price points.

The sales promoter is primarily concerned with promotions that last for a particular time period, take place in particular locations, have conditions attached to the deal and apply to some but not all versions of a product. This is what differentiates intelligent price promotion from wholesale, self-destructive discounting.[3]

IMMEDIATE DISCOUNTS

These are discounts off the normal price that are available immediately at the time of purchase. They take six main forms, from seasonal discounts to extra-fill packs. These very different forms can obscure the thing they all have in common: the consumer can buy a given amount of a product for less.

Immediate discounts have a number of important strengths. Everyone likes a bargain: the queues at the January sales in Oxford Street are living proof that people will go out of their way to seize a bargain. Immediate discounts are a tremendous sales clincher and a powerful and immediate incentive to buy in consumer markets where 70 per cent or more of purchase decisions are made in the shop.[4]

Their weaknesses, however, are very serious. Discounting can rapidly degenerate into price wars. It can be readily copied by your competitors. It often does not distinguish between those who would have bought without the discount and those who need it. It is also extremely expensive. An immediate discount tends to cost you exactly what it saves the customer. Discounting can also downgrade the value of your product or service and lead to a situation where no sales take place at normal price. Very rarely do the sales gains achieved by price reductions lead to a sustained increase in market share. Immediate discounts are powerful, but, like a powerful drug, they can quickly take over and destroy your business. Companies must also be aware of the substantial legislation governing the making of bargain offers that properly constrain the making of unreasonable price comparisons.

Seasonal discounts

The offer

These are price reductions designed to boost sales in off-peak seasons, move outdated lines or heavy stocks, bring forward purchases or improve cash flow.

How they work

In their familiar form of retail 'sales', they are now highly formalized, and have become a seasonal sales promotion far removed from their original purpose of moving end-of-season stocks. Some retailers have run 'closing down sales' continuously for several years, a practice that stretches the bounds of legality. Leisure companies use seasonal discounts very widely, charging different prices in their low, mid and high seasons.

What to look out for

The critical issue is the logic of the season. UK families who give presents on the feast of the Epiphany (6 January) rather than on Christmas Day can use the post-Christmas sales to buy their presents. That's not a problem while only a minority do so. Holiday companies found their margins severely squeezed in the early 1990s when consumers found that holidays could be bought cheap in a late-booking sale. Excessive use of sales ends up with consumers deferring purchase to the next sale.

Multibuys

The offer

These are a particular form of quantity discount offered by retailers (and funded by manufacturers) for multiple purchases of the same item. Consumers are offered a discount for buying two or more packs of the same brand. A long-established variant is the BOGOF – 'buy one, get one free' – that is flashed on-pack, on the shelf or in newspaper advertisements.

How they work

Multibuys normally work by means of barcodes. The shop's EPOS system counts up the number of items with a particular barcode and applies the discount automatically. Multibuys have become hugely significant. A study of the laundry detergent market by the London Business School found that multibuy promotions in the top multiples had nearly tripled in number between 1994 and 1996. Average discounts had risen from 18 per cent to 25 per cent.[5] Since 1990, the leading detergent firms had increased the proportion of their consumer promotional spending on multibuys from 20 per cent to 65 per cent.

What to look out for

Multibuys are easy promotions to set up and give quick and measurable results. They can be very effective for a manufacturer needing to combat competitor action. However, there are significant costs. Multibuys have become the standard mode of purchase for some consumers. The London Business School study found that 95 per cent of multibuys are bought by just 27 per cent of households – mainly larger families who are, in general, better off. The level of sales increase a brand enjoys when a multibuy is offered can be between 50 per cent and 200 per cent. The hangover after the party comes later – when the same consumers switch to your competitor's multibuy.

Used sparingly, multibuys are an effective way of stockbuilding in the consumer's home, and can encourage greater usage simply by virtue of greater volume. They also block purchases of competitors' products until stocks of yours are exhausted. However, they have become a millstone around the neck of manufacturers, blocking other forms of sales promotion. Also, the manufacturer often doesn't get the credit: 56 per cent of consumers think they are funded by the retailers.

Outside retail markets, multibuys exist in the form of quantity discounts. For example, magazines offer discounts for signing up for longer subscriptions. Here it is far easier to calculate the cash and loyalty benefit of signing people up for quantity and getting the money up front. The traditional BOGOF is an effective promotion when not over-used.

Banded packs

The offer

There are several options for banded pack offers, but they come to the same thing: two or more of the same product are banded together or placed in an additional outer wrap so that the consumer buys them together.

How they work

Drink and confectionery brands are regularly sold in a variety of banded packs, whether of 12, 24 or more individual units. The price normally falls as the quantity increases.

What to look out for

Unlike with multibuys, there are packaging costs associated with banded packs. There is also a need to negotiate additional line listings, and to hold stocks of the additional packaging variants. The benefits are that banded packs are clearly a manufacturer's initiative and tend to be less under the control of retailers. They can increase the amount of space available to the product in the shops and can encourage stockbuilding by the consumer. A banded pack can be a powerful incentive to volume purchase.

Reduced shelf price

The offer

This is the commonest form of price promotion. A standard product is on sale with a shelf sticker or poster showing a reduced price.

How they work

If a £1 item is discounted by 25p, it can be shown in a variety of ways: 'normally £1, now 75p'; 'only 75p'; '25p off'; 'our price, 75p'; 'save 25p'. Signs of this kind are commonplace in clothes shops, consumer durable retailers, food stores and pharmacies. They can be funded by the retailer seeking to shift stock or establish a price advantage on goods that consumers use to make comparisons between retailers. They can also be funded by the manufacturer via display allowances. Often they are jointly funded.

What to look out for

The important point is the credibility of the standard price. Since the demise of resale price maintenance, it has become ineffective (and now illegal) to claim price reductions against a recommended price that is not actually charged. The DTI's Code on bargain offers must be followed in justifying shelf price reductions.[6]

More generally, shelf price reductions are simple and effective to operate, but give discounts indiscriminately. They can serve to reduce the willingness of the consumer to pay the full price.

Reduced price offers

The offer

Reduced price offers (RPOs) are flashed on-pack, offering a saving ('10p off') or a price slashed through and a lower price given. They differ from shelf price reductions by being printed on-pack.

How they work

It is one thing for the manufacturer to print a reduced price on-pack, and quite another to ensure that the reduced price makes sense in all retail outlets. They require an additional line listing and separate stocks and packaging. Many retailers now refuse to take them, and will increasingly require that they receive the same margin as if the full price was charged.

What to look out for

For the consumer, RPOs are an attractive offer – volumes of sales certainly rise when an attractive reduction is made. It also gives the manufacturer control over the price charged to the consumer. However, it is an expensive promotion in terms of margins and packaging and, increasingly, difficult to run with major multiples. Used too often, it can devalue the standard price. It can also lead to rapid copying, resulting in almost all products in a sector being reduced in price.

Extra-fill packs

The offer

These are packs flashed '25% extra free' or '550ml for the price of 440ml'. They differ from RPOs in that the price remains the same, but the quantity of the product sold for that price goes up.

How they work

Extra fill appeals to existing users of your product, who can get more for the same price. They can also be useful in trading consumers up to larger sizes. The costs for the manufacturer include packaging origination and carrying additional stock. There can also be difficulties with some retailers in obtaining new listings and shelf space.

What to look out for

The major advantage of extra-fill packs over price reductions is that the perceived value to the consumer is more than the cost to the manufacturer. Once the packaging has been paid for, the cost of additional ingredients is often low. Extra fill does not devalue the product in the way that price reductions do. However, they are readily copied: in off licences it often seems as if every major lager brand is an extra-fill product.

DELAYED DISCOUNTS

These are forms of discount that are not immediately available at the point of purchase. The purchaser will normally have to do something after purchase in order to benefit from the saving. The crucial feature of delayed discounts is that not everyone who thinks they are going to take up an offer actually does so. Everyone is familiar with buying a product on the strength of a '20p off next purchase' coupon, sincerely intending to make use of that coupon and finding it in the kitchen drawer some months later – normally after its expiry date. This is the principle behind delayed discounts.

Delayed discounts enable savings to be targeted at people who fulfil the range of conditions that you wish to impose. The non-redemption level means that the size of the saving offered can be higher, and therefore more attractive. They also allow an opportunity for creativity that is not normally available with immediate discounts.

The weaknesses of delayed discounts include their lack of immediacy: a bird in the hand can be worth two in the bush. They also involve additional handling and postage costs for both the consumer and the supplier. A £10 voucher could well have added on costs of around 80p: 20p for both you and the consumer in postage, plus the costs of envelopes, handling and voucher redemption. These costs are great news for the Post Office, but can detract from the value of the offer you are making. There is also the danger that an excess of complexity can turn off participants: if a saving is being offered, it should be apparent that that is the case.

The major form of delayed discount is a coupon that can be used against a future purchase. These are discussed in the next section. Other common forms are cash rebates, cash share-outs and repurchase offers.

Cash rebates

The offer

In a cash rebate, the customer is invited to collect tokens from a number of packs and mail them in to receive a cash voucher. This promotion can also be used as a variant of the BOGOF, where a coupon is mailed for the full cost of another product. The value of the cash rebate can also be varied, as can the conditions of entry; for example, buy a complete set, and we'll rebate you £10.

How they work

Cash rebates require postage from consumer to mailing house, and from mailing house to consumer, which adds significantly to their costs. They have been overtaken in consumer goods markets by multibuys, but are effective in sectors where goods are more expensive and where EPOS systems have yet to make their mark. They are particularly popular in financial services – '£500 cash back when you take out a mortgage' is a typical example.

What to look out for

If the offer is less substantial than £500 (which everyone will take up), the cost to the manufacturer of a cash rebate will depend on the number of people who actually take up the offer. As there is always slippage between the numbers of people who are attracted by an offer and those who take it up, this enables a more attractive offer to be made. The size of the rebate must justify the postage and handling involved. In financial services markets, cash rebates are a highly effective way of incentivizing people with their own money.

Cash share-outs

The offer

In this offer, a sum of money is divided among all those returning the requisite number of proofs of purchase from a product or service. It is typically communicated as 'send in five proofs of purchase for your share of our £100,000 share-out'. Variants can include the option of sending in an unlimited number of POPs.

How they work

The predicted redemption rate is carefully calculated to ensure that participants will receive a reasonable sum of money, normally equating to that which they would receive on a cash rebate scheme.

What to look out for

The main advantage of the cash share-out is the scale of the sum that can be offered. This can be attractive. However, it involves a substantial amount of postage and handling and can cost more to administer than the benefit given to the consumer.

Repurchase offers

The offer

Purchasers of consumer durables, such as fridges or hi-fi, are offered a commitment by the manufacturer to buy back the product at a specified point in the future (often five years) for the same amount as they paid for it. A variant is to offer a lower guaranteed trade-in price.

How they work

This offer at first seems like a guarantee of bankruptcy for the manufacturer. It relies on three considerations:

- a great many people will forget to apply for repurchase in five years' time
- inflation will have eaten into the value
- those who do ask for repurchase form a good market for repeat purchase.

What to look out for

Offers of this kind need to be carefully calculated and insured, and low inflation levels are making them less attractive than they were. They can also seem too good to be true – certainly in the full repurchase form. However, as a means of making an offer with a higher perceived value than cost, they have their advantages in markets with repurchase cycles of five years or so.

COUPONS

The offer

Coupons are used to provide an immediate or delayed discount on a product or service to end-users or intermediaries. They can be distributed in a wide variety of ways, all of which have different redemption rates and vary considerably in popularity over time. They are used so extensively that they form a subject in their own right. As with delayed discounts, the critical factor is the level of redemption and the slippage between being attracted by the offer and taking it up.

How they work

A coupon is, in principle, a straightforward thing to organize: you print your coupons giving a specified saving on next purchase; you distribute them; retailers or other intermediaries accept them in part payment for your product or service; and you reimburse the intermediary. If there is no intermediary involved, it is even simpler: you simply accept your own coupons in part payment.

Coupons are the nearest most of us get to printing money, and we do so in huge volume. It is critical to think through questions of distribution, redemption and format.

There are six main ways of distributing coupons:

- on or in your product or service
- door to door
- in newspapers
- in magazines
- by direct mail
- in store.

These different ways of distributing coupons are described by the coupon industry as different 'media'. They have different shares of the total number of coupons distributed. This is shown in Figure 8: magazines and newspapers come out as clear leaders. It is a different picture if you look at how the different media compare for the number of coupons redeemed. This is shown in Figure 9 where we can see that in-pack and on-pack coupons are streets ahead of the rest.

The difference is the radically different levels of the redemption rates of the various media, which range from less than 1 per cent to over 20 per cent. The different redemption rates by media are shown in Figure 10. Note that there is also considerable change year-on-year. Although the general differences between different forms of media are clear enough, there is considerable variation over time.

So, how do you decide which way to distribute your coupons? It depends what you are trying to achieve. Different coupon 'media' have very different uses and characteristics.

- Coupons in or on a product or service are primarily a generator of repeat purchases and a reward for loyalty; they are not effective for new users.

- Door-to-door couponing is most effective for targeting a particular geographical area – for example, near a shop. It has relatively high distribution costs, but is effective in gaining new users, particularly when used in conjunction with a sample.

- Newspaper couponing is apparently wasteful (up to 99 per cent non-redemption), but the figures need to be related to the huge size of newspaper circulations. Whether it works on your product or service as a trial generator or as a reward to regular users can only be determined by experience.

- Magazine couponing is similar to newspaper couponing, but can be more carefully targeted.

- Direct mail is the most expensive and also the most targeted form of couponing, and has the highest redemption levels after in-store couponing.

- In-store couponing has the highest redemption levels of all categories. Its usefulness must be tested to establish whether or not it really does generate extra business for your product or service or simply provides a convenient discount to those who would have bought anyway.

Getting the format of a coupon right is vital for something that can be used as money. Clear guidelines have been drawn up for the grocery trade for the design, structure and organization of coupons. These are available from the ISP, and you should ensure you have an up-to-date copy.[7]

Any couponing activity requires a redemption system. If you are going to redeem your coupons yourself, the redemption systems are a matter for your own internal accountancy. If they are to be redeemed

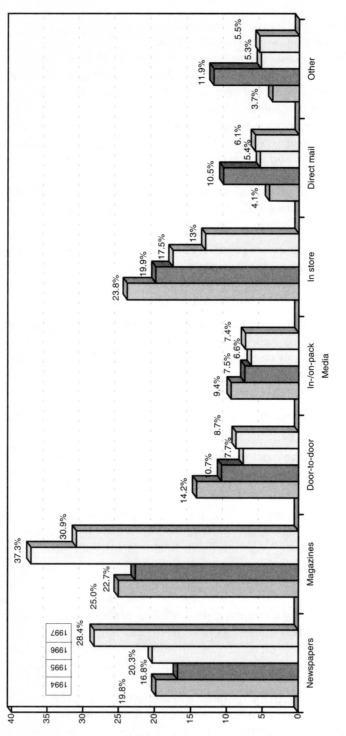

Figure 8   The share of distribution of coupons by media

Source: NCH Promotional Services

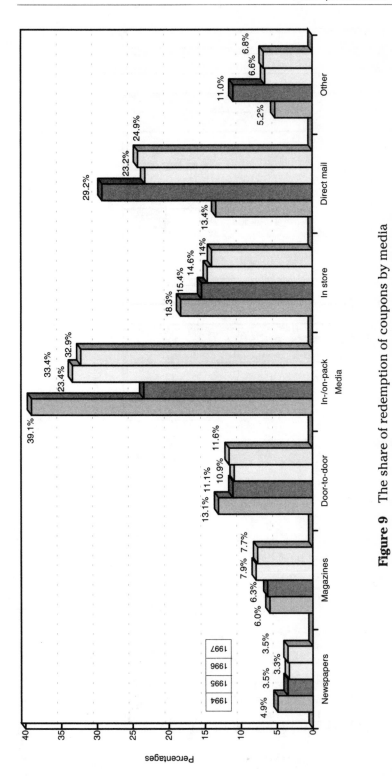

Figure 9   The share of redemption of coupons by media

Source: NCH Promotional Services

Figure 10   The different redemption rates of coupons by media

Source: NCH Promotional Services

by intermediaries, you need to ensure that all likely intermediaries will accept them and that they will be duly recompensed for their trouble in so doing. The best answer is to use one of the handling houses that specializes in coupon redemption and discuss your requirements fully with them. The leader in this field is NCH Promotional Services. NCH's experience is considerable, and has saved many a promoter from expensive error.

What to look out for

There are three major problems that can arise with any couponing activity.

- **Estimating redemption** The ranges given above are only averages and the cost difference between a high and low redemption can be huge. It is always best to test couponing on a small scale before you use it widely.

- **Malredemption** Malredemption is large-scale fraudulent redemption. It arises, for example, from a batch of newspapers being systematically cut for all their coupons and redeemed at a friendly retailer. There are ways of coping with it, and handling houses are best able to advise on this.

- **Misredemption** This differs from malredemption in that it is the result of individuals redeeming individual coupons against products or services they have not bought. It is almost impossible to act against without the support of retailers. For many years, major multiples accepted coupons irrespective of the products bought. In the mid 1990s, they agreed to check that the products on the coupon had been bought, but this is not something that is easy to police. An allowance must be made for a proportion of coupons (which cannot be accurately determined) to be misredeemed. If you are redeeming your coupons yourself, this will only arise as a result of human error on the part of your own staff.

Despite these difficulties, coupons are a promotional evergreen. They are a good way to provide a price benefit without making it available on every pack sold. The secret is to use coupons in a creative and carefully targeted manner, and to calculate in detail the redemption costs against the extra business you gain.

FINANCE DEALS

The offer

Consumer credit has grown by leaps and bounds in the last 20 years. It has accelerated dramatically during the 1990s as credit controls have loosened and financial innovation has increased. Popular resistance to buying on credit (if it ever existed except as a nostalgic memory) is certainly a thing of the past.

For these reasons, every business needs to understand how enabling customers to buy now and pay later can be used to its advantage. Fundamentally, this is a sales promotion operation.

If a customer pays by cash or cheque, it does not matter where that money comes from. Our interest as sales promoters is where the customer looks to us to help with the credit arrangements. This section is designed to tell you how to do it and how to evaluate the options.

Finance arrangements are one of the oldest sales promotional tools. It was commonplace until the 1960s for grocers, butchers and other tradesmen to run credit accounts for their customers. Popularly referred to as buying 'on tick', it had the benefit of any credit offer. Of course, credit arrangements of this kind never registered in the Treasury's money supply figures. It is one of the reasons the view that we live in a uniquely credit-based society today should be taken with a pinch of salt.

Zero per cent finance is one of the great sales-clinching offers of all time in 'high ticket' markets – those in which the consumer needs to lay out a substantial sum to make a purchase. It has been widely applied in the motor, furniture and consumer durables sectors. Like most creative finance offers, its application is potentially far wider.

Zero per cent is the pinnacle of a range of reduced interest offers. If bank loans are averaging 10 per cent and credit card interest is averaging 26 per cent, an offer of 6 or 8 per cent interest is also attractive, and very much cheaper to offer.

These offers share in common the fact that, at any one moment, money has a certain price. The price depends on who you are, how much you want, and over what period. The price of money can be found in the financial pages of the newspapers, and takes its lead from the rate set by the Bank of England. This is the benchmark against which, at any one time, reduced or 0 per cent interest offers can be set.

How they work

If a company lends money at less than the rate that it pays to borrow it, it has to make up the difference from somewhere.

For example, an electrical retailer offering an interest rate of 4 per cent on a £199 product, and paying interest at 9 per cent to the bank, must bear the difference of 5 per cent. What this amounts to requires fairly complicated calculations, which are best left to finance professionals. (It should be noted that here and elsewhere in this chapter interest rates are quoted at their flat or nominal rate, which is simpler for our purposes. The Consumer Credit Act requires, among other things, that the annual percentage rate (APR) is quoted for all interest rates.)

Having done the calculations, it is possible for the electrical retailer not only to put a figure on it, but to compare the cost to that of any other promotional offer. Let us assume that the offer we have described will cost the retailer £25. It is directly comparable to a £25 discount, insurance with a cost of £25 or a premium costing £25. Which works best? Different offers appeal to different people, and the finance offer will appeal most to those who have need of finance to make the purchase. For this reason, consumer durables retailers tend to ring the changes on the offers they make.

While the principle of subsidized finance is fairly simple, the forms it can take are immensely varied. There are four key forms of subsidized finance.

Manufacturer and finance house deals

These deals are normally set up by major manufacturers that sell through dealers – they most commonly occur in the motor trade. For example, Rover Group concluded a deal with Lombard to borrow on behalf of its customers a large slice of money at 8 per cent. It then constructed a range of interest rate options for its customers. These ranged from 4.1 per cent (for repayment in 12 months and a 50 per cent deposit) to 6.5 per cent (for repayment in 48 months and a 20 per cent deposit). Dealer and customer would agree the actual price of the car in the usual way. The net amount owing would then be repaid by the customer at the interest rate selected.

Rover Group, meanwhile, would pay Lombard the difference between 8 per cent and what the customer was actually paying. The calculations involved would not directly concern either the motor dealer or the customer, both of whom were benefiting from Rover Group's deal with Lombard.

Intermediary and finance house deals

Finance companies such as Lombard generally dislike concluding deals of this kind with companies other than major manufacturers. If you want to persuade them to do so, it is helpful to understand their criteria. These are the main ones.

- The item should be durable, identifiable and movable (DIM). This covers products that last, which have serial numbers on them and can be removed if the debt is not paid. Cars, boats and machinery obviously fit the bill.

- The debt outstanding should be less than the resale value of the item should they be forced to repossess it. The answer to that is to have relatively high deposits and relatively short repayment periods.

- You must be an honest, trustworthy, credible business.

Given that you can satisfy these criteria – and others of a more technical nature – there is no reason for not approaching a finance house to construct a finance deal that you can subsidize.

Personal loan deals

Items that are not durable, identifiable and movable – for example, furniture and carpets – cannot be financed by a finance house. The reason is that the item itself cannot provide adequate security against non-payment. One answer is for customers to take out a personal loan, normally secured against their house. The manufacturer or retailer can then subsidize the interest rate in the same way as with a finance house deal. There are many credit providers with whom these deals can be negotiated.

Unsecured finance

The final major form of subsidized finance involves the manufacturer or retailer providing the credit without direct recourse to any external source of money. It is commonly used by furniture retailers. Let us assume that a furniture retailer sells a three-piece suite on a no deposit, 0 per cent interest deal. The cash price is £1040, and the credit price is £10 per week for two years.

Applying discounted cash flow calculations to the repayments, the furniture retailer can calculate the value of the sale on the day it is made. Two of the crucial elements in this calculation will be the company's view of the movement of interest rates and inflation over the two-year period and the expected level of bad debts. Assuming these estimates are correct, it can identify the true value of the sale in profit and loss terms. The repayments then become a matter of cash flow.

Calculated incorrectly or with an over-optimistic assessment of likely bad debts, this method of providing subsidized finance is a sure-fire way of going bankrupt. It is a route that only the most hardened, experienced and cash-rich businesses should even think of.

What to look out for

Most marketing people do not need to be experts in consumer finance. Getting involved in 0 per cent finance deals or other subsidized interest rate offers calls for a fairly sophisticated knowledge of the potential, the pitfalls and the economics of our financial system. If you are willing to master the arithmetic and study the systems, the rewards can be considerable. However, even so, it is best to appoint a professional to do the job for you or at least to check your calculations. It is also vital to follow the requirements of the Consumer Credit Act and other legislation closely.

TRADE PRICE PROMOTIONS

In Chapter 2, we identified a critical feature of promoting via inter-mediaries such as retailers. A promotion that attracts the retailer but not the consumer may still work; a promotion that attracts the consumer but not the retailer is unlikely to get off the starting blocks.

The distinction is often made between 'push promotions' (aimed at pushing products via the retailer to the consumer) and 'pull prom-otions' (aimed at the consumer, pulling products via the retailer). The distinction is not an absolute one – most promotions need both pull and push if stock is not going to sit on the shelves (not enough pull) or not reach them in the first place (not enough push). This section looks at the push element in the mix – the use of price to give retailers reasons to support the promotion of your product or do the promotion themselves. There are five main forms of trade price promotion.

Overriders

The offer

An overriding discount is agreed at the beginning of a year between a supplier and a purchaser, and is payable by the supplier at the end of the year if the purchaser has achieved agreed targets.

How they work

Overriders normally relate to the volume taken over the year, but can also cover display, distribution and other business targets. If the targets are not reached, the overrider is not paid. They are heavily used by food and motor manufacturers and holiday companies supplying via retailers. Some motor dealers derive most of their profit from overriders, discounting the normal trade margin to their own customers.

What to look out for

Some purchasing professionals dislike overriders on the grounds that the cost to the supplier is simply built back into the price. Suppliers also dislike them because, over time, the targets can become ritualized and purchasers can expect their overrider as a right. Nevertheless, they are widely used, and in some markets cannot be avoided – they become a cost of doing business. The trick is to make sure that the targets set for the overrider in annual negotiations give some benefit to both parties over what would otherwise have been achieved.

Display and advertising allowances

The offer

These are allowances for a retailer to conduct some piece of promotion for the manufacturer. The allowances can pay for media support, stack ends, leaflets, coupons, window bills, display and any other form of retail support.

How they work

Most retailers have a tariff for almost every form of promotional support – from a stack end to a window bill. Increasingly, allowances are charged for listing a product, and investment in the retailer's in-house magazine or advertising is a required cost of doing business. Allowances that used to be at the discretion of manufacturers are increasingly at the command of the retailer. The growth of EPOS systems has enabled even medium-sized retailers to know exactly how much of a product can be sold from a given position in the store, and to charge manufacturers accordingly.

What to look out for

Manufacturers need to look closely at the total profitability of each product line in each retailer. Take away the total of all allowances, overriders, volume discounts and other trade discounts from the selling price to the retailer and you have the net selling price. Take your manufacturing and promotional costs away from that and you know the contribution to overheads you are achieving from that retailer on that product line. If possible – and it often is – allowances should be targeted to achieve particular results, such as extra display and advertising. In many cases, allowances have become part of an increasingly complicated calculation of the cost of doing business with a particular retailer. You need an equally complicated financial system to work out if it is worth while.

If you are a small- or medium-sized retailer, there is massive opportunity for increasing your margins by claiming allowances. The major multiples all have sophisticated EPOS systems that give them the power of knowledge. It is knowledge that gives the retailer power, and small retailers still have a long way to go in acquiring it.

Volume and case bonuses

The offer

These are short-term bonuses given by manufacturers to retailers. A case bonus is an amount of additional discount given per case bought. A volume bonus is an amount of additional discount given for buying a certain volume of product – more than would normally be bought at that time. Sometimes these take particular forms. For example, a baker's dozen is the practice of charging for 12 cases while supplying 13.

How they work

Volume and case bonuses are used by manufacturers to fill a pipeline into the trade, to make life difficult for a competitor by filling stockrooms or to encourage a retailer to offer shelf price reductions. They also work in some trade sectors as a means of encouraging display and support for promotional activity. The hugely successful 'Bass

Nights' developed by Bass in pubs across the country relied on this mechanism. Pubs were offered a kit comprising posters, quiz games, merchandise prizes and other items to run a themed fun night in the pub. These were good news for the consumer. What appealed to the landlord was the offer of a free keg of beer. This put extra margin behind the bar – and encouraged them to run Bass Nights as often as they could.

What to look out for

Nothing is easier than giving the trade additional discounts in the hope that it will increase sales of your product, but it is a slippery slope that leads to increased expectations of discounts and a steady lowering in your average selling price. It is essential to use volume and case bonuses intermittently and only in return for defined benefits. As retailer power grows in most sectors, it is easier to say that than to do it in practice. It is one of the main reasons promoters seek alternative promotional mechanisms that do not devalue the brand's price to the trade or consumer.

Count and recount

The offer

The name 'count and recount' derives from days when salespeople would habitually go into customers' stockrooms to count the stock. Count and recount gave the retailer a bonus on the difference between the count and the recount – in other words, on the amount that had been sold. In most sectors, it can now be done by EPOS counting the quantity sold through the till, but the principle is the same.

How they work

Count and recount puts the focus of the manufacturer's discount on what is sold to the consumer. It provides a good reason for the retailer to ensure that products are not just taken in, but sold on to the customers.

What to look out for

In major multiples, this technique has largely been replaced by mechanics such as the multibuy, which have a similar effect. In other trade sectors, count and recount is a way of giving trade discounts that do not simply end up increasing retailer margins. It gives an incentive to consumer sales.

Credit offers

The offer

The provision of credit is as important to the retailer as it is to the consumer. Providing the trade with enhanced credit terms can encourage earlier and deeper stocking of your range.

How they work

Multiple retailers derive a significant part of their profits and their positive cash flow by taking payment from their customers two months or more before they pay their suppliers. In these markets, the manufacturer is a key source of capital. In other sectors, trade payments can be faster, and the manufacturer can vary the payment period. This is particularly important in seasonal businesses, such as garden centres.

What to look out for

The cost of credit can be calculated for trade promotions in the same way as for consumer promotions. It is important to be aware of the risk of bad debts and to be clear that you have the financial resources to carry the delayed payment. If you can do so, using credit is a powerful means of trade promotion.

CASE STUDIES

The first of the three case studies in this chapter illustrates the long-range alternation of price and value promotions in Tesco's promotional strategy. The other two are examples of price promotion taking a far more focused form in the case of two particular brands than it is often assumed to do.

CASE STUDY 15: TESCO

During the mid 1970s, Tesco became the largest grocery user of Green Shield Stamps. These were stamps produced by a third-party operator, rather like a low-tech version of Air Miles. Consumers collected them at the checkout, stuck them into books and exchanged the books for merchandise at the equivalent of Argos catalogue shops. They were widely available at petrol stations and other retailers as well as at Tesco. Green Shield Stamps were a central element in Tesco's strategy for customer loyalty. They were also costing 2 per cent of turnover, and were spiralling out of control. Double, even quadruple stamps were becoming commonplace.

On 9 June 1977, Tesco signalled the end of Green Shield Stamps and plunged the grocery trade into a bitter price war with the launch of 'Operation Checkout'. Shops were closed on a Saturday night, windows were covered and the Sunday press predicted a major development. When they opened the next day, they revealed deep, long-term price cuts in every department. Other retailers were forced to respond in kind. The price war continued into the early 1980s, radically increasing the major multiples' market share, depressing their profits and forcing a wave of closures, mergers and rationalizations. Tesco's own market share shot up from 8.5 to 12 per cent.

The recession of the early 1990s brought a new spate of price wars, with retailers competing with discount shops and the expected development of warehouse clubs by developing a secondary range of low-priced own-label 'value' lines. As the economy improved from 1993 onwards, so the threat of the discounters proved to be less serious than commentators had expected.

Tesco again rocked the grocery world with the launch of Clubcard in February 1995. It initially offered a 1 per cent saving on spends of over £10, plus a range of product offers. Clubcard quickly attracted over 5 million customers and was credited with driving Tesco's market share up to 18.5 per cent and producing a 16 per cent rise in sales in the first year. It was also quickly followed by competitors, including Safeway's ABC card and Sainsbury's Saver Card. In 1997, Boots took loyalty cards a stage further with the launch of an electronic card offering a 4 per cent discount. A number of co-operative retailers, which had originated rebates to consumers in the form of the 'co-op dividend' in the 1840s, also experimented with new electronic forms of dividend.

Where does Tesco go next? There are two safe predictions: that it is unlikely to retain the same formula forever and that it is unlikely to let its competitors be the first to make the change. What is less clear is the direction of the change. A new concept in 'loyalty'? Back to price competition or something quite different? The delight of sales promotion is that everything changes, but over a 20-year period, some things look much the same.

- What would you expect those consumers most attracted by the promotional policy adopted by Tesco in 1978 to do today?

- How has Tesco organized its total product and promotional mix to keep them on board?

CASE STUDY 16: GALE'S HONEY

In 1994, Nestlé's long-established honey brand, Gale's, faced a classic brand squeeze. It was 15 per cent more expensive than own-label honey's, and there was a price increase in the offing. Consumers viewed honey as . . . honey! Sales were slipping, brand loyalty was diminishing, a major multiple was threatening to delist, and there was little money in the budget. Cutting the price may have worked in the short term, but would have made the premium charged over own-label versions, ultimately, unsustainable. So, what could Gale's do?

The Nestlé brand manager set their sales promotion agency SMP a long list of objectives – reduce the rate of sales decline, avoid delisting, create impact on-pack, increase distribution, encourage multiple purchase, build loyalty – and keep the cost of the promotion under control. There's virtually everything in that list of objectives, but they boil down to one thing: provide an interesting reason for Gale's buyers to buy more. Also, one major constraint: keep the cost under control.

Getting to the heart of a long brief is a major challenge in sales promotion, and that was the first part of the agency's job. The agency built on the idea of buying more by opting for a 20p off next purchase coupon as the basic offer. It is a tried and tested mechanic for repeat purchase, but hardly exciting. It can also be expensive. So, the agency devised a novel multiple choice.

The 20p on-pack coupon was printed on latex. It could be scratched away and, if you were lucky, reveal a prize of £10. The consumer was then faced with an interesting choice: the chance of £10 or the guarantee of 20p. Once scratched off, the 20p coupon became invalid. The problem then was what to offer the majority of consumers who opted to win £10 but didn't win it. Instead of nothing, they found a beehive logo, which could be collected, for a range of Gale's pottery items.

The promotion worked. Distribution increased from 80 to 85 per cent, delisting was avoided, sales increased by 15 per cent, and coupon redemption was kept to less than 2 per cent. Also, the database of Gale's collectors was dramatically increased.

When you're in a tight corner, promotions need particularly careful thought. This could so easily have been a standard '20p off next purchase'. By asking consumers to have a bet on a £10 prize and not leaving them with nothing if they lost, Gale's hit every part of the brief.

The promotion also illustrates the difference between a marketing and a promotional brief. Nestlé's list of objectives was a wish-list. The promotion was a very well-targeted answer to the question 'Who do I want to do what?'

- If Gale's Honey put out a brief with the target of attracting new users, what promotional mechanics would be appropriate?

- When you look at the list of promotional offers allowed in different parts of the EU in Chapter 12, what parts of this promotion would you have to change if you wanted to run it across the EU?

CASE STUDY 17: WORCESTERSHIRE SAUCE

Lea & Perrins' Worcestershire Sauce is one of those products more likely to be found at the back of many people's cupboards than in everyday use. Yet, a wide range of daily dishes could be spiced up by a dash of Worcestershire Sauce if only it could be brought to the front of their minds.

The agency Lovell Vass Boddey sought to do this with a multilayered campaign that won an ISP Award in 1995. Data from previous promotional responders was profiled against a lifestyle database to target two million households with a minipack. This contained a sample of the sauce, a 10p off next purchase coupon and a free mail-in offer for a recipe book.

The coupon usage rate was 10 per cent, and uptake for the recipe book 6 per cent. Responders also received an additional coupon against next purchase and a lifestyle questionnaire, which received a 25 per cent response. This fed into planning and profiling for further promotions.

Door-drop samples, money off next purchase coupons and mail-in offers of recipe books are all standard promotional mechanics. The characteristic of this promotion was their intelligent integration and the use of database profiling to increase targeting accuracy before and after the promotion.

- What alternative means of coupon distribution were available to Worcestershire Sauce and what benefits/disadvantages would they have over the one chosen?

- What factors would you take into account in calculating the proof of purchase requirement to make for the recipe book?

SUMMARY

Price promoting is playing with fire. All the surveys show that consumers prefer it to any other form of promotion. They also show that it devalues brands and leads to an expectation of even more price promotion. The same holds true for the trade.

Promoters are most likely to use price promotion effectively if they think in terms of segment pricing, look for concrete benefits from each discount they give and use price promotion intermittently. One of the key challenges of sales promotion is to find value promotions that work as well as (or nearly as well as) price promotions and add to, rather than devalue, brand values. However, price promotion continues to be a benchmark for promotional effectiveness and is often made unavoidable by trade pressures and competition.

10

PREMIUM PROMOTIONS

Premium promotions are offers in which the benefit comes in the form of an item of merchandise. Why a 'premium'? The reason for the choice of name is lost in the mists of time. It can cover anything from a potted plant to a virtual pet to a magazine. It can be a standard item or uniquely created, branded by the promoter or off the shelf. Indeed, all merchandise and all products are potential premiums.

Sales promotion agencies and promotional suppliers are more frequently involved in this type of promotion than in price promotions because selecting and sourcing the premium, organizing handling and redemption and conveying the attractiveness of the merchandise is an industry in itself. Because of this, premium promotions play a big role in the sales promotions that are discussed in the marketing press.

Premium promotions are the most frequently used value offer. They are particularly good at giving the opportunity to enhance brand communication in a tangible way. There is considerable scope for originality, too, for creating something unique to your product or service that the competition cannot copy. There is scope for creating real consumer excitement and for placing in consumers' homes items that will be used for years to come. The relationship this can create with the brand is one of the longest-lasting effects of sales promotion.

There is a permanent tension in sales promotion between offering money off (price promotions) and offering a material, preferably brand-enhancing, benefit (value promotions). Case Study 18 at the end of this chapter details how Procter & Gamble moved from one to the other – and back again. The basis of premium promotions is competing without tampering with the price.

This chapter looks first at the four main premium promotion mechanics: on-pack offers, with purchase premiums, free mail-ins and

self-liquidators. It is important to understand the different characteristics of these mechanics, but, in practice, they are blurred by a fifth
category – the brand extension promotion.

An example of this is the *Dedicated To Pleasure* CD sponsored by
Haagen-Dazs in 1996.[1] Produced by EMI, the CD used the company's
distinctive press advertising on the cover, and included the Sarah
Vaughan track 'Make Yourself Comfortable', used in its TV advertising.
It sold over 60,000 copies, gave the brand a presence in 3500 music
stores and reached the Top 20 for compilation albums (itself constituting over a third of total music sales).

What else could the CD be used for? It could be made available free
for a large number of proofs of purchase (a free mail-in), sold at cost
price (a self-liquidator) or offered in company ice-cream parlours free
with multiple purchases (a near-pack). For practical reasons it probably could not be attached to cartons of ice-cream in the freezer (an
on-pack), but it could certainly be given to trade customers (a business
gift). In other words, the different types of premium promotion are
self-contained, but can be combined with the right premium to carry
the values and advertising images of the brand in a series of different
contexts.

Thinking this way has its dangers: always remember that the
premium must grip the promotional objective. Using a premium simply
because you've got it to hand is a mistake – it must justify itself against
each of your objectives.

ON-PACK OFFERS

The offer

This is a form of premium promotion in which the premium is
physically attached to the product. If it is in the product, as with
breakfast cereals, it is sometimes called an 'in-pack' promotion. If the
premium surrounds the product, replacing its normal packaging,
as with a storage jar for coffee, it is sometimes called a 'container'
promotion. An example of a straight on-pack is a magazine covermount
– a premium taped or bound to the magazine cover.

How it works

These promotions have similar characteristics to the immediate
discounts discussed in Chapter 9: they have instant appeal, give an

immediate benefit and do not divert resources into handling and postage; they are also quite expensive to run.

Whether it is appropriate to put a premium in, on or around the product depends very much on the nature and size of both the premium and the product, and the characteristics of your packing processes. It would be evidently impractical to include a paintbrush in a tin of paint and unnecessary to go to the trouble of taping a toy to the outside of a cornflakes packet. All things being equal, it is best to put the premium in the product; next best to attach it to it. These steps prevent consumers taking the premium but not buying the product. However, there can be considerable costs in creating new shipping containers and in disruption to high-speed packing lines. Retailers can also be resistant to non-standard pack sizes, particularly in the grocery trade. The use of on-pack offers is thus a matter of carefully weighing costs and benefits.

Covermounts are universal in the magazine market. There are periodic statements that they have gone too far, and that magazines will start competing on editorial quality instead, but use of cover- mounts goes on increasing.[2] As with much sales promotion, the value is two-way. In every sector of the magazine market, there are increasing numbers of interchangeable products and consumer loyalty is low. For manufacturers of certain products – notably book and music publishers – gaining exposure for the product on a magazine cover can be a very good means of sampling potential customers.

Ideal covermounts are flat, cheap, attractive and useful – which is why calendars, diaries and books are found on magazines as different as *FHM*, *Yachting Monthly* and *Options*. However, there is a limit to the use of paper. IPC claimed sales increases of 10–15 per cent from using confectionery as covermounts – a Chocolate Orange bar on *Essentials* and low-sugar Canderel on *Healthy Eating*.[3] In both cases, the products were new to the market, so gave their manufacturers a targeted sampling opportunity. In the case of Canderel and *Healthy Eating*, the consumer match was particularly good.

Use of on-pack premiums in the child and teens markets include pens, make-up and badges on magazines and the extensive use of character merchandise on confectionery. Nestlé uses figurines of Disney characters from the *Lion King* to *Pocahontas* in the place of caps on larger Smarties tubes. Once the Smarties have been eaten, the figurine forms part of a collection of characters that the child can keep. This collector element in on-pack premiums is less developed in the magazine market, but could be applied there too.

The reusable container form of on-pack offer makes the premium the packaging and the packaging the premium. Familiar examples include glass storage jars with instant coffee. They offer high perceived value, and can be made as a range that encourages repeat purchase. It is not a concept that would work in the service sector, but it is an excellent (and often quite cheap) promotion for any product that needs packaging.

What to look out for

Immediate free premiums suffer from the cost of giving away anything worth while on a low-priced product. They do not discriminate between those who would have bought without the incentive and those incentivized to buy, meaning that some of your promotional spending will be wasted. There is often an extra cost of new outer packaging and adjustments to packing processes to take into account, which is not of benefit to the customer. Used extensively, however, as with covermounts, they can simply become a cost of doing business rather than an additional offer.

On-pack offers are best compared with immediate price offers, and here the advantages really show. They do not devalue the product's price and they can develop and reinforce brand identity. If you have selected the right item, immediate free premiums can be a very powerful incentive to buy. The principal factors to look out for are that the premium should be right and the offer cost-effective in margin terms.

WITH PURCHASE PREMIUMS

The offer

These are promotions in which the premium is not physically attached to the product, but is available at the point of purchase. They are sometimes called 'near-packs' as a result of the retailers' habit of locating the premium near to the pack or product being promoted, and sometimes 'gift with purchase' (GWP).

In the service and retail sectors, these promotions all roll into one: when you buy the service, you collect the premium. Examples include a free portable TV when you buy a car, a free personal filing system when you appoint an estate agent and a free carnation at the conclusion of a restaurant meal.

These promotions are very common in duty-free outlets and at cosmetics counters in department stores where vanity bags or other items are given away when a purchase of a particular brand is made.

They also work well in the pub trade, so long as great care is taken not to overburden bar staff. Case Study 18 at the end of this chapter describes a classic grocery near-pack promotion in the 1960s, and Case Study 21 a near-pack used in the pub trade.

How it works

As with all premium promotions, a number of factors have to brought into balance: the attractiveness of the premium for the target market, its relevance to the brand, its cost, and the practicality of handling it. With near-packs, handling is a critical issue because arrangements have to be made for the product to be available at the point of purchase without being taken by those who do not buy the product. For these reasons, near-packs work best in outlets where there is counter service (as in the case of cosmetics counters) or where it is possible and worth while to use field marketing staff (as in duty-free outlets – see Chapter 4 for details of field marketing). It is generally not possible to use near-packs in grocery multiples today.

The premium can simply be a one-hit reward, such as a vanity bag with a purchase of cosmetics. It is also possible to include in the bag samples of other products, and to include coupons to be used against the purchase of full-size packs. That way the gift with purchase feeds into subsequent sales.

What to look out for

Near-packs give a direct and immediate incentive to buy one brand in preference to another without devaluing the retail price. The right incentive – such as a cosmetics vanity bag – can add real value to the brand proposition, but they are expensive, involve careful arrangements at point of purchase and reward those who would have bought without the incentive. They are, in practice, restricted to high-margin products.

FREE MAIL-INS

The offer

Free mail-ins are premium promotions in which the customer collects one or more proofs of purchase and sends them in for the item on offer entirely free or at no cost beyond postage. The benefit is delayed and not immediate. It is also subject to action on the part of the consumer after purchasing the item. Unlike on-packs and with-purchase premiums, not everyone who is encouraged to buy by the promotion will send in for the premium.

How it works

The word 'free' is one of the most compelling and powerful in our vocabulary. Rightly, it is subject to stringent restrictions. An offer is 'free' only if the customer pays nothing to obtain the item other than collecting the requisite number of proofs of purchase or pays only for postage in one or both directions. It is fair enough to say 'free with 30p for postage' if that is the cost of the postage, but it is not allowable to say 'free with 50p for postage and packing'. Promotions that require a telephone entry can be 'free' only if a non-premium telephone line is used – in other words, if the promoter is not recouping some of the costs by making profits on the telephone service.

A critical question in the structuring of a free mail-in promotion is the number of proofs of purchase that your customers must collect in order to obtain the item. This is a rule of thumb exercise, and follows these criteria.

■ The number must reflect the typical purchase frequency of your product category. Note that it is category frequency, not brand frequency: the purpose of a free mail-in is to encourage consumers to use your brand rather than your competitors' for more of their purchases of that type of product. If more than one was required for a free mail-in on a hi-fi or life assurance policy, that would be absurd, but for cat food or a visit to a pub, ten or more would be wholly reasonable.

■ The number must also be influenced by whether or not you are seeking to influence trialists, light users, medium users or heavy users of your product or service. The higher the number, the more you move along the spectrum towards heavy users. The lower the number, the less likely it is to make any difference to the purchase frequency of heavy users.

■ The level of redemptions is directly proportional to the number of proofs of purchase required. Raise the number of proofs of purchase and you lower the redemption level, and vice versa. This has obvious budget implications. The decision on the proof of purchase level is often taken in response to the level of redemption that is affordable.

The level of consumer redemption is naturally affected by the attractiveness of the premium (which you will want to maximize) and the closing date for applications (which you should set so that no products will be on retail sale after the closing date).

Two further factors are more amenable to alteration. You must decide whether or not to make any charge for postage and whether or not to offer a Freepost facility for customers to mail in their proofs of purchase. Note that the lower the postage costs are in each direction, the higher the response rate will be. You must also decide whether or not to restrict the offer to one application per household: this can unfairly restrict the reward to heavy and loyal users, but it also cuts out people exploiting an attractive offer aimed at less regular purchasers.

Free mail-ins can be used as part of a bigger promotional package. Remember, Gale's offered branded collectibles as a consolation offer to those who failed to obtain a £10 instant win (Case Study 16). SmithKline Beecham did the same with a promotion for Ribena in 1995, themed on the *Casper* film.[4] Consumers were invited to look under bottle ring pulls or inside cartons to see if Casper had 'spooked' their pack and given them a cash prize or a special Casper bubble watch. If not, they could collect tokens for the watch or, on the bottles, for a Casper beaker that revealed ghostly characters as it was filled.

Using free mail-ins in this way means that a promotion works at two levels: as an instant-win incentive for light users and as a collector offer for heavy users.

What to look out for

The operational planning of free mail-ins is critical. Things can go wrong with the handling, with the design of the premium, with delivery dates and so forth. Getting them right is a matter of sound organization and attention to detail.

The most difficult issue is organizing a supply of premiums to match your expected redemption level. It is embarrassing to be so optimistic that you have a warehouse full at the end, and equally embarrassing to be unable to meet demand. This leads many promoters to seek over-redemption insurance or to contract with a company prepared to supply all the premiums redeemed at a fixed fee (this aspect is covered in Chapter 4).

Unless you contract out the promotion for a fixed fee, you will need to develop a contingency plan to deal with the twin problems of over-redemption and under-redemption. Make an estimate of the likely flow of redemptions over the promotional period, then monitor the flow over the first few weeks to give you early warning of what the final redemption level will be.

If a free mail-in redeems at less than its expected level, you may be left with surplus premiums. You have three options: agree a sale-or-return arrangement with your premium supplier at the beginning (difficult if the premium is specially branded); sell off the surplus to a company specializing in the disposal of unwanted premiums (normally at a significant loss); or keep them for another (but probably equally unsuccessful) promotion.

If a free mail-in redeems at above its expected level, you may be faced with difficulties in obtaining sufficient extra premiums in time. Clearly, your early warning system should help here. It is also advisable to make arrangements for rapid extra deliveries with your premium suppliers at the beginning. Section 35 of the Sales Promotion Code makes it clear that 'phrases such as "subject to availability" do not relieve promoters of the obligation to take all reasonable steps to avoid disappointing customers'. If you cannot supply the premium you promised, 'products of a similar or greater quality or a cash payment should normally be substituted'. The best option is to order slightly fewer items than your expected redemption level, and have good arrangements for rapid re-supply with your suppliers.

Finally, you will need to organize the system for warehousing the premiums, receiving customer applications, sending out the premiums, banking the postage contributions (if any) and handling any subsequent customer complaints. There are specialist companies called 'handling houses' that can provide this service if you decide not to do it yourself, and these are discussed in Chapter 4.

SELF-LIQUIDATORS

The offer

A self-liquidator promotion (SLP) is one in which the customer pays for all (or almost all) of the cost of the premium and its associated handling and postage. Such an offer cannot be described as 'free'. At best, it can be described as a 'bargain' when the cost is still below what customers would pay in the shops. A typical example of a self-liquidator would be a 'Super kitchen knife – just £1.99, plus 50p postage and packing'.

How it works

A self-liquidator works in exactly the same way as a free mail-in, except that the customer pays for all or most of the cost of putting on the offer.

What to look out for

Self-liquidators were popular in the days of resale price maintenance, before the widespread development of retail discounting and mail order. In the 1970s, they fell out of favour. It became less and less possible to price a self-liquidator at a level that made it worth while for consumers to send in for it. Redemption levels of 1 per cent or less became common. Hugh Davidson, the former European Vice-President of Playtex, is scathing about them: 'Usually has no effect on consumer or trade sales; usually has nil level of interest for trade; a very over-used promotion technique; absorbs management and sales-force time to no object'.[5]

So, why do companies go on using them? The reason is that there are some cases in which they can be valuable. Nestlé, for example, created a series of watches that it offered as an SLP in France, Spain and Portugal on its Nesquick and Chopaquick brands. Produced in bulk in Switzerland, they featured an N instead of pointers and a rabbit and a dog respectively, which lit up when a button was pressed at night. They sold at significantly less than comparable watches.[6] Many book and CD products can work as SLPs because the retail margins remain very high. Collectibles such as branded merchandise can also be effective among regular users of a brand.

Self-liquidators work if one or more factors are present: you locate a premium at a radically lower price than that at which it is available anywhere else; you create an image for your premiums that makes it a desirable, full-price item; and if the margins in the category are very large. With these exceptions, self-liquidators are an attempt to run an extra benefit offer without actually giving an extra benefit. It is not surprising that customers give them the thumbs down.

BRAND EXTENSION PROMOTIONS

The offer

Forty years ago, businesses relied on resale price maintenance and branding was in its infancy. No one walked round in Brylcreem clothing, however much they put it on their hair. No one wore Burtons labels on the outsides of their shirts. Elvis Presley releases were not accompanied by a merchandise deal. The same change in the nature of business competition that has led to the decline of self-liquidators has led to the increase in brand extension promotions. The Haagen-Dazs promotion cited earlier in this chapter is a typical example. Many of these make a profit for the promoter.

An offer that makes a profit is a particularly attractive form of promotion. It adds to, rather than uses, your marketing budget, and turns the normal worry about redemption rates on its head. If each redemption makes you money, the more the merrier!

How it works

Brand extension promotions began when companies realized that people would pay high prices for merchandise carrying their brand names. Early entrants into this business were soft drinks brands (Coca-Cola), alcoholic drinks (Guinness) and motor cars (BMW). Items were sold by coupons on the product, mail-order catalogues and off-the-page advertising. During the 1980s, Coca-Cola extended the principle to retail shops selling only Coca-Cola-branded merchandise. They became a profit centre in their own right.

Confectionery companies have followed the same principle in a different way. Nestlé's Christmas stockings have long contained a tape, book or toy in addition to a selection of confectionery items. Once the premium exceeds the cost of the confectionery, it is questionable which is product and which is premium. The inclusion of collectible self-assembly plastic or other models is a permanent feature of Kinder Surprise eggs and several brands of yogurt aimed at children. Cosmetics companies, such as Revlon, have created bags containing a complete nail-care kit, and sold them as a temporary special product.

Confectionery companies, notably Cadbury's, have also been successful in licensing their brand names for use on a range of items, including lunchboxes and rucksacks, in return for a royalty on each item sold. The line between the premium purchased by the company for promotional use, the product manufactured under licence by a third party and the brand extension jointly marketed by both in their mutual interest has become blurred.

Customer magazines are a form of premium. A 1996 Mintel survey identified 246 customer magazines in the UK, among which financial services with 43 magazines, travel with 34, IT with 26 and retailing with 25 were particularly well represented.[7] Customer magazines are a promotional benefit in themselves, a platform for further promotional offers and a means of engaging other firms in joint promotion. Their scale is colossal – *Ford Magazine*, published in four variants, has a print run of 800,000 copies, putting it among the top 20 UK consumer titles.

Is this sales promotion? In Chapter 1, sales promotion was defined as a range of price and value offers designed to achieve marketing objectives by changing any part of the marketing mix to influence the behaviour of end-users or intermediaries, normally for a defined time period. Changing the product by including things in it or creating new products by putting your brand name on them is a sales promotional activity. It requires the promoter to think laterally about the brand – not just as a bar of chocolate, but as a bundle of values that can be expressed equally well in clothing, bags, watches, albums and magazines.

What to look out for

The critical question to ask yourself if you are considering this type of promotion is 'What business am I in?' The danger is that managers become overexcited about what are often marginal profit opportunities in branded merchandise and neglect the marketing of their core product.

Be aware of the point at which an activity ceases to be promotional and becomes a business in its own right. *The Guinness Book of Records* began as a promotional premium for Guinness. It has become an entirely self-standing product that many will not even associate with the dark liquid that gave it birth.

BUSINESS GIFTS

The offer

Business gifts are items given to trade customers to promote goodwill. In the grocery trade, they are often known as 'dealer loaders' – a reference to their historic use in persuading dealers to load up with stock beyond their requirements in return for an item of merchandise.

How they work

A survey by Mintel in 1997 of large- and medium-sized companies showed that existing customers are the main focus of business gift activity – cited by 63 per cent of respondents.[8] Branding of items was seen as essential by 70 per cent of respondents. Few companies spent more than £20,000 a year on business gifts and most were not wholly clear as to why they were doing it. Yet, judging by the level of advertising for clocks, calendars, ties and leather goods in the marketing press, business gifts are big business. Not knowing why you're doing it simply isn't good enough.

Some specialists in the industry draw a firm distinction between a premium and a business gift. A premium is seen as an item designed to persuade a consumer to buy one brand rather than another. A business gift is seen as something that has impact, attractiveness, usefulness and longevity, but has no such focused objective.[9] This is a false distinction. Eversheds used a highly imaginative premium item to encourage firms to contact it about intellectual property law (Case Study 7). Electrolux used a tape recorder in a special box to encourage buyers to list a new product (Case Study 20). Chapter 3 described the use of a single wellington boot to encourage commercial property agents to visit a new development. These are examples of items of merchandise being used in imaginative ways to persuade business customers to do something. The key sales promotional question 'Who do I want to do what?' therefore applies to business gifts as much as to any other area of sales promotion.

The public sector and many large organizations have rules preventing their staff receiving gifts of more than token value from suppliers, and these must be respected. However, 80 per cent of businesses are small operations run by their owners and there is no conflict of interest between owner and buyer. If this is your market, an item of merchandise can be a perfectly reasonable way of persuading them to buy one brand rather than another. When NatWest wanted to encourage start-up businesses to choose it rather than another bank, it teamed up with BT to offer what was, essentially, a consumer promotion (Case Study 12).

Approaching business gifts in this way enables you to use them in a cost-effective and focused way. Avista has sometimes given well-made and distinctive soft toys with discreet branding to our clients at Christmas. They seldom cost more than £10, and have this objective: 'we want our clients to think of us as people who are imaginative, know about premiums and care about families'. Business gifts can be used to achieve other objectives, too:

- ■ 'we want personnel managers to have our telephone number on their desk at all times'

- ■ 'we want leisure centre staff to carry their personal kit in one of our sports bags'

- ■ 'we want shipping managers to put a map of the world on their walls that shows our shipping routes'

- ■ 'we want marketing executives to come to our seminar on opportunities on the Internet rather than to those of our competitors'

- ■ 'we want chief executives to understand that we are at the leading edge of thinking in our business'.

Note that the promotional objectives in all these cases are specific and deliverable. If the objective in the first example is specified as 'we want personnel managers to telephone us every time they need temporary staff' it cannot be delivered by a business gift. Having your telephone number on their desk is helpful, but the objective is not then a foregone conclusion. You will need to use it as part of a promotional campaign, not as the campaign itself.

The objectives cited above could be delivered, respectively, by a branded desk clock, an up-to-the-minute sports bag, an overprinted map, a free book on the Internet and a reprint of an article discussing your firm that appeared in an industry magazine. None of these items is particularly expensive. Some, such as the magazine article reprint, demand imagination and effort, but cost almost nothing at all.

When you are looking for business gifts, there are three sources. The first is to go direct to the many companies that advertise in the marketing press or to your local *Yellow Pages*. This can take time, but is the cheapest way of doing it if you know exactly what you want. The second is to use a business gifts catalogue. There are very many of these, often syndicated to local agents. Burostat, for example, produces a 124-page annual catalogue of gifts that local agents overprint with their own name. The advantage of this is that you have a single source of supply, can order in small quantities and that many items are available from stock. The third approach is to use a premium sourcing house. These were discussed in Chapter 4, but they are only really interested in large quantities or wide ranges of items. The advantage of using them is that they know about the latest technologies and designs and can search out and design something original for your company.

What to look out for

There are rules governing VAT and income tax on business gifts, particularly those given internally. Make sure you have a copy of the latest Customs and Excise advice and are in touch with your Inland Revenue office if you have any doubt.

Make sure you have also understood the internal rules of the companies you do business with. Violating a rule that puts the recipient of a gift in an embarrassing position is bad business: no one can have as a promotional objective 'I want my customer to be embarrassed'.

That said, make sure you apply to business gifts the same rigorous thinking about promotional objectives that you use in other areas. Don't expect them to do more than they can do, but make sure they do that job well.

CASE STUDIES

The four promotions in this chapter specifically focus on near-packs, on-packs and business gifts. Other relevant case studies for premium promotions are Kleenex Facial Tissues (Case Study 4), Eversheds (Case Study 7) and NatWest/BT (Case Study 12).

CASE STUDY 18: PROCTER & GAMBLE

Some promotions are remembered for years, if not decades. Test this out by asking someone over 50 if they remember the plastic roses promotions of the early 1960s. This is the story behind it.[10]

In the late 1950s, Procter & Gamble and Lever Brothers were locked in trench warfare. Daz was an innovative synthetic detergent when it was launched by Procter & Gamble in 1953. Two years later, Lever Brothers responded with Omo. By the late 1950s, there was no functional difference in washing performance between the two brands. Price promotion was rife and ultimately unproductive. Up to 70 per cent of packs carried a '3d off' flash, weakening the perceived value of the brands. There was continuous heavyweight TV advertising. Despite all this activity, market shares seemed locked at 12 per cent for Daz and 9 per cent for Omo.

How could Procter & Gamble break through the 12 per cent share ceiling? How could it escape the price warfare? The answer when it came was a classic of promotional marketing. Nearly 40 years on it carries lessons for any brand in any sector facing similar market conditions.

Procter & Gamble tested alternatives to the '3d off' packs in a panel of 88 stores across the country. Dozens of alternatives were tested – and the clear winner was the offer of plastic roses as a near-pack. Rolled out nationally in 1961, 8 million roses were given away and Daz's market share increased to 18 per cent. Costing around 3d against a perceived value of 6d, the flowers made sense both to the company and the consumer. The scope for retail prominence was immense. The promotion was repeated in the next two years, scoring brand shares of 16 per cent and 14 per cent respectively. By then, Omo had responded with plastic daffodils, effectively turning the detergent price war into a flower war.

Plastic flowers were then – as now – considered naff by many people. They had very little to do with brand values, but rigorous testing showed that they worked. And they did – for a while. Price warfare then resumed and, by the mid 1970s, was again normal.

The lesson of the Procter & Gamble roses is that promotional innovation can have massive impact on brand share, but no single promotional technique lasts forever.

■   What parallels to the Procter & Gamble and Lever price warfare can you see in the market today, and how could premium promotions change the situation?

■   What retail sectors could you now use near-packs in, and in what retail sectors would it be impossible?

CASE STUDY 19: CLEARBLUE ONE STEP

What kind of promotion is right for a pregnancy test? Women hope for very different outcomes, and can approach the test with considerable anxiety. By 1994, the pregnancy testing market was crowded with technically similar products. Clearblue One Step faced a major competitor that had recently been relaunched with a full support programme. In a crowded market, loss of brand share soon leads to loss of distribution and a cycle of decline sets in.

Clearblue One Step identified four objectives for the promotion: to offset competitor activity; add value to the product; affirm the brand's position on women's health issues; and offer an item of relevance irrespective of the test result. The product cost £10.75 and the cost of any promotional item had to be in proportion to that price.

SMP's promotion had both trade and consumer targets. In pharmacies, it is often the pharmacy assistant who recommends which pregnancy test to buy, so the promotion had to appeal to them. In multiples, such as Boots, consumers self-select, so if the offer was to work, it had to be clearly marked on the pack.

The solution was to band a Well Woman diary to the pack. This featured relevant and helpful information, irrespective of the test result, and a host of other health advice. It worked: sales in autumn 1994 were up 20 per cent on the same period in 1993 – a volume increase of nearly 12,000 units a month.

This was a workable, practical solution rather than a piece of creative genius. What shines through is the clear link between market conditions, brand values, promotional objectives and the promotional solution. It deserved to work and to win an ISP Award for the company and its agency, SMP.

■   What other options for an on-pack premium could have been considered by Clearblue One Step? What would their advantages and disadvantages be?

■   Why would a free mail-in promotion or a price offer not be appropriate for this product?

■   Are there other promotional mechanics Clearblue One Step could have considered?

CASE STUDY 20: ELECTROLUX

Convincing buyers to stock a product is crucial for any new entrant. These 'gatekeepers' are the first hurdle any new product has to overcome on the road to success.

In 1994, Electrolux launched a new micro cleaner, the X8. 'It is very difficult to create buyer interest in the vacuum cleaner market and to make the product promise that bit different', commented Simon Mahoney of sales promotion agency SMP. The objectives of the trade launch were, nevertheless, to create interest and awareness among buyers, gain listings and increase market share.

Building on the name X8, Electrolux sent out a series of Xtraordinary mailers to buyers. The rep then visited the buyer carrying a security box that looked as if it was made of stainless steel and which was emblazoned with top secret messages. On removing the lid, a cassette player played a personalized message to the buyer about the top secret mission he was about to embark on. After the message was played, the box revealed the X8 in all its 'micro' glory. The cassette player was left with the dealer.

Daft or what? It certainly worked, creating a great deal of interest and amusement in the trade. All existing Electrolux outlets listed the X8, and the firm gained several new accounts. Electrolux's share in the cylinder cleaner sector increased by 50 per cent over 1993, and overall it moved into brand leadership.

Marketing is a serious business. Electrolux no doubt had a stack of technical and market research reports to show just how successful X8 would be, but you can't bore someone into buying – amusing people often works better.

- Does leaving the tape recorder with the dealer create a conflict of interest in companies where there are rules against gifts? If so, what steps could you take to deal with it?

- In what kinds of markets does creating a special premium of this kind make sense, and in what kinds would it not work?

CASE STUDY 21: SMIRNOFF

Smirnoff is the UK's leading brand of vodka, but it faces a constant battle to persuade its core 18–24-year-old consumers to ask for it by name in pubs and clubs. It's not an easy market: there are severe restraints on the involvement of staff in promotions at a crowded bar and the age group is promotionally sophisticated. It is often immune to promotional incentives and easily bored.

The agency Marketing Principles looked closely at the question 'Who do I want to do what?' The key answer was to encourage groups of friends to talk about Smirnoff. This is how the objective was achieved.

On asking for Smirnoff, consumers were given a foil sachet that contained a pin badge replica of a Smirnoff bottle. The consumer then 'cracked' the badge to turn it from opaque to one of four luminous colours. It literally glowed for up to four hours. Two of the colours could also be exchanged over the bar for a baseball cap or T-shirt.

The promotion achieved its objectives. Outlet participation was 60 per cent and sales of Smirnoff's vodka were up by an average of 16 per cent. Nearly a million Smirnoff consumers participated.

Two things characterize this promotion. First, the mechanic was simplicity itself – a small item handed over the bar to those who asked for Smirnoff. The bright and extensive promotional material had a simple message: 'Ask for it!' Second, the promotion relied on conversation among consumers to reveal its real nature and they were all asking questions. Why is your badge red? Why have you won a T-shirt? Are there any other colours? How long will this go on glowing? The promotion picked up the key nature of youth pubs: a busy bar, a great deal of chat among friends and a keen interest in working out something that is not immediately obvious.

- What other premiums could Smirnoff have considered as items for the bar staff to hand over?

- What particular issues in the Codes of Advertising and Sales Promotion Practice did Smirnoff have to take into account in designing this promotion?

- In what other markets is it crucial to encourage groups of friends to talk about the product?

SUMMARY

Premium promotions are the most important way companies can compete promotionally without altering the price. There are four main mechanics – on-pack, near-pack, free mail-in and self-liquidator. The boundaries between them are becoming blurred with the growth of brand extension promotions.

There are considerable opportunities for promoting, enhancing and extending brand value, but companies must be careful to remember their main priorities. Business gifts should not be considered a separate category, but an extension of thinking about 'Who do I want to do what?' in the business-to-business field.

There are practical and operational issues to consider in sourcing premiums, organizing handling and dealing with redemption rates, further details of which are given in Chapter 4.

11

PRIZE PROMOTIONS

Prize promotions differ from every other mechanic discussed in this book in that the benefit to the consumer depends on whether they win or not. A 20p coupon is a guarantee of 20p off the product specified on it. A free mail-in is an undertaking by the promoter to provide a premium in return for a certain number of proofs of purchase. With prize promotions, there is no such guarantee. Three other characteristics distinguish prize promotions:

- they are offers where the maximum cost can be predicted in advance and does not vary with the numbers who participate

- a far bigger benefit can be given in a prize promotion than in a promotion where the benefit is available to everyone who participates

- they are heavily regulated by the British Codes of Advertising and Sales Promotion, by the Lotteries and Amusement Act 1976 and by other legislation, which is far from simple to interpret.

There is a difficult balance to be struck in writing about prize promotions. On the one hand, they are staggeringly successful. The chance to win a car, a holiday or a substantial sum of money at little or no cost is permanently attractive to consumers. *Reader's Digest* has built its business on this basis, giving away nearly £3 million a year. On the other hand, they are a legal minefield. The complicated pattern of law regulating lotteries and gaming recognizes its attractiveness. Historically, government has restricted the opportunity to gamble. Although government is easing restrictions on casinos and betting shops, and has gone into the business itself with the National Lottery, the older laws still remain.

Too much stress on legal niceties can lead promoters to regard it as a no-go area. Too much stress on promotional effectiveness can lead promoters to forget the need for caution. This chapter is designed to show you that it is a minefield, but one that is worth getting through – just watch your step.

There are five types of prize promotion – competitions, free draws, instant wins, games and lotteries. They are distinct in legal terms, subject to different legal and code of practice restrictions, and offer different mechanisms for winning the prize. The distinctions are not immediately obvious, and it is worth spending some time making sure you fully understand them.

- Competitions offer prizes for the successful exercise of a significant degree of mental or physical skill or judgement. Participants may be required to pay or make a purchase to enter.

- Free draws make available prizes by distribution of random chances. The selection of the winning ticket is separate and later, not instantaneous with its distribution. No skill or judgement is involved, and participants cannot be asked to pay or make a purchase to enter.

- Instant wins offer prizes by distributing a predetermined number of winning tickets. Consumers know instantly whether they have won or lost. No skill or judgement is involved, and consumers cannot be asked to pay or make a purchase to enter.

- Games are forms of free draw or instant win that give the appearance of requiring skill, but, in fact, rely on probability. They can be based on brand name games, such as Monopoly or Trivial Pursuit, or on generic games, such as Bingo or snakes and ladders. Because no significant degree of skill or judgement is called for, no purchase or payment can be required in order to enter.

- Lotteries work in the same way as free draws or instant wins, but participants pay to enter. They are strictly regulated under the Lotteries and Amusements Act 1976, and are, in practice, restricted to small-scale, local, non-commercial schemes.

These distinctions become clear if we take an example of a prize promotion a local travel agent might put on. The promotion could be headlined 'Win a weekend break with Sunshine Travel'.

- It would be a competition if it required entrants to identify the capitals of five countries and to complete a tie-breaker. It would be legal to subhead the promotion 'when you book your next holiday with Sunshine Travel'.

- It would be a free draw if it said 'just drop your name and address in the box'. It would be illegal to subhead it 'when you book your next holiday with Sunshine Travel'. Anyone walking through the door must be allowed to enter.

- It would be an instant win if Sunshine Travel overprinted its booking confirmation with numbers that could be revealed by scratching off a latex panel, and a particular combination of numbers instantly won the prize. To be legal, anyone walking through the door should be given an equal chance of winning.

- It would be a game if the promotion read 'Play snakes and ladders at Sunshine Travel and win a weekend break'. The game may require the use of a dice, even a certain amount of skill. The rules for a free draw would still apply to it.

- It would be a lottery if the subheading read 'raffle tickets available at just 10p each'. It would be legal only if it was promoted by a local charity or voluntary association registered with the local authority.

To all intents and purposes, lotteries are a no-go area for commercial promoters. The only exceptions are small-scale lotteries, held at a single event (such as a dinner) with non-cash prizes below £50 in total value, and where the proceeds are entirely devoted to charity. For this reason, lotteries are not considered further in this chapter.

The other four types of prize promotion are subject to specific rules relating to the closing date, the judging process, the description of prizes, the announcing of winners, and so forth. The key features are described in the sections that follow, and in more detail in section 40 of the British Codes of Advertising and Sales Promotion Practice. Philip Circus, the Director of Legal Affairs at the Institute of Practitioners in Advertising and legal adviser to the ISP, has written an invaluable book entitled *Sales Promotion Law: A practical guide* and writes a regular column in *Incentive Today* that provides a running commentary on legal developments. Anyone running prize promotions needs to be absolutely clear that they follow the complicated laws that govern them, and the best way to do that is to have your copy checked by the ISP, the ASA or a specialist lawyer.

COMPETITIONS

The offer

To qualify as a competition – and therefore for it to be legal to ask for a purchase to be made – the winner must be determined by the skill or judgement shown. There are many forms of competition, the main ones being:

- **order of merit** 'List the following five items in order of importance.'

- **complete a slogan** 'Complete this sentence in not more than ten words.'

- **question plus slogan** 'Answer these five questions and complete this sentence in not more than ten words.'

- **spot the difference** 'Identify 12 differences between pictures A and B.'

- **estimate** 'Estimate how many packs of this product will fit inside this car.'

- **spot the ball** 'Mark the position of the football on this photograph.'

- **identify** 'Identify these famous people from the photographs of their eyes.'

- **be creative** 'Draw a picture or take a photograph or write a story.'

- **treasure hunt** 'Use the clues to find the hidden treasure.'

By far the most common type of test is the question plus slogan. It is the easiest to fit into the limited amount of space available to communicate most competitions, the easiest to explain and the easiest to judge. Its benefit over a slogan-only test is that the questions filter the number of slogans that have to be judged.

That said, there is a simplicity to promotions that do not have a filter to reduce the number of tie-breakers. It makes the competition easier to enter for consumers, and can increase participation. Captioning a photograph is a good one-shot test of skill and judgement that many people enjoy entering.

About 3 per cent of the population always enter competitions and 40 per cent do so from time to time.[1] The scale of competitions used to be enormous. *Reader's Digest* estimated in 1988 that, at any one time, there is £1 million in competition prizes waiting to be won. The November 1988 issue of *Competitors Companion* listed 27 competitions running in Tesco alone over the autumn, and 63 competitions with a closing date of 30 November. Prizes included 40 holidays, £60,000 in cash, 12 cars and 40,000 smaller prizes.

Today, competitions are much less frequent, having been replaced in many cases by instant-win promotions and put in the shade in respect of the prizes they offer by the National Lottery. Radio stations frequently run competitions that ask a number of simple questions, but have no tie-breaker: the winning entry is the first correct set of answers drawn from a hat. These are, in reality, free draws. It is the skill and judgement in the tie-breaker that is the criterion of skill and judgement in the competition as a whole.

Competitions are known for attracting the professional competition entrant. These are obviously small in number, but it is wrong to think of a clear divide between professional competition entrants on the one hand and non-entrants on the other. The secret of good design is to make your competition attractive to the 40 per cent who sometimes enter, and not just the 3 per cent who always do.

How they work

Competitions tend to have a low level of entry – 0.5 per cent of opportunities to participate would be considered high. Hugh Davidson, the former European Vice-President of Playtex, considers that they 'absorb management and salesforce time to no object'.[2] However, this ignores 'promotional slippage' – the number who are attracted by an offer, but do not enter. Competitions can be effective in creating awareness, interest and impact at point of purchase well beyond the number who enter. These are legitimate sales promotion objectives, and they do have a bearing on sales. Unusual prizes can attract significant levels of publicity, and there is still scope for more run-of-the-mill prize publicity in local papers. Competitions are beneficial on these grounds.

Competitions can also be useful ways of drawing attention to a product's characteristics. The Zantac 75 promotion (Case Study 5) used an imaginative competition mechanic for exactly that purpose.

There is a major benefit in running a promotion that has a fixed level of costs and makes limited demands in terms of premium supply. Once you have established the competition prizes and paid for the communication materials, you know the limit of your costs. This is a characteristic shared by other types of promotion described in this chapter, and is of particular value when a company's budgeting procedure makes it difficult to cope with open-ended costs.

There are various guidelines it is wise to follow when designing a competition. Remember that it is not a mastermind test. Some competitions require entrants to jump through hoops that would leave Magnus Magnusson gasping. There is no point in making the test obscure and difficult. There is, however, considerable purpose in making it fun and amusing for your target audience. Competitions continue to be attractive to children, and very often in specialist markets, for these reasons.

Once you have selected the type of competition you want to run, design it so that there is an identifiable winner. A competition that consists of only a series of questions is likely to result in a great many correct solutions. The winner cannot be selected at random, otherwise it becomes a draw. This is the reason for the common use of the tie-breaker slogan. Creative tests are also capable of yielding a single winner. Every other kind of test needs a method of judging between those who get the correct answer to the estimate, the identification, the order of merit or the questions.

It is essential to set it up from the beginning so that a judge is able to judge. The requirement in a competition is for the exercise of 'skill and judgement'. These are prone to subjective interpretation. It is therefore important to indicate on what grounds 'skill and judgement' will be assessed. This is the reason for the inclusion in tie-breaker instructions of phrases such as 'in the most apt and original way' or 'in the most amusing way'. Any independent judge will want to know the grounds on which the selection of a winner is to be made, so it is sensible to build this into the structure of the competition from the beginning.

When you come to write the copy, make sure everything that the entrant has to do – from obtaining the necessary number of proofs of purchase to completing a tie-breaker – is as clear as possible. The events that follow – from the judging process through to any obligation to participate in publicity activity – must also be made clear from the beginning. Section 40 of the British Codes of Advertising and Sales Promotion sets out what must be included.

The level of response to competitions is strongly influenced by the prizes on offer. The best starting point is to fix the budget available. There are then several ways in which you can think about the prizes you offer.

There is an argument that a single, major prize creates the greatest interest; another, that the greater chance of winning one of many lesser prizes is more attractive. There is no absolute answer to this. Partly in response to the National Lottery, there has been a decline in the conventional system of a complicated and graduated prize structure: a big first prize, three second prizes, five third prizes, and so forth.

This structure dissipates impact and increases costs. The best solution is probably a single, major prize and a large number (perhaps 100 or more) of runners-up prizes. It can be possible to use a variant in which everyone gains an item of some value – for example, a coupon for money off future purchases. If you are doing this, be careful not to describe it as a prize. Something that every entrant obtains is not a 'prize' but a 'gift'.

There are several tried and tested prizes. Holidays and cars are always top of the list because everyone likes them, and it is easy to provide a better version than most people would buy of their own accord. However, your holiday does tend to be lost among the many other holiday prizes simultaneously available. Hence the reason for specials, such as Golden Wonder's offer of 'your own tropical island' or the prize of becoming Lord of the Manor of an English village. Specials tend, by their nature, to be things no one really wants, however. The best solution is probably a twist to a standard prize – for example, 'get your hair cut in New York'. This combines a good standard prize with a special that (importantly) relates to the item in question – in this case, a haircare product.

Many competition rules specify that there is no cash alternative. There are two reasons for doing this: that you have already bought the prize in question or that you will be buying it at a substantial discount to the normal price, and prefer not to disclose the actual cost to you. If the rules do not exclude a cash alternative, arguments about the value of a prize can be difficult, and a refusal to give a cash alternative can seem unreasonable. Conversely, there are cases where a cash alternative is essential, for example, in the case of the delightful but impractical tropical island. In that case, the amount of the cash alternative should be specified upfront.

It is worth seeking publicity for the prizewinner. Local papers are normally happy to run a photograph and caption of a local prizewinner, and it is generally possible to obtain coverage in your relevant trade press. Prizewinners are sometimes reluctant to be used in this way, and it is important to respect their sensitivities. However, if you intend to use the prizewinner for publicity purposes, it is important to make this point in the competition rules, and to specify it as a condition of entry.

What to look out for

There are several things to look out for when running a competition, and some require very careful thought. Asking entrants to predict a future event, such as the outcome of a football match, is considered forecasting, and is illegal in a competition. Asking them to predict when the first goal will be scored is also illegal in a competition, but on the different grounds that it is a matter of chance. Asking them to predict the weather at the London Weather Centre on the day the match will be played may not be illegal because the weather is a state of affairs and not an event; its legality will depend on whether or not a substantial degree of skill is required.[3] No wonder lawyers are needed!

Judging is an area of administration that causes headaches, particularly if you are faced with thousands of entries. Resist the temptation to treat it as a draw – choosing the first tie-breaker slogan that catches your fancy. You could find a dozen other entrants providing evidence that they had submitted the same slogan. Be clear before you start judging how you are going to interpret the rules. Is '100' two words ('one hundred'), one word or not allowed because it is not a word? Do hyphenated words count as one word or two? A good guide is to reduce the number of potential winners by making a strict interpretation of the instruction to complete a sentence in '12 words or fewer'. Being strict also protects you against those who may complain that, if they had known that 'words' meant 'words or numbers' they would have submitted a different entry.

Slogans are often required to be 'apt and original'. There is a trap for the unwary here. If two entries use the same slogan, neither can be the most original, for how do you choose between the two? Slogans that echo the long-established advertising of a brand ('I love Cadbury's Roses because they grow on you') are unlikely ever to be original, however flattering they may be to the advertiser.

James Porteous, a veteran of the judging business, advises using a team of eight people in a judging session. The first stage is to take a pile of entries, choose the ones you like and pass those you have rejected to your neighbour to do the same. When the process has been carried out by five of the eight, that is a majority. The shortlisted entries have been shortlisted by a majority. The second stage is to go through all the individual favourites and reverse the process – putting to one side any that any single judge dislikes.

These two stages will have produced a crop of entries that could all be winners. The third stage is to choose the winner or winners by asking the question 'Is this entry better than that?' This is done by all the judges together. If you need to select one winner, take the entry at the top of the pile as the provisional winner and read out the slogan. Take the next entry, read the slogan and ask 'Is it better?' If not, discard it. If it is, it becomes the provisional winner. The process continues until all entries that have reached stage three have been reviewed, and the last remaining provisional winner becomes the actual winner.

If there are ten winners to be selected, follow the same process, but select the ten entries at the top of the pile as provisional winners. If any subsequent entry is better, discard the least good of the ten and replace it, continuing until all entries that have reached stage three have been reviewed.

A large and apparently daunting task quickly and fairly becomes manageable using this method. Normally, judges come to a consensus choice of the final winner. If you need to take a vote, allocate each judge ten points to distribute among the entries that are in contention for the prize. Often, everyone's second preference will emerge the winner.

The Code of Practice requires that both an expert and an independent judge are involved in the judging process. They can be one and the same person – for example, a teacher for an art-related competition, a travel agent for a travel competition. They can prove a help in managing the judging as well as demonstrating that the process is fair and seen to be fair.

A large number of entries is a reasonable test of the attractiveness of a competition, but not of its promotional effectiveness. The number of entries can be quite unrelated to the promotional objectives. Attracting entries depends on presenting the competition in the most compelling way for your particular audience – offering a free or low-cost means of entry and making the competition easy. Clever word games will be attractive to some groups, if not to most. It may be, however, that your promotional purpose is trade-related – for example, to gain display. Once that is achieved, the number of entries makes no difference at all. The question 'Who do I want to do what?' discussed in Chapter 3 is the basis on which you can determine the style of competition you use and how easy and attractive you make it to enter.

FREE DRAWS

The offer

In a free draw, winners are determined entirely by chance and it is not permissible to require any payment or proof of purchase from entrants. Free draws differ from instant win promotions in that people do not know immediately whether they have won or not. Second stages in free draws vary, and include waiting until the closing date to see if your entry is selected; posting a set of numbers into a handling house to be checked against a predetermined list of winners (a practice much favoured by direct mail magazines); and hoping to find the matching half of (for example) a banknote on your next visit to the outlet that hands them out.

Why should promoters use free draws rather than competitions and lose the ability to ask for a proof of purchase? What is the advantage of issuing prizes at random to people who may never be customers? There are four reasons for using free draws.

- They can be highly effective in generating interest, awareness and participation. In particular, free draws are a strong traffic-builder for retailers and a proven readership-builder for newspapers. The absence of tie-breakers means that free draws attract up to 20 times as many participants as do competitions.

- They are easy for the promoter to administer, easy for consumers to enter, involve a fixed prize fund and are a quick and easy way of building a customer and prospect database.

- They can involve an implicit encouragement to purchase. This needs to be treated carefully. Newspapers invariably state (as they are required to) that consumers can check their tickets without buying the newspaper; petrol stations invariably state (as they are required to) that tickets are issued to all those who visit the petrol station, not just those who buy petrol. This is the 'plain paper entry' route. In practice, between 80 and 90 per cent of those who enter also make a purchase.

- They allow substantial opportunities for creativity. In comparison with competitions, the main alternative for those seeking a mechanic with fixed costs, free draws require far fewer rules, do not require questions or tests, but do allow free rein for games of every kind.

Free draws share some of the features of competitions: a fixed prize fund; a range of prizes; the need to make conditions of entry clear. These points are therefore not repeated here. This section looks at the characteristics particular to free draws, those relating not to the offer itself, but to how it works.

How it works

The simplest way to operate a free draw is to have a pile of cards on which consumers can write their names, addresses and any other information you want to collect from them, a box for them to make their entries and a declared date on which the winner will be drawn from the box. For business customers it is even simpler – simply provide a box into which they can drop their business cards. When you make the draw, it is important that it is done by an independent person and that it is done with witnesses so it is seen to be independent.

Another way is to issue consumers with a card printed with a unique set of random numbers. These numbers are openly displayed and not covered by latex. The winning numbers are announced separately – on a board in a shop or in the pages of a newspaper. Consumers have to check the winning numbers against the number of their card and, if they are the same, contact the promoter to claim the prize. Most newspaper cards operate in this way, with winning numbers displayed daily in the paper. There is a clear advantage of a double hit – first, obtain the card, then check the winning numbers. Note that, to be legal, consumers must have a no-cost way of checking the winning numbers.

Predetermined number cards are a variant on the random number system. Each card is uniquely numbered, but instead of the winning numbers being announced for consumers to check, cards must be returned to the promoter to be matched against predetermined winning numbers. *Reader's Digest* and other direct mail operators often use this format because it encourages consumers to respond to direct mail.

A fourth method is to distribute a series of different cards that have to be matched together to create a set. Only a limited number of the cards needed to complete the set are distributed. Once the set is complete, the win is instant. Petrol stations have used this format to good effect with matching halves of banknotes. The left-hand halves were plentiful and right-hand halves very rare.

These are very much the bare bones of each type of free draw offer. Actual free draws can be very complicated, and can have characteristics of two or three of these types. For example, you can have an instant win card that is also (when mailed in) a predetermined number card and gives the opportunity to match and complete a set. Numbers can be replaced with symbols or words and a whole range of other variants introduced.

What to look out for

Out-of-the-hat draws are perfectly straightforward. They are regularly used by retailers, motor dealers and companies holding exhibitions as a traffic-builder, as a way of capturing names and as a focus of attention. As long as the guidelines in the Code of Practice are followed, they present no terrors. Indeed, they are one of the fastest and simplest forms of promotion to organize, and highly attractive on those grounds alone.

Other types of free draw need careful attention to the mechanisms that prevent fraud and ensure an equitable distribution of winning tickets. You need to use a security printer to make sure that you do not have multiple winning tickets in circulation. A means of verifying the winning ticket via hidden but unique marks is also advisable. You need to carefully seed the winning tickets so that they do not all turn up in the same outlet at the same time. Also, you need to ensure that there is no one involved with the distribution of winning tickets who can take advantage of their knowledge. A good way of doing this is to ask an independent person to do the seeding. That way you are also protected if you are publicly accused of fixing the scheme.

All these factors are manageable if you do three things. First, use a specialist printer (this is discussed in Chapter 4). Second, consider the use of promotional insurance (also discussed in Chapter 4). Third, make sure your copy is checked by the ASA, the ISP or a specialist lawyer. A good sales promotion agency can help you with all of this as well. These three golden rules for successful prize promotions apply even more strongly to instant wins.

INSTANT WINS

The offer

Instant wins have been around for a number of years in the form of scratch cards overprinted with latex or with perforated windows to hide the winning or losing combinations. Only a limited number of winning cards are distributed, and the consumer knows instantly whether or not the card they have is a winner.

Instant wins took a major step forward with the launch of the Heinz 'Win a car a day' and Pedigree Petfoods 'Is there a car in this can?' promotions in the late 1980s. They are seen by some promoters as the only truly new promotional technique in the last ten years.[4] The great advantage of these promotions over free draws is that consumers know if they have won a prize as soon as they open the can. The hope that there will be a line drawing of a car on the inside of the lid creates an element of excitement and expectation every time the can is opened. The first time it was used, the consumer interest was colossal. Instant wins converted prize promotions from a delayed to an immediate offer – and the latter is always more effective.

Why had instant wins not been used on grocery products before the late 1980s? The reason was that promoters thought it was illegal because consumers would have to buy the can to see if there was a picture of a car under the lid, making it a lottery. What made these promotions possible was careful legal advice that offering consumers the opportunity to have a can opened by the manufacturer on their behalf meant that they did not have to make a purchase in order to participate. Prior to the Heinz and Pedigree Petfoods promotions, an opportunity to 'Win a car a day' printed on a tin was thought to need a competition mechanic. Free entry or 'plain paper entry' made instant wins a promotional offer that could legally be made on-pack.

Promoters still have to be careful. It is vital that there is a genuine, realistic and unlimited method of free entry. In 1995, Interactive Telephone Services (ITS) was convicted of operating a lottery under the Lotteries and Amusements Act 1976. The promotion was called 'Telemillion' and consisted of phoning a premium rate telephone line, answering a simple question and, if the answer was correct, being entered in a draw. ITS claimed the promotion was not a lottery, because there was a free entry route. The court disregarded this as free entries never exceeded more than 0.184 per cent of entries in any month. If there was a genuine, realistic and unlimited free entry route, the proportion would be much higher.[5] Promoters are cautious about releasing figures for the proportion of free entries they receive, but a figure of 10 to 20 per cent would be considered reasonable.

How it works

Instant wins work best on low-cost, high-volume products that have relatively low product differentiation. This enables large prizes to be offered and for the possibility of winning the prize to be a major factor in the purchase decision. Walkers Crisps lifted its market share in groceries from 57 to 63 per cent between August 1992 and August 1994 on the basis of three separate instant win offers.[6] Walkers' device for the instant win was a twist of blue paper in the crisp packet – a harkback to the days when crisps were plain, and the salt was contained in a twist of blue paper. The company went on to achieve further gains by integrating 'Dial-a-prize', 'Instant cheque' and other essentially similar promotional activities with its Gary Lineker theme advertising in 1995/6.

Walkers also noted a decline in response to its instant win promotions each time it used them. This is a standard promotional experience. It has been shared by Camelot with its 'Instants'. To continue working, the instant win principle needs constant refreshing with new formats. Among the best people to advise on new ways of delivering the same concept are the specialist printers of scratchcards and games discussed in Chapter 4. Another good way of keeping at the leading edge of promotional practice is to watch what *Reader's Digest* does: a technique is not worn out the second time it is used, though it may be by the twentieth time.

What to look out for

The considerations that apply to free draws also apply to instant wins, notably in respect of security and seeding. An additional issue to take into account is the possibility that the top prize is won early on in the promotion. From then on, consumers are, in effect, being misled about the possibility of winning. The same applies if the promoter keeps back the pack containing the top prize until late on. It can be advisable to have two or three big prizes, though this militates against the attractiveness of the mega prize.[7]

GAMES

The offer

'Games' in sales promotion are anything from a newspaper fantasy football league to a wordsearch with prizes to a scratch-off game of Monopoly to predicting the temperature on Christmas Day. Some require proofs of purchase and some do not. They are distributed variously on-pack, door-to-door, in advertising and as free-standing cards. Everyone knows what these games look like, and they can be hugely successful. However, as we will see below, they are really versions of a free draw, instant win or competition.

How it works

Most people think of a game as something that involves skill. In fact, English law defines a game of skill very restrictively. Most games, including complicated card games such as whist and bridge, count in law as games of chance. Only in such games as duplicate bridge, chess, darts and snooker does the element of skill predominate over the element of chance. If it is a game of chance, as you will know by now, you cannot ask for payment or purchase.

Don't people pay to enter games of chance such as bingo, roulette and the football pools? Yes they do, and these are regulated under the Gaming Act 1968 and other legislation. The general purpose of that legislation is to restrict the availability and attractiveness of gambling and to subject it to taxation and detailed regulation.

Games used in sales promotion are generally of two types. They are a form of instant win or free draw dressed up as 'playing' a version of Monopoly, Scrabble, Trivial Pursuit, ludo or snakes and ladders. Alternatively, they are a form of competition dressed up as 'playing' a word game, predicting a future state of affairs or some other test of skill and judgement. What they are not (because that would be illegal) is the sort of game that the Gaming Board regulates. It follows that 'games' do not really exist as a separate category of prize promotion, but, rather, they are a version of either a free draw/instant win or a competition.

This distinction has been tested in law. In 1995, News International won a case against Customs and Excise, which wanted to charge it pool betting duty of 37.5 per cent or general betting tax of 7.5 per cent on its 'fantasy' promotions.[8] These varied from 'fantasy fund manager' in *The Sunday Times* to the 'Dream team' in *The Sun* and two cricket competitions in *The Times* – a classic case of versioning the same concept for the different interests of different readers. Three of the four promotions operated by premium telephone line. The crucial question was whether the payment that this involved amounted to a bet. If it did, News International would have to pay up. The tribunal held that it did not.

What to look out for

If you are going down the free draw/instant win route, games are in practice a clever and interesting way of dressing them up. All the considerations given in the sections on those two mechanics apply. Above all, ensure there is a free entry route that is genuine and realistic. The opportunities for a great promotion rely on your skill and ingenuity in devising a game theme that is original, simple and exciting.

If you are going down the competition route, and requiring a proof of purchase, the considerations in the section on competitions apply. Be careful not to ask for any payment other than the proof of purchase. It is here that you can take advantage of promotions that are based on probability. These are discussed in the next section.

PROBABILITY PROMOTIONS

The offer

Golf clubs have long enjoyed 'hole-in-one' competitions where an enormous prize is made available in the unlikely event of a hole-in-one being achieved. The possibility is insured against by specialists who have calculated the probabilities and are prepared to underwrite the risk for a fee. Exactly the same principle can be used in sales promotions that require a series of ten items to be listed in order of priority or the temperature on a given day to be predicted.

How it works

The basic form of this offer requires the entrant to list a number of items in order of importance, such as the world's best cricketers or the factors that make for a good holiday. The 'correct' solution is chosen in advance by an independent judge and placed in a sealed envelope. Skill and judgement must be required on the part of those entering. It would be wrong, for example, to ask entrants to list a series of numbers in order of importance, because that would only require guesswork.

Who can objectively place in order of importance the all-time best cricketers or the factors that make for a good holiday? Objectively, no one can, in the sense that they could list the countries of the world in order of size or population. However, the judgement of an expert amounts to an objective test. It is fair enough, therefore, to ask a cricketing journalist to determine the all-time best cricketers and a top travel agent to determine the list of the factors that make for a good holiday and to use your expert's answer as the correct solution.

The basis of a promotion in which ten items are listed in order of priority is the probability (or unlikelihood) of anyone listing any set of items in any particular order. The chances of so doing depend on the numbers of items to list, and these are as shown in Table 4.

The exponential shape of the curve is obvious. If there are ten items to list in order of importance, the chance of someone getting it right is 1 in over 3.6 million. It should be possible, therefore, to risk offering a prize of £1 million for the inverse of the probability – just 28p. The risk in letting 1000 people enter is around 1000 times greater, but should still only cost £278. Of course, an insurance company needs to cover its administrative costs, security, re-insurance and the possibility of more people entering than expected. The normal minimum for

Table 4 *The probabilities of listing items in a certain order for given numbers of items*

Numbers of items	Probabilities of being right
2	1 in 2
3	1 in 6
4	1 in 24
5	1 in 120
6	1 in 720
7	1 in 5040
8	1 in 40,320
9	1 in 362,880
10	1 in 3,628,800
11	1 in 39,916,800
12	1 in 479,001,600

insuring a £1 million prize is £25,000. A rule of thumb for working out the insurance cost is to divide the expected number of entrants by the odds, multiply by the prize value and double the resulting number.

Increasingly imaginative ways are being found to integrate high-value prizes with high odds and lower-value prizes with lower odds. For example, an offer with a football theme could promise a huge prize for getting three questions right:

- the number of goals in a match (odds 4 to 1)
- how many players will be booked in the match (odds 20 to 1)
- the time in minutes before the first goal (odds 90 to 1).

The odds of getting all three questions right are several million to one, but you could offer a voucher or merchandise prize to those getting one or two of the questions right. You could also risk – and insure – the possibility of offering more than one huge prize on the basis that fewer than half the people who win a prize actually check that they have done so.

What to look out for

Promoters using this mechanic should remember that these offers can produce substantial negative publicity and give an impression of sharp practice. Case study 23 shows how Faber & Faber dealt with this possibility by offering a prize of such high value and high odds that it was unlikely anyone would win.

Brooke Bond was less fortunate with its 1995 promotion headlined 'Millionaire tomorrow?' Consumers were asked to select their own combination of numbers and letters and enter them in a free draw. If their sequence matched that drawn on TV, the winner would receive £1 million. Complaints were made to the ASA that the probability of winning was 6760 million to one. Brooke Bond was censured by the ASA on the grounds that 'Readers would neither readily appreciate the substantial odds against selecting the correct combination nor realize that unless this was achieved no prize at all would be awarded'.[9]

Particular care needs to be taken with promotions that involve predicting the future. The distinction between predicting an event (illegal) and predicting a state of affairs (legal) needs to be borne in mind if a competition format is being used and a proof of purchase is asked for. Note that if no proof of purchase is required, both are legal. In all these cases, a specialist insurer, such as PIMS, can quote a price for insuring the prize you want to offer. It can also work the calculation backwards, telling you, for example, what prize and what odds you could offer if you had (say) £30,000 available to pay for the insurance and a reasonable estimate of the likely number of entrants (how these firms work is described in Chapter 4).

The golden rule, as in any other promotion, is to think about the people who will enter the competition as being people with whom you want to build a long-term relationship. People don't mind high odds – they are high enough in the National Lottery – but they do mind being misled.

CASE STUDIES

An element of prize promoting comes into many of the case studies in this book: the main mechanic in the Maxwell House promotion (Case Study 1) was a free draw; a competition was used by Zantac 75 (Case Study 5) and by Rover Group (Case Study 8); Gale's Honey used an instant win technique (Case Study 16) as did Smirnoff (Case Study 21). These all give a sense of the wide variety of prize promotions.

The two case studies selected for this chapter focus on a particular way of integrating an instant win into a product and on an effective probability promotion.

CASE STUDY 22: SARSON'S

Vinegar is not an exciting product. Sarson's, the brand leader, is constantly looking for reasons to maintain its grocery display and justify its price premium over own-label vinegars. Its one distinguishing characteristic is its 'shaker' top, reflected in its advertising line, 'Shake on the Sarson's'.

This, plus the emergence of new ink technologies, gave the basis for a promotion by SMP that won an ISP Award in 1995. Collarettes were printed with a special ink that reacted with vinegar. When sprinkled with vinegar, they revealed cash prizes of £1 to £1000, a £1 McCain's voucher or a 20p off next purchase coupon.

The promotion had extensive objectives: increase sales, arrest market decline, add interest, justify price premium, encourage repeat purchase, add value, differentiate from own-label vinegars, and reinforce the advertising message. It succeeded in lifting share. It's characteristic was a clever use of emerging ink technology to deliver a standard range of prizes in an interesting and relevant way.

- Could Sarson's have referred to the 20p off next purchase coupon as a prize?

- If Sarson's had wanted to offer a £1 million top prize, what would it have needed to do?

CASE STUDY 23: FABER & FABER

Some sectors are relatively low users of sales promotion and so give an opportunity for the creative use of techniques that are familiar elsewhere. One of those is the book trade. Publishers face the challenge that 60 per cent of bookshop visitors leave without making a purchase, that consumers buy on impulse and that the saliency of individual titles on bookshelves is low. The solution is to provide your range of key titles with maximum in-store prominence and encourage consumers to browse among them and make a purchase.

Triangle Communications addressed this for Faber & Faber with a self-assembly 'book tower' containing four copies of each of 25 titles heavily flagged 'How to become a millionaire'. Consumers were asked to enter a competition based on clues among the books and complete a tiebreaker. This was to write the title for a book with a given synopsis. The winner was guaranteed a £10,000 prize and the opportunity to turn this into £1 million at a prize-giving event hosted by Melvyn Bragg. At this event, the winner was asked to select from a tower containing 100 books, 99 of them containing £10,000 cheques and 1 a £1 million cheque.

The need to grip intermediaries was not neglected and followed the theme of the promotion. Retailers were invited to submit photographs of their displays for a £500 reward, which they could turn into £10,000 by means of the same mechanism used with consumers. The highest achieving rep also won £500 that could be turned into £10,000.

The promotion took the book trade by storm, increasing Faber & Faber's sales during the period of the promotion by 15 per cent. Support from both independents and multiples was considerable, with Dillons featuring it for a two-month period. It also received extensive PR coverage – including speculation about whether or not TS Eliot, one of the featured authors, would have approved of the promotion (his widow said he would have done).

Competitions are a relatively unusual mechanic today as consumers are considered not to enjoy the literary effort involved. However, book buyers are among those for whom writing tie-breakers is a pleasure. Using a competition enabled a proof of purchase to be required. The mechanic required them both to browse and make a purchase – central to the promotion's objectives.

Faber & Faber made no secret of the low probability of anyone winning £1 million. The press carried stories of how the risk was being offset by the company having placed a bet with Ladbrokes. The firm was right to be up-front about this: book buyers would have worked it out anyway, with potentially negative PR coverage. Being upfront avoided this and added to the positive PR coverage.

In many sectors, this promotion would have seemed old hat. In the book trade, it was both innovative and effective – and closely focused on the firm's objectives at every point.

- ■ What other retail sectors can you see using the type of promotion Faber & Faber used, and in what ones would it not work?

- ■ Do you think an instant win would work with books, and a tie-breaker competition with vinegar?

SUMMARY

The five types of prize promotion each have their strengths and can be used to achieve different promotional objectives. It is vital to be clear about the differences between them. They are among the most powerful promotional techniques, but are subject to quick wear-out.

The administrative rules are well covered in the codes of practice and should be followed in detail. Copy should always be checked, and insurance is often a good idea.

Prize promotions offer particular opportunities for creativity, and have the major advantage of largely fixed costs.

The law in this area is particularly complicated and uncertain. Parliament has legislated separately for gaming, lotteries and betting, and in none of this law did it specifically address the needs of sales promoters.

Prize promotions are an enormously successful promotional device, as major national newspapers from *The Times* to *The Sun* have discovered. Like them, you should take specialist advice before using all but the simplest forms.

Part 3

Context

12

INTERNATIONAL SALES PROMOTION

When we speak of international promotions, we usually think of major, worldwide activity promoting a branded product in many countries, at the same time, under the same theme. Pepsi-Cola's worldwide link-up with the Spice Girls in 1997 is an example. However, a great deal more international promotion comprises activity that is designed in one country and then also implemented in another. It is multi-local rather than global.

In the early 1970s, it was quite common for companies throughout the world to employ UK sales promotion consultants to create promotions in their own countries – rather as UK TV producers were recruited in the 1990s to develop soaps in Eastern Europe. This was because UK consultancies were far more experienced than the non-specialists in other countries. Such promotions are not truly international as they appear in only one country, but we shall include them in this chapter as they still occur quite frequently, particularly in emerging markets.

A truly international promotion should appear in a number of countries, though not necessarily at the same time, nor in exactly the same form. This is the direction in which promotional activity has developed in multinational companies.

TYPES OF INTERNATIONAL PROMOTION

International promotions started with a highly successful, transferable promotion run in one country. The success of this promotion becomes known throughout the sales and marketing community, both within the company and often its competitors. Quite quickly the promotion, or a very close approximation, is run in another country, either by the original company or, perhaps, by its competitor. If it is successful again, it is repeated again and again in as many markets as possible. This is how the famous Shell 'Make Money' promotion first travelled the world in the 1950s, long before internationally integrated marketing was an everyday topic.

It is not a long step for marketing people within the company to recognize that they should meet or at least communicate with their opposite numbers in other countries in order to pass on details of their successful promotions. These promotions may then be replicated in other countries by the originating company before their competitors can do so. Relationships between these marketing people soon form to the point at which one manager discusses a potential promotion with one of their colleagues in another country. The usual stimulus for this discussion is money: the desire to split the origination costs with another group of people. Three things can be a particular focus of cost-saving promotion activity: the development of unique premiums, the use of character licenses, such as Disney, and the exploitation of celebrity links, such as the Spice Girls.

Corporate pressure for the standardization of promotions has also been powerful.[1] This has been driven by concern about the impact of varied promotional strategies on international brand identity, doubts about whether or not all subsidiaries have an equal capability to design, implement and evaluate promotions and the integration of retail customers on a regional basis.

The increasing importance of sales promotion in the marketing mix and the growing sophistication of promotional techniques led many companies during the 1980s to conclude that it was no longer possible to regard it as a locally determined activity supported by a certain amount of cross-frontier information sharing. However, the pace of internationalization has been slower than was forecasted. There are aspects of sales promotion that remain determinedly local.

By the late 1990s, the structure for managing the local/global balance in sales promotion had taken one of two forms. In one model, a worldwide promotions planning group is created that is responsible for all promotions throughout the world – a pattern followed by Coca-Cola and Pepsi-Cola. In the other, an essentially country- or region-based network becomes more proactive and, as a group, tries to find promotional solutions that will fit the needs of several countries. This is the pattern followed by Nestlé and a number of other leading companies. In both cases, the promotions will be planned in concept and outline in one country, allowing other countries to manage the local details within a global theme.

The primary difference is not one of sales promotional effectiveness, but of corporate culture. The first structure tends to dictate global strategy, while the second is far more consultative. In the one, there is a strong belief in the efficacy of central control, while in the other of the value of harnessing diversity.[2] What has been proven in both circumstances is that the economies of scale can be very attractive.

Whichever structure a firm has adopted, there remain three quite different forms of international promotion activity. These are promotions that are planned in one country, but run in another country; the almost, but not quite, mythical pan-European or pan-world promotions; and the relatively new phenomenon of promoting within a well-defined market that just happens to be global. These three types can be described in shorthand as 'single country', 'multiple country' and 'borderless'.

The difference is very important. The approach you will have to take initially will be different in each case. After that the details of creation and implementation will be the same.

Single country

The process for promoting in another country is no different to that for promoting in your home country. The only difference is that you have to imagine a totally different 'village' to answer the question 'Who do I want to do what?' Crucially, you must make sure that you really know what that village is like. You need to know the people, the way they do business, their expectations and what is allowed by law and by custom, just as you do automatically at home.

Not all that long ago, an English company decided to promote its products in an Irish chain of supermarkets by offering a free draw for a tea set to be won in each store, every day for one week. By 11 o'clock on the first day, all the free draw entry forms had been used up. All the stores were so jammed with people that no business could be done until new entry forms had been delivered and the crowds dispersed. It is hard to believe, but it is true. Not a good promotion! If only the promoter had realized that housewives in Eire were far less promotionally sophisticated than in the UK.

Another example can be found in the fashion mail-order business. Freemans has agents in many different countries, all using a modified form of the UK catalogue. An important sales opportunity is presented each year by the need to buy new clothes for growing children at the beginning of the school year in September. Thus, a form of 'Back to school' promotion has proved successful in every market. The promotion itself may be simple and similar in every market. What is different is the timing. In Japan and Europe it is possible to promote in August, when mothers are beginning to think of the peace and quiet that lies ahead when the children return to school. In the Middle East, families tend to stay abroad on holiday until much later and therefore the timing of the promotion needs to be as much as two months later, in late September/early October.

Multiple country

If a promotion is to run across several countries, it is likely that the greater the number of countries that you include, the simpler will be your promotion. Often it will become a basic theme that may then be implemented locally using a variety of techniques. Coca-Cola and Pepsi-Cola are well known for their global promotional themes.

In 1996, Shell became the world's largest distributor of die-cast model cars, selling over 26 million via its worldwide 'Colleczione' promotion. The international objective was to reinforce Shell's sponsorship of the Ferrari Formula One team. The model Ferrari cars were offered by the local Shell companies in any appropriate way they saw fit. Some gave them away with oil purchases, some redeemed them free on petrol sales while others offered only a discount on the car in return for a smaller purchase of petrol. The promotional objectives were selected locally as the local situation dictated. In this type of international promotion, the global theme provides a stronger tool than any of the individual companies could afford to provide for themselves as advantage can be taken of tremendous economies of scale.

In 1997, this promotional activity was researched in South America, the Far East and in Europe, and a new range of variations on a theme was developed for 1998. You can expect to collect your Lego Ferrari toy, only at your local Shell station, wherever you are in the world.

Multiple country promotions on a regional basis are becoming increasingly possible as trading groups harmonize their laws and companies set up a single structure to market their products across a group of countries. This has long been the pattern in Northern Europe, and will be extended by the completion of the Single Market. It is also more and more the case in South East Asia. If, as some argue, the fundamental building block of the future is regions rather than individual countries, sales promotion will increasingly take place on a multiple country basis rather than either globally or nationally.[3]

Borderless

The world is shrinking rapidly. There are now well-defined markets that cross geographical borders. While the customers may be from many different countries, they are often more similar to each other than they are to their fellow citizens.

These markets may well increase rapidly once the Internet becomes a true marketplace, but, until then, perhaps the best example is that of the frequent business traveller. These people stay at the same hotels and fly on the same aeroplanes. The brands to be found in international airports are already identical across the world, and hotel chains are similarly interchangeable from country to country. Loyalty is what the hotels and airlines want to promote, and they do this by a variety of frequent flyer and frequent visitor promotions. The key point is that the structure for truly global promotion is in place. The communication appears mainly at the point of use or by direct mail. Customers are more similar than different. 'Who do I want to do what?' can be asked and answered of frequent business travellers as a single 'village' across the world, and campaigns can be implemented on a truly global basis. All that needs changing is the language – and, in some cases, not even that.

Other well-defined, cross-frontier markets are achieved by the spread of identical retail formats. Benetton, Marks & Spencer and McDonald's are among three very different retail formats that are identical across frontiers and appeal in each location to fundamentally similar people.

However, it remains the case that there are fewer markets that are truly global than was expected ten years ago, and that the cultural factors governing behaviour remain persistently different. Even within business-to-business markets, there are radically different approaches to the relationship between groups and individuals, the taking of personal benefits from business transactions and the use of time.[4] The disparities are even greater in consumer markets. For these reasons, sales promotion more than any other part of the marketing mix needs to be planned globally, but implemented locally.

LOCALIZING THE GLOBAL

Once you have identified which of the three types of international promotion you are to implement, you will be able to set realistic and achievable objectives. As with all promotions, it is better to keep it simple, especially when it is to happen halfway around the world. When you start getting down to the details, you should follow exactly the same process as outlined elsewhere in this book. However, you must take account of the particular characteristics of culture and law that continue to differ between countries in most consumer markets.

Every country has laws that may affect your promotion. Table 5 (see page 237) indicates what is legal and what is not in some European countries. It is a guide, but no more. You will see that in Germany it is possible to run a competition or a sweepstake, but not a free draw. The rules are more subtle. If you run a competition, the answers must be easy to find on the competition form. You may then award the prize to the sender of the first correct entry received – a free draw in all but name. What's more, you are not supposed to have the entry forms near to the promoted product. That's the law, but it is normally flouted. Thus, to operate promotions effectively, you need not only a knowledge of the law, but also that of local practice and culture.

Again, in Germany, if you wish to band a premium to your product, you must ensure that it is very product-related and worth not more than a small percentage of the price of the main product. As a consequence, banded offers are hardly used and the consumer's expectation is that such offers may well be useful, but are of limited value. Should you introduce a banded offer that is more exciting than is allowed, then not only will you have broken the law, but you will run the risk of generating an unusually high demand that could create an 'out of stock' situation.

There are also differences in trade expectations and in the logistics required to support promotions. If a market is experienced in promotions, the trade will be equipped to handle and implement them. If not, your best ideas may never see the light of day due to confusion and lack of discipline.

It is surprising how many support services we take for granted when we run promotions – post offices that are reliable, retailers who will redeem coupons fairly, literate consumers. The absence of these are just a few of the things that could sink your promotion.

If you decide to supply the promoting companies with promotional items, find out about the customs regulations and the way the customs people really work. It is not unknown for items that are known to be urgent to fall into some suddenly created and highly expensive import category if they are to be released within a year. If you use local suppliers, and it is often a good idea, make sure you have a local contact capable of managing them if things go wrong.

Often cultural differences require different techniques. In some countries, people want, and expect, an immediate reward: they live for today, not tomorrow. Thus, a collector scheme is less likely to succeed than a banded or free product offer. A free mail-in might seem attractive, but will be totally useless in most developing countries.

Differences in practices of payment for drinks affect the way in which on-trade promotions can be run. The Smirnoff promotion (Case Study 21) assumed UK practice – that people go to the bar to order their drinks and then pay for them immediately. In France, the traditional practice is to sit at a table and be waited on or, if at the bar, to remain there. It is also the practice to collect a number of receipts and pay for them all when you leave. These differences in behaviour would have meant a fundamental rethink of the Smirnoff promotion.

However, different practices also create different opportunities. There are greater numbers of small, counter-service retailers in some countries than in others – the UK included. This means that promotions no longer possible in countries where the grocery trade is dominated by superstores can still be run in countries where the former situation persists. Great promotions of the past in one country can be a new opportunity in another. How can you make the most of them and avoid the other pitfalls we have discussed? The answer is to know the behaviour of your 'village' – both intermediaries and final consumers.

If you are promoting in a foreign country, you need allies who will act as your eyes and ears. Providing you ask the right questions, they will be able to come up with the answers. The difficult part is knowing which questions to ask. Also, whether you are promoting in a single country, across a range of borders or dealing with a truly global market, the additional challenge makes promoting even more fun than on your home ground.

CASE STUDIES

The following two case studies illustrate the two primary forms of international promotion – one that is borderless because the market makes it possible to be so and one that operates across multiple, but different, markets.

CASE STUDY 24: TONY STONE IMAGES

Tony Stone Images has long been the UK's leading supplier of stock photography, used by generations of art directors. By the mid 1990s it faced a classic marketing challenge. Competition was increasing and it had little brand differentiation. The solution, devised by agency IMP, was to demonstrate that the company understands creative needs and was not just another stock photography supplier. The strategy was to associate Tony Stone Images with 'creative visual solutions' and to position the company as a partner rather than a supplier.

The core idea was the 'scamp', or scribbled drawing that 'creatives' use to indicate the picture they have in mind – it being a poorly kept trade secret that drawing is not always their greatest strength. The campaign began in April 1996 with a series of trade press ads featuring single-colour scamps in place of the traditional full-colour photography used by competitors. It was extended to a range of merchandise incentives such as Post-it Notes and a sweatshirt with a rough outline of a jogger helpfully arrowed 'jogger'. The campaign continued at Christmas 1996 with a calendar for the following year showing both scamps and the photographs that matched them, one for each month.

To launch Tony Stone Images' 1997 generic stock photography catalogue, IMP devised a competition offering a two-night break in New York. It featured a scribbled drawing of a skyline marked 'sunrise/sunset, wide angle skyscrapers'. Entrants were asked to identify the matching photograph in the catalogue, mark on a map where it had been taken and fax back their entries. A follow-up mailing offered a night out for two for identifying a 'lovey dovey shot' in the catalogue and, as a tie-breaker, completing a half-drawn scamp. These competitions meant that the catalogue was browsed and that the product therefore stood out.

The mailing was translated into French, German, Danish and Flemish. It worked internationally because creatives are creatives the world over, photography is similarly international and the creative concept had universal appeal to the target audience. This is more than an illustration of international sales promotion: it is a fine example of using carefully thought-out and relevant incentives to make a whacky but deeply serious point about the positioning of a company and its relationship to its customers.

- How did IMP answer the question 'Who do I want to do what?' in this promotion?

- What other ideas could you suggest to extend the campaign for future years?

CASE STUDY 25: UMBRO

Every football fan dreams of walking out of a tunnel into a stadium filled with 80,000 supporters. If you can't achieve that, at least you can enjoy the gear that goes with it. This is the background to Umbro's positioning itself as being as passionate about football as the fans. It was the specific impetus for an in-store promotion devised by IMP to run internationally with the retail chain Footlocker in the run up to Euro '96.

The objectives were to extend the Umbro brand personality through sales promotion and to increase sales through Footlocker on a pan-European basis to the benefit of both companies. The promotion was to use the humorous, mickey-taking tone of voices familiar on terraces and in dressing rooms.

The core idea was to give purchasers of Umbro products an electronic swipe card that they took through a free-standing 'tunnel' in the shop. It would play one of two messages: 'You came, you won, you're walking out a winner. Claim your Euro '96 T-shirt from the cash desk'. Alternatively, 'What grief, what pain, you haven't won, but you can still win Euro '96 T-shirts with your gamecard'. Messages were recorded by recognizable football commentators from each country.

Football is a game of two halves whatever the country. Footlocker would not operate across Europe if specialist retailing was not remarkably similar. After all, fans watched the same games during Euro '96. However, sales promotion is not yet similarly international. In Germany, cards had to be made available to shoppers who did not make a purchase. In Italy, the promotion had to be registered with the Finance Ministry for tax purposes. In Holland, winners would hear a cheer in the 'tunnel' and then had to go to the cash desk and answer a simple question before they could obtain their T-shirt.

The variances are important, but so is the transferability of the core concept of tunnel, swipe card and football razzamatazz. The promotion worked for Footlocker and Umbro because the hard work had been undertaken to devise an offer that simultaneously worked across countries and adapted to their specific rules. It also illustrates a feature of the internationalization of sales promotion: that promotions are increasingly tailor-made to specific retailers, which know the particularities of their own markets as well or better than the promoter.

- What dangers, if any, do you see in trying to devise retail promotions that will work in several different EU countries?

- If budgets had allowed, are there any other marketing activities that you would have recommended to support this promotion?

SUMMARY

International sales promotion came about to achieve cost savings and ensure consistency. It differs depending on whether companies are centralized or decentralized in their structures, but the nature of sales promotion means that there are always cultural and legal factors to take into account.

Borderless promotions work where there is a single international target audience. In most cases, international promotions are multiple-country ones, and vary in terms of timing and detail from country to country.

Succeeding requires close attention to be paid to the behaviour and culture of each market you are promoting to.

13

SELF-REGULATION AND THE LAW

Promotional activity has long operated within the dual context of self-regulation and legal constraint. As early as 1890, the leading poster companies set up a Joint Censorship Committee to exclude objectionable posters. In 1907, Parliament passed the first of the modern pieces of advertising legislation, the Advertising Regulations Act, which gave local authorities power to control poster hoardings.[1] Both these developments concerned posters – the most publicly intrusive form of advertising. Both derived from an active public campaign. They are a measure of the close relationship between self-regulation and law and the impetus that public and political opinion gives to both.

The balance between self-regulation and law has varied over time, and varies considerably between countries. Within the EU, Germany has tended towards law, the UK towards self-regulation. However, the picture is not black and white – all countries have a mixture of both. Since the 1986 Single European Act, it has been an open question as to whether or not EU practice would tend towards one or the other. In autumn 1997, the European Commission published a Green Paper on Commercial Communications that will lead to an EU directive with legal force. Soon after, the European Promotional Marketing Alliance – the umbrella body for the industry – announced the preparation of a European Code of Sales Promotion Practice, to be published during 1998.[2] The outcome is likely to be a continuing balance between the two.

That balance is moving steadily towards greater protection of the consumer from unsupported claims. Chapter 1 discussed the basis of business in building long-term customer relationships, the foolishness of campaigns that undermine relationships, and increasing public concern about the ethical status of the company behind the brand. Promoters who understand that will have little trouble with either the codes of practice or the laws. However, both the codes and the laws include details that are not obvious at first sight. You need to take account of them in the letter as well as the spirit.

UK CODES OF PRACTICE

The British Code of Sales Promotion is a self-regulatory code written by people in the business in their own long-term self-interest. It is based on the view that self-regulation is preferable to laws for promoter and consumer alike. It is supported by the Code of Advertising Practice (CAP) Committee, and is under the supervision of the Advertising Standards Authority (ASA). First introduced in 1974, the sixth edition of the Code was published in 1995, and a seventh is expected in 1998. Since 1995, it has been sent out with its advertising 'cousin' as the British Codes of Advertising and Sales Promotion. Its fundamental requirements are that all promotions should be:

- legal, decent, honest and truthful
- conducted equitably, promptly and efficiently
- seen to deal fairly and honourably with consumers
- in line with accepted principles of fair competition
- not bring the industry into disrepute
- in line with the spirit, as well as the letter, of the rules.

The Code is not a substitute for the legal protection of the consumer, producer or distributor against fraudulent practice, but a complement to the law. Promoters are expected to stay within both. Implementation of the Code is in the hands of individual sales promoters, whether they be companies or agencies. As with the law, ignorance of the Code is no defence for not following it. If you have not already obtained a copy, phone the ASA for one now (see under Trade associations in the Useful addresses section at the back of the book).

The implementation of the Code is monitored by the ASA. It used to send out 'mystery shoppers' to buy promoted products and check them against the Code, but now it relies entirely on people writing in to complain, and on a certain amount of research on different aspects of the Code. In 1995, it received 1243 complaints and upheld 307; in 1996 it received 1169 and upheld 268. About 13 per cent of the ASA's work is accounted for by sales promotion.

The 300 complaints typically upheld by the ASA each year represent a fraction of the total number of promotions, but they involve some big names and some consistent failings. Every month, the ASA publishes a monthly report that details the complaints it has upheld, and some of those it hasn't. A sample of complaints upheld over the last few years highlights the issues at stake and forms the case study in this chapter.

The ASA Council, which ultimately adjudicates, is a committee of the great and the good chaired by the former Labour and SDP politician Bill Rodgers (Lord Rodgers of Quarry Bank). Its decisions can be (and are) criticized from two directions – as being overly fussy and as being toothless. Its August 1997 report was delayed because Direct Line Financial Services took out a High Court injunction in protest against a criticism of the company in it. The ASA published the report without the Direct Line case.

Injunctions have only been taken out 3 times in more than 20 years, but many other companies (notably tabloids) appear year after year for the same or similar infringements. The Press Complaints Commission has had a similar experience. In the final analysis, companies have to decide if they support a self-regulatory system or not. If they do, they need to take what the ASA says seriously, even if they think it is overly fussy (which it can be) and toothless (which it can be).

There are several regulars in the ASA's reports. Many relate to availability, participation and administration. Promoters are expected to have sufficient quantities of their promotional products to meet likely demand. Phrases such as 'subject to availability' do not relieve you of your responsibilities. Demand should be estimated in advance, and you should also have plans to meet unexpected demand. If all else fails, an item of equivalent value must be offered. If there are limitations on participation, or any costs that consumers may incur in taking part, they must be clearly stated. Also, arrangements must be made to dispatch goods within 30 days.

Promotions directed at young children are an area of particular sensitivity – not least because children are such keen participators in promotions. The Code requires that they should be for products that are suitable for them. They should not take unfair advantage of children's lack of experience, encourage them to make excessive purchases, or cause conflict between them and their parents. Obtaining parental permission for a child's participation is often a good idea.

The word 'free' is one of the most powerful available to promoters, and its use is closely governed. If the consumer has to pay for anything other than postage, it may be a fine promotional offer, but it is not 'free'. This applies to a contribution towards a mail-in item, the cost of premium rate telephone lines as much as the requirement to make a purchase before taking up the offer.

The most unnecessary area of complaint relates to the rules of promotions – unnecessary because it is not difficult to get the rules right. The Code provides a list of rules that should be included in competitions, free draws and instant win offers. Keep them simple if possible, but always include entry conditions, the closing date, a description of the prizes, the criteria for judging entries and the availability of a winners list.

As an annexe to the Advertising and Sales Promotion Codes, the CAP has produced specific rules for the advertising and promotion of alcoholic drinks, cigarettes, financial services, vitamins, health products, slimming products, cosmetics and medicines. There are also specific rules about environmental claims, distance selling, employment and business opportunities.

How do you make sure you stay within the Code? The CAP, which writes the Code, operates a fast, free and confidential Copy Advice Service, dealing with over 10,000 enquiries a year (for the telephone and fax numbers for this service, see under Advertising Standards Authority, under Trade associations in the Useful addresses section at the back of the book). However, there is a downside to this: if you fail to follow the advice of the CAP because you disagree with it, you will not have a leg to stand on if there is a subsequent complaint. For this reason, members of the ISP often prefer to use the ISP's Legal Advice Service. Going to the CAP is a bit like going to a policeman to ask whether or not what you want to do is within the law. There are also various legal practices offering advice on sales promotion law.

Producing codes of practice has become a growth industry. Many of them are turgid, repetitive and entirely without teeth. Just as clubs think they need ties, so trade associations think they need codes. You should make your own judgement about what codes matter in your business. There are references to sales promotion in codes produced by the Consumers Association for business sponsorship of educational materials, for financial services promotion produced by the various financial regulators, by the pharmaceutical industry and by many other industry associations. The following codes can be particularly relevant to sales promotion.

- British Promotional Merchandise Association Code of Practice

- Direct Marketing Association Code of Practice

- DTI Code of Practice for Traders on Price Indications

- International Code of Sales Promotion Practice

- Institute of Purchasing and Supply Code of Practice

- Mail Order Traders' Association Code of Practice

- Promotional Sourcing Association Code of Practice

- Promotional Handling Association Code of Practice

- Independent Committee for the Supervision of Standards of Telephone Services Code of Practice.

John Williams reprints many of these codes in his *Manual of Sales Promotion* – and they extend to more than 80 closely printed A4 pages. They frequently change, but are generally free, so it makes most sense not to reprint them here. However, I suggest that you get hold of up-to-date copies of those that affect you, using the Useful addresses section at the back of the book.

UK LAW

More than a hundred UK laws affect the conduct of sales promotion, along with a growing number of EU directives. Some types of promotion – particularly involving packaging, product safety and statements at point of sale – are subject to Local Authority Trading Standards Officers. Legislative teeth has been given to the ASA by the 1988 Control of Misleading Advertisements Regulations, which gives the Director-General of Fair Trading the power to take out a court injunction against an advertiser or promoter who continues to use an ad or promotion that the ASA has ruled against.

These regulations are some of the very few that were actually designed to control sales promotional activity. Most of the other acts and regulations were designed to control consumer credit, gambling, trade descriptions and so forth. It is not surprising, therefore, that the legal framework for sales promotion derives from small sections of a large number of acts, and that it is sometimes contradictory.

There are slight differences between England and Scotland, in that the Scottish legal system and some of the relevant legislation differs in details from that pertaining to England. However, for all practical purposes, the UK can be considered a single unit for sales promotion.

EU AND INTERNATIONAL LAW

Promoters thinking of running promotions in other countries – including the Republic of Ireland – must take account of the very different legal frameworks that apply in these countries.

Only in Greece, Spain and Portugal (among EU countries) are all the many UK techniques allowed. Germany is a graveyard for sales promotion: free draws, share-outs, collector promotions and next purchase coupons are among the techniques that are disallowed. The Benelux countries are fairly restrictive as well.

A rough guide to what is allowable in different EU countries is given in a table prepared and regularly updated by IMP (see Table 5). It is only a guide and promoters should always seek advice before applying a UK technique elsewhere.

CASE STUDIES FROM THE ASA

The following five case studies taken from ASA reports, deal with typical infringements of the Code. Some are obvious, some less so. In answering the questions that follow each example, bear in mind that the ASA Council is not infallible – it may make judgements that you or others want to dispute.

COCA-COLA

Coca-Cola ran a promotion in January 1990 headlined 'Free music – 10,000 music vouchers to be won'. To take part, consumers had to phone a premium rate telephone number, at that time charging 38p per minute at peak times. People complained that this meant it was not 'free', that consumers effectively paid to enter and Coca-Cola benefited from that payment.

The ASA upheld the complaint. Although there was an option to participate by post, it was only possible to do so after 30 April – three months after the promotion began. (ASA Report 184, August 1990.)

■ What steps could Coca-Cola have taken to keep this promotion within the Code if they still wanted to use the word 'free'?

■ If they didn't use the word 'free', how else could they have described the promotion?

Table 5 *Which countries allow which kinds of promotion?*

Promotions	UK	Irish Republic	Spain	Germany	France	Denmark	Belgium	Netherlands	Portugal	Italy	Greece	Luxembourg
On-pack price reductions	●	●	●	●	●	●	●	●	●	●	●	●
Banded offers	●	●	●	?	●	●	?	●	●	●	●	?
In-pack premiums	●	●	●	?	?	?	?	?	●	●	●	?
Multibuys	●	●	?	?	●	●	?	●	●	●	●	?
Extra product	●	●	●	●	●	●	●	●	●	●	●	●
Free product	●	●	●	●	●	●	●	●	●	●	●	●
Reusable/alternative use pack	●	●	●	●	●	●	●	●	●	●	●	●
Free mail-ins	●	●	?	○	●	●	●	●	●	●	●	●
With purchase premiums	●	●	○	○	●	○	?	?	●	●	●	?
Cross-product offers	●	●	○	○	●	?	○	●	●	●	●	○
Collector devices	●	●	○	○	●	?	?	●	●	●	●	?
Competitions	●	●	?	?	●	?	?	●	●	●	●	●
Self-liquidating premiums	●	●	●	●	●	●	●	●	●	●	●	?
Free draws	●	●	○	○	●	○	○	○	●	●	●	○
Share-outs	?	●	○	○	?	○	○	?	●	?	●	○
Sweepstake/lottery	?	?	○	○	?	?	○	○	●	?	●	○
Money off vouchers	●	●	○	○	●	?	●	●	●	?	●	●
Money off next purchase	●	●	?	?	●	○	●	●	●	?	●	●
Cash back	●	●	●	●	●	●	●	●	●	○	●	●
In-store demos	●	●	●	●	●	●	●	●	●	●	●	●

Key: ● Permitted   ○ Not permitted   ? May be permitted

Source: IMP

VAUXHALL MOTORS

The company offered '£1500 cash back' on its Astra GTE and £1000 or £500 on other Astra and Nova models in a series of press ads in 1991. People complained that when they went to the showroom, they found that the £1500 cash back didn't apply to the GTE Convertible, and that some of the other models featured in the ads were not available.

The ASA criticized Vauxhall for not making it clear that different cash back arrangements applied to the GTE Convertible than to other GTE models. It also criticized the company for not extending the cash back offer when it ran out of stock during the promotion, particularly as it was continuing to run ads for it. (ASA Report 9, February 1992)

- How could Vauxhall have ensured that the consumer offer on the GTE Convertible was clear within the meaning of the Code?

- Assuming all the ads were booked, what steps could Vauxhall have taken to ensure that it stayed within the Code when stocks ran out?

THE EXPRESS

The paper ran an offer in 1993 headlined on the front page 'Free ice-cream for every reader'. In fact, the voucher inside the paper entitled them to a double scoop of Thornton's ice-cream for the price of a single scoop, as long as one scoop was a specified flavour.

The ASA upheld the complaint. (ASA Report 31, December 1993)

- What words could *The Express* have used in its front-page headline to keep within the Code?

- Would it have been acceptable within the Code for the restriction to specified flavours to have been in small print on the inside?

THE SUN

In 1996 *The Sun* ran an offer headlined on the front page 'This paper gives you a FREE go in tonight's £30m lottery . . . YOUR FREE National Lottery Syndicate ticket is inside *The Sun* today . . . and it could win you a share of tonight's £30m roll-over jackpot. That's right, it could be you!'

On page 3, the paper continued 'Play SYNDICATES for £30m tonight'.

In fact, *The Sun* had not bought its readers a 'free go' in the Lottery. It had bought 40,000 tickets, one for every hundred copies of the paper sold. Readers could, at best, expect one-hundredth of any prize. Also, the forecast jackpot was not £30 million, but £23.8 million.

The ASA said the promotion was misleading. (ASA Report 61, June 1996)

- How do you think this promotion differs from the Sellotape promotion (Case Study 14), which was not criticized by the ASA?

- How could *The Sun* have rephrased its promotion to keep within the Code?

BALKAN HOLIDAYS

The company ran a brochure ad in 1996 claiming 'Free up to age 12! All two-week beach holidays and two-centre beach/mountain holidays to Bulgaria'.

Unfortunately, it was not true. People complained that some holidays did not have free child places.

The ASA upheld the complaint. (ASA Report 67, December 1996)

- Would consumers have a case in law for holding Balkan Holidays to its offer of a free child place on all holidays?

- How effective do you think the ASA has been in persuading advertisers not to make misleading offers of this kind?

SUMMARY

Sales promotion is a practical, nuts and bolts affair and there are a lot of detailed rules to follow in both the Codes and in legislation. There are also some broad principles that reflect good business practice. The collective need of promoters to avoid intrusive legislation makes it important to follow both the spirit and the letter of the Code. Following the Code is not difficult if you use one of the copy-checking services available to help you. If in any doubt, contact the ISP (if you are a member) or a specialist legal practice. Each country has different laws governing sales promotion, and you need to understand and respect them.

14

LEARNING MORE ABOUT SALES PROMOTION

Considering the scale of sales promotion, there are still relatively few books about it, a relatively low level of teaching about it in university and professional courses and relatively little academic research into it. However, the situation is better than it was ten years ago, and can only go on improving. This chapter gives you a guide to finding out more in books and magazines and from exhibitions, conferences and courses. It ends with a series of self-study questions that you can use to check that you've made the most of this book.

BOOKS

Dr John Williams has written an A4 format book of nearly 500 pages entitled *The Manual of Sales Promotion*. First published in 1983, and completely revised in 1996, it is privately published by his company, Innovation Licensing Limited, and costs £40. It provides checklists for techniques and administration, reprints most codes of practice and provides draft copy for many types of promotion. It is an excellent source of reference for the details of sales promotion.

Alan Toop, founder of The Sales Machine, is one of the most prolific writers on sales promotion. His first book, long out of print, entitled *Choosing the Right Sales Promotion* was published by Crosby Lockwood in 1966. Kogan Page published his *European Sales Promotion: Great campaigns in action* in 1992, which is comprised of more than 40 case studies under broad headings such as awareness, brand value and repeat purchase. The examples are good, and his comments are pithy.

If you can find it anywhere, his earlier book *Just £3.95?!* published privately by The Sales Machine in 1978, contains powerful case studies of brand-enhancing promotions that are still relevant today. Together with Pran Choudhury and Ricky Elliott, he wrote *Successful Sales Promotion* (Sangram Books 1992), which mainly consists of 26 sales promotions from India on brands including Horlicks, Palmolive and Bournvita.

Christian Petersen, co-founder of KLP, wrote one of the best of the earlier generation of books – *Sales Promotion in Action* (Associated Business Press, 1979). Shortly before his untimely death, he teamed up with Alan Toop to write *Sales Promotion in Post-modern Marketing* (Gower, 1994). It is expensive to buy, but well worth borrowing for its intelligent discussion of the changing face of marketing and the evolution of sales promotion techniques.

For the legal side, you cannot do better than Philip Circus' *Sales Promotion Law: A practical guide* (Butterworth, 1996).

The publisher of this book, Kogan Page, has also published Chris Brown's *Sales Promotion Handbook* (1993). It is complementary to this book, containing useful checklists for many aspects of sales promotion.

One of the few academics to take sales promotion seriously is John Quelch of the Graduate School of Business Administration at Harvard. His book *Sales Promotion Management* (Prentice Hall, 1989) is mainly concerned with price promotion, is wholly US-focused, and fairly demanding. If you like statistical analysis, it provides an important basis for thinking seriously about price promotions.

Knowing more about a subject needs to go hand in hand with knowing how it fits into a broader scheme of things. Here there is a problem. The established industry view is that sales promotion is just one part of one of the four Ps. In the seventh edition of his classic book *Marketing Management* (Prentice Hall, 1997), Philip Kotler is less dogmatic about this classification than in earlier editions, but he still goes on using it. Kotler does not refer to the alternative way of seeing sales promotion in the marketing mix advanced by Waterschoot and Van den Bulte (see note 6 to Chapter 1 in the References and further reading section, page 250). The mechanical model of marketing developed in the 1950s and 1960s is collapsing under the weight of reality, but the textbooks have yet to develop a new model. In the interim, readers have to develop their own way of fitting the various elements of marketing into a coherent whole, and refer to books such as *Sales Promotion in Post-modern Marketing*. The textbooks get longer and longer, but don't give the answer.

One popular model is 'integrated marketing'. PR Smith's *Marketing Communications: An integrated approach* (Kogan Page, 1993) provides an accessible example covering all the communications tools. The trouble is that integration is easier to talk about than to do, and you still have to know what the separate bits are that you are trying to integrate. In practice, integrated marketing is a buzzword that cuts little ice with most companies. Far better to understand sales promotion thoroughly, and then try to ensure that your campaigns reinforce and do not undermine everything else the company is trying to do. Integration is wider than marketing, and absolute integration a dream we seldom achieve.

MAGAZINES

If you've got time to look at academic marketing magazines, there are, periodically, articles on sales promotion in the *Journal of Marketing* and *Journal of Marketing Research*. Most of them are mind-numbingly statistical, US-based, focused on price promotions and very difficult to draw practical conclusions from. If that doesn't put you off, the easiest way to access them is not through electronic media, but by going into a business school's library and looking in the index of the bound volumes.

There are several popular magazines published in the UK that are relevant of which *Promotions & Incentives* and *Incentive Today* are the best. Both are controlled-circulation magazines, so you should try to get yourself on their distribution lists. However, beware the bias that their dependency on advertising creates. There is almost nothing in them on price promotion (other than coupons) because price promotion does not attract advertisers. There are endless, repetitive features on vouchers, travel and luxury gifts because they do attract advertisers.

The features on sales promotion that occur in *Marketing* and *Marketing Week* follow a similar pattern, but occasionally carry very useful in-depth analysis.

The ISP publishes a useful newsletter, which is particularly good on developments in EU regulations. It also publishes an awards brochure each year, which gives photographs and brief write-ups of that year's winners. It is an excellent way of keeping in touch with what the industry regards as best current practice.

There is, sadly, no equivalent in sales promotion of the monthly magazine *Admap* or the biennial *Advertising Works*, both published by NTC Publications and containing serious analysis of advertising effectiveness that is accessible to practitioners. Unfortunately, these publications have a dual role: serious research and advancing the cause of advertising. They tend to underestimate the significance of sales promotion, if they mention it at all.

EXHIBITIONS AND CONFERENCES

The major event in the sales promotion calendar is the *Incentive Today* exhibition held in London in May. Other exhibitions are held in different parts of the country, notably the Sales Promotion and Incentives exhibition held every two years in Manchester. These are particularly good for keeping up to date with the latest in premiums.

Conferences are organized periodically by the ISP, the SPCA and by commercial providers. These tend to be expensive, but bring out the insights of those at the leading edge of the business. If you want to keep up-to-date in this way, meetings of the ISP (mainly in London) are particularly useful.

COURSES

The top-level course in sales promotion is run by the ISP with support from Kingston Business School. In 1997, it cost £500 for ISP members and £600 for non-members. It is a correspondence course run over a three-month period commencing in January, and is supported by a series of mainly London-based seminars and tutorials at further cost. It is a well-structured course, combining detailed knowledge with its application in practical conditions, and culminating in a real-life set brief.

The ISP also run an intensive three-day course entitled (from its town of origin) The Brighouse Weekend. Sadly, it has migrated from West Yorkshire, but it continues to provide a first class training and the opportunity to devise and present a promotion to senior marketing managers.

The Chartered Institute of Marketing (CIM) runs three-day residential courses – Sales Promotion and Sales Promotion for Retail – at intermediate level (two to five years' experience) at its headquarters near Maidenhead. In 1997 these cost £1150 all-in, and were each run three times a year. CIM also runs a one-day course on sales promotion in various parts of the country.

The CIM's Diploma and Certificate include sales promotion within their papers on Marketing Communications. This only provides the most general introduction to each of the communications disciplines. The CIM courses are valuable for their strategic approach to marketing and for putting what you know about communications in a broader context.

The Communications Advertising and Marketing Foundation (CAM) offers a course culminating in a Certificate for which you need to sit six papers that focus more on the communications disciplines – respectively, marketing, advertising, PR, media, sales promotion and direct marketing, and research and behavioural studies. In 1997, it was taught at 30 centres throughout the UK and on six different distance learning programmes.

The CAM Diploma allows students who have taken the certificate to specialize in one of the communications disciplines. The ISP Diploma is recognized by CAM as the specialist qualification in sales promotion. To achieve the CAM Diploma you need to take the ISP Diploma and the CAM paper in Management and Strategy.

The Marketing Standards Board published a substantial set of NVQ standards for marketing, advertising, market research and other aspects of the marketing mix in 1995. They have not been widely adopted, and, at the time of writing, the Sales Promotion NVQ standards had not been finalized.

SELF-STUDY QUESTIONS

If you are doing one of the courses on sales promotion, you'll find that these questions help you meet the course requirements. If you're using the book to help you in your day-to-day work, you'll find they help you get the most out of what you've read. You can also use them as a 'trivia quiz'!

Chapter 1

- What is the difference between price and value promotions, and what sort of promotions fit into each category?
- What are the main reasons for the growth in sales promotion?
- How can sales promotion be planned strategically?

Chapter 2

- What are the main points to include in a promotional brief?
- What sorts of promotion are best for encouraging trial?
- What sorts of promotion are best for encouraging repeat purchase?
- What are the pros and cons of delayed and immediate promotions?

Chapter 3

- What are some of the leading techniques for developing creative ideas?
- How would you go about answering the question 'Who do I want to do what?'

Chapter 4

- What issues should you take into account when organizing a pitch among sales promotion agencies?
- What are the main things needed in a brief for a handling house?
- What things can you use promotional insurance for, and why should you do so?

Chapter 5

- What are the different ways in which you can set a budget for sales promotion?
- If you offer a premium with three proofs of purchase on 150,000 packs, how many opportunities to apply will there be?
- What are some of the main issues to watch in contracts for sales promotional supply?

Chapter 6

- What are the main types of research you can use in sales promotion?
- What must you record for effective evaluation?
- Why do you think so little research goes on into sales promotion?

Chapter 7

- What do you need to watch for if you are organizing a free flight offer?

- How do free rooms offers work?

- What issues do you need to take into account if you are using discount coupons?

- Why can insurance be offered in a promotion at a much lower cost than the consumer would pay for it from a broker?

- How do fixed-fee promotions work?

Chapter 8

- What major problems tend to arise in joint promotions?

- What should you take into account in looking for a joint promotion partner?

- What can you do and what can't you do if you want to promote on the back of a major event licensed to another company?

- What particular rules apply to promoting with charities?

Chapter 9

- What are the key features of segment pricing and how does it differ from other types of pricing?

- What are the pros and cons of multibuys?

- What are the pros and cons of reduced price offers?

- What alternative means of coupon distribution are available, and what are the typical redemption rates for each?

- If a 10p coupon is placed in a newspaper with a circulation of 2,300,000 and a readership of 3,900,000, and you expect a 1 per cent redemption rate, how many coupons will be redeemed?

- What are the main types of trade price promotion?

- What key things should you look out for if you are using a 0 per cent finance offer?

Chapter 10

- What are the pros and cons of on-pack offers?
- What do you need to take into account if you are planning a near-pack?
- What contribution can you ask the consumer to make if you are running a free mail-in?
- Why have self-liquidators fallen out of favour?
- How can sales promotion extend a brand into new distribution outlets?

Chapter 11

- What are the main differences between a competition and a free draw?
- What is it essential to include in an instant win if it is not to be considered to be a lottery?
- What types of prize promotion do games actually consist of?
- What sorts of lotteries are legal for promoters to run?
- How can companies offer a million pound prize without having a million pounds to give away?

Chapter 12

- What are the main types of international promotion?
- What must you take into account in planning a promotion that is going to run in several countries?

Chapter 13

- How do you make sure your promotional copy accords with the codes of practice?
- What are the most frequent causes of promotions being criticized by the ASA?

■   What are the main principles of the Codes of Advertising and Sales Promotion Practice?

SUMMARY

If sales promotion is a major part of your job, there's a lot to be said for doing the full range of courses arranged by CAM, the CIM and the ISP. Together, they give you a good grounding in communications, a good grounding in marketing, and specialist knowledge in sales promotion. If sales promotion is less central to what you do, at least make sure you keep up with the magazines.

If this all seems like a lot of work, do not worry. This book has been designed to help you design and implement promotions that really work. There's no substitute for experience and for keeping your eyes open, and the best form of learning is doing.

REFERENCES

INTRODUCTION

1 Kotler, P (1997) *Marketing Management: Analysis, planning, implementation and Control* (9th Edn), Prentice Hall, Englewood Cliffs, New Jersey.
2 Harris International Marketing (November 1987) 'Do Promotions Promote Sales?' *Marketing Week.*
3 General Household Survey, HMSO 1996, quoted in the *Marketing Pocket Book 1997*, NTC Publications, Henley-on-Thames, p41.
4 (1996) *The UK Coupon Market*, NCH Promotional Services.
5 Data from the *Advertising Statistics Yearbook 1996*, Advertising Association, the Direct Mail Information Service and RSL Sportscan, as quoted in the *Marketing Pocket Book 1997*, pp113, 122, 124.
6 (October 1997) *Promotions & Incentives*, p13.
7 Fletcher, W (1992) *A Glittering Haze: Strategic advertising in the 1990s*, NTC Publications, Henley-on-Thames.
8 Roberts, A (February 1996) 'What do we know about advertising's short-term effects?', *Admap*, pp42–5 (the survey, a MediaSpan Advertising Assessor analysis, fused AGB Superpanel data with BARB TV audience data).

CHAPTER 1

1 Kay, J (1993) *Foundations of Corporate Success*, Oxford University Press, Oxford, pvii.
2 For a summary of changes in marketing structures, see Kashani, K 'Why marketing still matters', in, Bickerstaffe, G (Ed) (1997) *Mastering Management*, Financial Times/Pitman Publishing, London, p165.
3 Feldwick, P (April 1996) 'What is brand equity anyway, and how do you measure it?', *Journal of the Market Research Society*, **38**, 2, pp85–103 argues that 'brand equity' means 'how healthy is this

brand?' – in other words, all the things that make it a valuable asset now and in the future.

4 A very good summary of the pros and cons of the persuasion and involvement models can be found in McDonald, C (1992) *How Advertising Works: a review of current thinking*, Advertising Association/NTC Publications, Henley-on-Thames, pp91–108.

5 The research behind this is in Finney, J (1992) *Finding Faith Today*, Bible Society/Churches Together in England, London. The application of 'belonging' rather than 'believing' strategies by the churches is evident in Warren, R (1995) *Signs of Life: How goes the Decade of Evangelism*, Church House Publishing, London.

6 van Waterschoot, W, and Van den Bulte, C (October 1992) 'The 4P Classification of the Marketing Mix Revisited', *Journal of Marketing*, **56**, pp83–93.

7 Ehrenberg, ASC, Hammond, K and Goodhart, CAE (1991) *The After-effects of Large-scale Consumer Promotions*, Centre for Marketing and Communications, London Business School, London.

8 Ogilvy, D (1983) *Ogilvy on Advertising*, Pan, London, p169.

9 Boulding, W, Lee, E and Staelin, R (May 1994) 'Mastering the Mix: Do Advertising, Promotion and Sales Force Activities Lead to Differentiation', *Journal of Marketing Research*, **XXXI**, pp159–72, provide evidence that the critical factor is whether or not any of these activities is unique. So a price promotion will add to brand value if it is unique, and not if it is not.

10 Quelch, J (1989) *Sales Promotion Management*, Prentice Hall, Englewood Cliffs, New Jersey, p7.

11 RSA (1995) *Tomorrow's Company: The role of business in a changing world*, Gower, Aldershot.

12 Collins, JC, and Porras, JI (1996) *Built to Last: Successful habits of visionary companies*, Century Business, London.

CHAPTER 2

1 Joachimsthaler, E and Aaker, D (January/February 1997) usefully summarize these and other cases in 'Building Brands Without Mass Media', *Harvard Business Review*, pp39–50.

2 Fletcher, W (1992) *A Glittering Haze: Strategic advertising in the 1990s*, NTC Publications, Henley-on-Thames.

CHAPTER 3

1   There are now nine volumes in the series, which is published every two years. The latest is Duckworth, G (Ed) (1997) *Advertising Works 9: Advertising Effectiveness Awards 1996*, IPA/NTC Publications, Henley-on-Thames.
2   Mahoney, S (February 1995) 'The Carrot and the Stick', *Sales Promotion*.

CHAPTER 4

1   (July/August 1997) *Incentive Today*, p17. *Promotions & Incentives* publishes details of four agencies each month as the 'P&I Portfolio'
2   (January 1996) *Promotions & Incentives*, p20.

CHAPTER 5

1   Broadbent, S (1989) *The Advertising Budget: The advertiser's guide to budget determination*, IPA/NTC Publications, Henley-on-Thames (sales promotion is not considered specifically, but the approach can be applied to it). For a discussion on price promotional budgets see Quelch, J (1989) *Sales Promotion Management*, Prentice Hall, Englewood Cliffs, New Jersey.
2   *Business Promotion Schemes* (VAT Notice 700/7/94), *Retail Schemes* (VAT Notice 727) and *Business Gifts* (VAT Notice 700/727) and *Business Gifts* (VAT Notice 700/35/88), available from your local VAT office or VAT Communications, HM Customs and Excise, 4th Floor West, New King's Beam House, Upper Ground, London SE1 9PJ
3   Baguley, P (1995) *Managing Successful Projects*, Pitman Publishing, London.

CHAPTER 6

1   Chisnall, P (1991) *The Essence of Marketing Research*, Prentice Hall, Englewood Cliffs, New Jersey; Hague, P, and Jackson, P (1992) *Marketing Research in Practice*, Kogan Page, London.
2   Hague, P, and Jackson, P (1996) *Market Research: A guide to planning, methodology and evaluation*, Kogan Page, London.
3   Wicks, A (1990) 'Advertising Research', in Burn, R, Hague, P, and Vangelder, P, *A Handbook of Market Research Techniques*, Kogan Page, London, pp317–20.

CHAPTER 8

1   (March 1997) *Promotions & Incentives*, pp34–8 talks of divergent views on this, and notably the possibility that the reason for Sainsbury's departure from Shell's scheme is that 'Sainsbury's is trying to be a filling station and Shell is trying to be a shop'.

2   This is the Dirichlet theory, tested with 30 food and drink products, 20 personal care products and many other sectors in several countries over a 45-year period. For a summary of it, see Ehrenberg, ASC, and Uncles, MD (1995) *Dirichlet-type Markets: A review* (Parts 1 and 2), University of Bradford Management Centre Working Paper Series 9501 and 9502.

3   Uncles, M (1994) 'Do You or Your Customers Need a Loyalty Scheme', *Journal of Targeting, Measurement and Analysis for Marketing*, **2**, 4, pp335–50 – a criticism of loyalty schemes based on this approach.

4   Wood, A (February 1997), *Incentive Today*, p2.

5   (17 April 1997) *Marketing*, pp32–4.

6   The *Financial Times* (20 September 1995) was attributing Tesco's success to its Clubcard within six months of its launch.

7   Westoby, P (July 1995) *Sales Promotion:* 'The bottom has fallen out of the loyalty market in the USA – it could happen here too'.

CHAPTER 9

1   Publishers feared that the demise of the net book agreement would lead to a discount war. In fact, retailers such as Tesco implemented a range of techniques, including merchandising books with other products and changing its bestseller section every two weeks – a totally different approach to that adopted by booksellers, and one in which price is only one of the promotional tools used (Fiona Kennedy (Spring 1997) *The Author*.

2   NCH Promotional Services offers a segmentation of consumers into Branded EDLP seekers (19 per cent), Low Price Fixture Ferrets (23 per cent), Promotion Junkies (18 per cent), Stockpilers (21 per cent) and the Promotionally Oblivious (18 per cent). Targeting price deals at the last category is a waste of time (24 April 1997, *Marketing*, pp30–3).

3   Dahar, SK, and Hoch, SJ (January 1996) 'Price Discrimination Using Instore Merchandising', *Journal of Marketing*, **60**, pp17–30.

4   Mulhearn, FJ, and Padgett, DT (October 1995) 'The Relationship Between Retail Price Promotions and Regular Price Purchases',

Journal of Marketing, **59**, pp83–90, provides evidence that people who buy on price will transfer to purchases at the regular price.

5   I am indebted to The Blue-Chip Marketing Consultancy for a summary of this research.

6   DTI (November 1988) *Code of Practice for Traders on Price Indications*.

7   (May 1997) *Notes for Guidance on Coupons: Recommended Best Practice* (Revised edn), ISP, London.

CHAPTER 10

1   (6 September 1996) *Marketing Week*, p52; (January 1997) *Incentive Today*, p17.

2   'A year ago the publishing industry was hinting covermounts would be eased out in favour of promotions rooted in editorial', reported (September 1995) *Promotions & Incentives*, p51, but (February 1997) *Incentive Today*, p21, reported 'Covermounts in kids and teens markets are practically part of the product'.

3   (February 1996) *Incentive Today*, p28.

4   (November/December 1995) *Promotions & Incentives*, p48.

5   Davidson, H (1987) *Offensive Marketing*, Penguin, Harmondsworth, Middlesex, p260.

6   (March 1996) *Incentive Today*, p24.

7   (8 May 1997) *Marketing*, p23.

8   (May 1997) *Promotions & Incentives*, pp28–31.

9   Reid, T (May 1995) *Sales Promotion*, pp31–3.

10   Marshall, C (October 1993) *Promotions & Incentives*, pp20–26.

CHAPTER 11

1   BMRB/Mintel 1994, quoted in Williams, J (1997) *The Manual of Sales Promotion*, Innovation Licensing Limited, 58 Jermyn Street, London SW1Y 6LX.

2   Davidson, H (1987) *Offensive Marketing*, Penguin, Harmondsworth, Middlesex, p261.

3   Circus, P (April 1996) *Incentive Today*, p10.

4   Hyslop, R (May 1996) 'Ten Years Remembered', *Incentive Today*, p56.

5   Circus, P (November/December 1995) *Incentive Today*, p6.

6   Duckworth, G (Ed) (1997) *Advertising Works 9: Advertising Effectiveness Awards 1996*, IPA/NTC Publications, Henley-on-Thames, pp203–

230. This is one of the very few examples of an advertising effectiveness case study acknowledging the positive effects of sales promotion.

7 Circus, P (February 1996) *Incentive Today*, p10.

8 (January 1996) *Promotions & Incentives*, p6; ISP's response to Gaming Board criticisms of prize promotions, (June 1996) *Incentive Today*, p4.

9 (November/December 1995) *Incentive Today*, p22.

CHAPTER 12

1 Kashani, K, and Quelch, J (May/June 1990) 'Can Sales Promotion Go Global?', *Business Horizons*, pp37–43.

2 Trompenaars, F (1993) *Riding The Waves of Culture: Understanding cultural diversity in business*, Nicholas Brealey, London.

3 Ohmae, K (1996) *The End of the Nation State: The rise of regional economies*, Free Press Paperbacks, Simon & Schuster, New York.

4 Hampden-Turner, C, and Trompenaars, F (1993) *The Seven Cultures of Capitalism*, Piatkus, London.

CHAPTER 13

1 Nevett, TR (1982) *Advertising in Britain: A history*, Heinemann, Oxford.

2 (October 1997) *Promotions & Incentives*, pp4–13.

USEFUL ADDRESSES

TRADE ASSOCIATIONS

Advertising Standards Authority (ASA) and Code of Advertising Practice Committee (CAP), 2 Torrington Place, London WC1E 7HW; ASA: tel 0171-580 5555; fax 0171-631 3051; web site http://www.asa. org.uk; CAP's Copy Advice Service: tel 0171-580 4100; fax 0171-580 4072

Association of Promotion Marketing Agencies Worldwide (APMA Worldwide), 750 Summer Street, Stamford CT 06901, USA; tel 00 1 203 3253911; fax 00 1 203 969 1499; web site: http://www.apmaw.org; e-mail mccapma@aol.com

British Advertising Gift Distributors Association, 1 West Ruislip Station, Ruislip, Middlesex HA4 7DW; tel 01895 622154; fax 01895 631219; e-mail the-associaton@bagda.demon.co.uk

British Committee of the International Chamber of Commerce, 14–15 Belgrave Square, London SW1X 8PS; tel 0171-823 2811; fax 0171-235 5447; web site http://www.iccwbo.org.uk; e-mail 106142.2273@ compu serve.com

British Promotional Merchandise Association, Bank Chambers, 15 High Street, Byfleet, Surrey KT14 7QH; tel 01932 355660; fax 01932 355662; web site http://www.artex.co.uk/bpma.htm; e-mail: bpma@martex. co.uk

CAM Foundation, Abford House, 15 Wilton Road, London SW1V 1NJ; tel 0171-828 7506; fax 0171-976 5140; web site http://www.cam.uk.com

Chartered Institute of Marketing, Moor Hall, Cookham, Maidenhead, Berkshire SL6 9QH; web site http://www.cim.co.uk

Code of Advertising Practice Committee (CAP), see under Advertising Standards Authority, above

Direct Marketing Association, Haymarket House, 1 Oxendon Street, London SW1Y 4EE; tel 0171-321 2525; fax 0171-321 0191; web site http://www.dma.org.uk; e-mail dma@dma.org.uk

European Marketing and Promotion Association, PO Box 47, Banbury, Oxfordshire OX15 6AS; tel 01295 678150; fax 01295 678155

Incorporated Society of British Advertisers (ISBA), 44 Hertford Street, London W1Y 8AG; tel 0171-499 7502; fax 0171-629 5355; web site http://www.isba.org.uk; e-mail info@isba.org.uk

Institute of Practitioners in Advertising, 44 Belgrave Square, London SW1X 8QS; tel 0171-235 7020; fax 0171-245 9904; web site http://www.ipa.co.uk; e-mail mark@ipa.co.uk

Institute of Purchasing and Supply, Easton House, Easton on the Hill, Stamford, Lincolnshire PE9 3NZ; tel 01780 756777; fax 01780 751610; web site http://www.cips.org.uk; e-mail info@cips.org.uk

Institute of Sales Promotion, Arena House, 66–68 Pentonville Road, London N1 9HS; tel 0171-837 5340; fax 0171-837 5326; web site http://www.isp.org.uk

Point of Purchase Advertising Institute (POPAI) Europe, 16 Avenue de Messine, 75008 Paris; tel +33 1 53 75 16 87; fax +33 1 53 75 16 88

POPAI Europe – UK Office, Devonshire House, Bank Street, Lutterworth, Leicestershire LE16 4AG; tel 01455 554848; fax 01455 554421

Sales Promotion Consultants Association, 2nd Floor, 47/48 Margaret Street, London W1N 7FD; tel 0171-580 8225; fax 0171 580 8189

Voucher Industry Federation, 5 Grafton Street, London W1X 3LB; tel 0171-647 1510; fax 0171-647 1599

AGENCIES THAT HAVE SUPPLIED CASE STUDIES

Ammirati Puris Lintas, 84 Eccleston Square, London SW1V 1PX; tel 0171-932 8888; fax 0171-932 8421

The Blue-Chip Marketing Consultancy, St Peter's Court, 8 Trumpet Street, Manchester M1 5LW; tel 0161-237 5050; fax 0161-237 5060; e-mail bluechip,mcr@compuserve.com

Clarke Hooper Consulting, Parliament House, St Lawrence Way, Slough, Berkshire SL1 2BW; tel 01753 577767; fax 01753 823664; web site http://www.chc.co.uk; e-mail info@chc.co.uk

The Communications Agency, 11 Bingham Place, London W1M 3FH; tel 0171-224 3456; fax 0171-224 3565; e-mail The_Communications_Agency@compuserve.com

The Continuity Company, Unit 5, Washington Centre, Halesowen Road, Netherton, Dudley DY2 9RE; tel 01384 242442; 01384 242432; e-mail name@contco.com

IMP, 123 Buckingham Palace Road, London SW1W 9DZ; tel 0171-931 8000; fax 0171-931 8800; web site http://www.dmbb.com

Lovell Vass Boddey, Centurion Court, 85 Milton Park, Abingdon, Oxfordshire OX14 4RY; tel 01235 833844; fax 01235 833811; e-mail 100321.3430@compuserve.com

Marketing Principles, Frewin Chambers, Frewin Court, Cornmarket, Oxford OX1 3HZ; tel 01865 791854; fax 01865 791852; e-mail info@marketing-principles.co.uk

Promotional Campaigns Group, Forest Lodge, Westerham Road, Keston, Kent BR2 6HE; tel 01689 853344; fax 01689 862517; e-mail pcw@pavilion.co.uk

SMP, Castle House, 27 London Road, Tunbridge Wells, Kent TN1 1BX; tel 01892 548282; fax 01892 538996; e-mail smp@smp.uk.com

Tequila Option One, 82 Charing Cross Road, London WC2H 0BA; tel 0171-557 6100; fax 0171-557 6111; e-mail info@tequilaoptionone.co.uk; web site http://www.tequilaoptionone.co.uk

Triangle Communications Limited, 17 Newman Street, London W1P 3HD; tel 0171-637 0322; fax 0171-255 2021; e-mail triangletriangle.com.co.uk

PROMOTIONAL SUPPLIERS

Brevis Marketing Services, Hille House, 132 St Albans Road, Watford WD2 4AG; tel 01923 255355; fax 01923 235324; e-mail name.surname@ brevis.sprint.com

The Continuity Company, Unit 5, Washington Centre, Halesowen Road, Netherton, Dudley DY2 9RE; tel 01384 242442; fax 01384 242432; e-mail name@contco.com

Fotorama, Fotorama House, Icknield Way Estate, Tring, Hertfordshire HP23 4JF; tel 01442 828383; fax 01442 822415

Granby Marketing Group, Causeway Park, Wilderspool Causeway, Warrington WA4 6QF; tel 01925 234684; fax 01925 241206

PIMS, Quadrant House, 80–82 Regent Street, London W1R 5PA; tel 0171-434 3046; fax 0171-434 0384; web site http://www.pims.promo.co.uk; e-mail ideas@pims.promo.co.uk

GENERAL

Article Number Association, 11 Kingsway, London WC2B 6AR; tel 0171-836 3398; fax 0171-240 8149; web site http://www.ana.org.uk

Central Statistical Office, Press and Information Office, 1 Drummond Gate, London SW1V 2QQ; tel 0171-233 9233; fax 0171-533 6261

Consumers Association, 2 Marylebone Road, London NW1 4DF; tel 0171-486 5544; fax 0171-830 7667; web site http://www.which.net; e-mail which@which.net

National Consumer Council, 20 Grosvenor Gardens, London SW1W 0DH; tel 0171-730 3469; fax 0171-730 0191, e-mail admin@nccuk. demon.co.uk

MAGAZINES

Incentive Today, Blenheim House, 630 Chiswick High Road, London W4 5BG; tel 0181-742 2828; fax 0181-742 0329

Marketing, 174 Hammersmith Road, London W6 7JP; tel 0171-413 4150; fax 0171-413 4504; web site http://www.marketing.haynet.com; e-mail 100433.2576@compuserve.com

Marketing Week, St. Giles House, 50 Poland Street, London W1V 4AX; tel 0171-439 4222; fax 0171-434 1439; web site http://www.marketing-week.co.uk/mw0001

Promotions & Incentives, 174 Hammersmith Road, London W6 7JP; tel 0171-413 4152; fax 0171-413 4509

Sales Promotion, Market Link Publishing, The Mill, Bearwalden Business Park, Wendens Ambo, Saffron Walden, Essex CB11 4JX; tel 01799 544200; fax 01799 544203

INDEX